MW01505134

9-
0-

P-1

1- Very busy day

2- People from Georgia, Indiana —

1- Pet + Pontiac,

2-

3- We have caught up on our back

4- bills and I have received

5-

EVENING a ck regularly

Wednesday, July 31

9-
10-

P-1   Q – 10

11- Joe went out on the road today

12- his first main day out.

1- Jim + Barb stopped in today on

2-

3- their way north

4-

5-
EVENING

THERE MUST BE A BETTER WAY

Other books by Henry Dominguez

The Last Days of Henry Ford

Edsel Ford & E. T. Gregorie

The Cellini of Chrome

The Ford Agency

Golden Jubilee

Edsel

THERE MUST BE A BETTER WAY

**The story of how Al Thieme invented the Amigo and
helped mobilize people with walking disabilities**

by
HENRY DOMINGUEZ

Endsheets: Copies of pages from Al Thieme's journals.

LCCN 2022916688

ISBN 978-0-9777701-3-7

Printed in China by WKT Company Limited

Planet Ink, Van Bagley • 415-260-3267 • van@planetinkusa.com

First Edition

Book cover design by Brennan Doan

Book layout and design by Jason Chacon

To all Amigo Company employees:
past, present, and future.

CONTENTS

THERE MUST BE A BETTER WAY

Foreword

by Jim Van Tiflin

Former President, Second National Bank, Saginaw, Michigan

As everyone knows, Michigan was the hub of the automotive industry. People such as Henry Ford, Walter Chrysler, Ransom Olds, and David Buick all founded their companies in Michigan, and their stories are legendary. It was out of that environment, in a small village called Bridgeport, that a journeyman plumber was faced with a dilemma. His wife had just been diagnosed with a debilitating disease, which would compromise her mobility, and he was determined to do something to make her life more manageable. That man was Al Thieme.

Al spent countless hours developing the first Amigo wheelchair, a story that will be fully described in the pages that follow. What I wish to share here are the challenges that Al and all entrepreneurs face, since approximately 90 percent of all business start-ups fail. As a banker, my job was to try to figure out which one of the ten loan applications I had before me was likely to be successful, and then reject the other nine. In fact, I once turned down one of Al's loan requests. Part of the decision process requires a banker to consider the three *C*'s: Character, Collateral, and Cash Flow, and Al's challenge was that he had only one of those C's: Character.

Of course, Al was not the first entrepreneur in history with that problem. Henry Ford, who also lacked collateral and cash flow in the beginning, failed twice before he founded the Ford Motor Company that we know today. Ford had the passion to finally succeed, and Al Thieme has always had plenty of passion, too.

My wife, Janis, and I have become friends with Al and Beth Thieme, traveling widely with them, so I have witnessed firsthand their passion for each other and their business. They are both constantly looking for opportunities to expand the horizons of Amigo Company. As a result, they have built an international corporation.

This book is a must-read for anyone who is even *thinking* about starting a business, and I am convinced that it will provide ample case study material for many business schools.

Prologue

by Jennifer Thieme Kehres

Christmas Eve 1984 was one of the most pivotal moments of my family's life. One phone call set in motion a chain of events that included a cross-country move, growing up in my parents' hometown, and being part of the next generation of our family business.

Who called? The bank.

"We're putting you out of business!" they said.

My dad, Al Thieme, does not have an engineering or manufacturing background, or even a college degree. He was a high school dropout (and actually a kindergarten dropout before that), a grocery store bagger, a painter, and a plumber, before he invented the Amigo in 1968. His relentless optimism, grit, and persistence drove him to fulfill the American dream—inventing a product in his garage that would lead to an international business and improving the lives of thousands of people.

Even though the business became worldwide, his success has been hard-earned. In the early 1980s, sales topped $13 million. There were two manufacturing plants—one in Michigan and one in New Mexico. My dad was named National Businessperson of the Year and was honored at the White House.

But then that phone call came.

Amigo Company was hemorrhaging money. There were problems left and right and, to save the business my parents had to make a decision—Michigan or New Mexico?

My mom and dad have said they always had each other to lean on, and with their faith and determination, they could do anything.

This time, however, they had everything on the line.

Closing the Albuquerque plant, which had more than 100 employees, was excruciatingly painful for them, as was selling their house, packing their belongings, leaving my birthplace, and driving 1,600 miles, with me in the back seat, to their hometown, Saginaw, Michigan, where they weren't exactly welcomed back with open arms.

But that's what they felt they needed to do to save the company, to hold on to the business my dad had created almost two decades before, and to fulfill his promise to the banker who called.

"No!" my dad proclaimed. "You're not putting me out of business."

Introduction

I have known Al Thieme for over forty years and worked for him between 1979 and 1987. My wife, Pat DeHerrera, and I are godparents to Al and Beth's first child, Jennifer.

One day in April 2020, Al called me and asked if I would write the story of his beloved Amigo Company. At first, I thought he just wanted a simple commemorative book to celebrate the company's fiftieth anniversary, but he wanted a full-blown, detailed history of the Amigo Company.

•••

I was born and raised in Ogden, Utah, so I am a westerner—used to blue skies, dry air, and majestic, snow-capped mountains. But I also have a love of automobiles, and that is what took me to Michigan. After graduating from college in 1976, I began working at Saginaw Steering Gear, a division of General Motors, located in Saginaw. At that time, General Motors was the world's largest automobile manufacturer.

On my first day at work, I learned why the locals called it *"Generous Motors"* because of all the benefits GM gave to its employees: health insurance; dental insurance; free eyeglasses once a year; two weeks of vacation to start (five weeks over time); a lucrative 401(k) plan, where the company matched your contributions (dollar-for-dollar in some instances); and the coveted GM pension. With its high wages, investment plan, and retirement package, GM chairman Roger Smith once said: "There's no reason why every GM employee shouldn't retire a millionaire."

To General Motors, money was no object. One time, I was chided by my boss for not spending *enough* money during a business trip!

•••

I loved my work, but I hated Michigan. The sky was always overcast, the humidity was unbearable, and no mountains! And Saginaw wasn't what I had envisioned, either. As a Utahn, I thought everything east of the Mississippi was one big city! It wasn't. In fact, Saginaw was *smaller* than Ogden, and there were fewer things to do in Saginaw than in my hometown. One of my friends at work, who was a native Saginawian, made fun of that.

"Are you married?" he asked me when we first met.

"No," I replied.

"Well, you will be," he replied confidently.

"Why's that?" I asked.

"Because there's nothing else to do in Saginaw!"

So, although I had one of the most coveted jobs in the area, I had second thoughts about having moved to Michigan and began thinking of ways of getting back west.

•••

In the meantime, two of my fellow engineers at Saginaw Steering Gear, Robert Hoppe and Bud Paffrath, were moonlighting at Amigo Company, helping to develop a new product, and they asked me if I would like to help them. That is when I first met Al Thieme.

Handsome, dynamic, and energetic, Al was the quintessential entrepreneur, and I had never met anyone like him before. In fact, he was the opposite of most of the managers at Saginaw Steering Gear, who were intelligent and competent but hardly dynamic. Al was having fun working, and it appeared that he was providing an environment for his employees to have fun at work as well.

At that time, his company was growing, and he was looking

for college-trained people to join his company. It wasn't long after I had started working for him part-time that he asked me to join the company full-time. I was hesitant at first, but when he learned that I was from the west, he closed the deal when he told me that he would eventually open a plant in the West and that I could work there.

I liked Al's dynamism and the product his company was making, so I quit General Motors in July 1979 and went to work for the Amigo Company.

•••

When I started at Amigo, the company was expanding, and sales were growing at 50 percent per year! As the company grew and more people were added in every department, I was able to move around in the company, learning different aspects of its operations. When I started, Al put me in charge of purchasing, then, after a year or so, I became manager of production and eventually director of engineering. That's what I was doing when Al opened a plant in Albuquerque, New Mexico. I got married in June of 1982, and a few months later, Al moved me and Pat to his new western plant, just like he said he would.

Eventually, I became his right-hand man at the western plant.

As one of his executives, we traveled a lot together, many times sharing a hotel room to save money, and that's when I found out about some of his other entrepreneurial traits. When the morning alarm went off, he wouldn't roll over and hit the "snooze" button—he'd immediately jump right out of bed, anxious to start the day. And he'd sing in the shower. When he was home, he'd get to work around 6:00 in the morning and would practically have a full day's work done before anybody else arrived! He'd still be at work long after everybody else had left, go home, and have dinner, and then work some more. In other words, Al Thieme was always working. And he pretty much expected the same thing from his executives.

Taking the cues from my years at General Motors, I'd get

to work just before 8 o'clock and leave at five. But I was subtly informed by Al's brother, Alden, that Al expected his salaried personnel to be at work by 7:30, leave no earlier than 5:30, and work Saturday mornings! I got the hint.

The extra-long workday wasn't too bad, but I could never get used to working through part of "my" weekends.

Al continued to give me more responsibility, but I was not trained in business. Therefore, to learn what I didn't know and to become a better manager, I started working on an MBA at night at the University of New Mexico.

•••

Not long after, however, troubles began. Sales of Amigos, for some unknown reason, began to drop. It was then that I learned that no company earns a penny unless something is sold! That was true at General Motors, too, of course, but it sold so many cars a day that money seemed to fall from the sky! And sales were so removed from engineering that nobody gave it much thought. The common notion was that sales had always been strong and always would be.

However, at Amigo Company, *everybody* knew how precious each Amigo order was. We all cheered when sales were good, and we became a little despondent when sales didn't quite meet expectations because we knew that our jobs depended on the sales of Amigos. And that feeling was palpable.

Even though Al was perpetually optimistic, he understood his employees' anxiety. He told them repeatedly in company meetings that no company, not even the great General Motors, was immune to downturns and troubles.

"There is no such thing as job security," he said, "not even at General Motors!"

Everybody just rolled their eyes when he said that—me included.

Unfortunately, Amigo sales continued to fall, and Al Thieme was forced to shutter the Albuquerque plant and move back to Michigan. That is when I left the company. Pat and I loved Albuquerque, and I wanted to finish graduate school. After I did that, ironically enough, I once again joined General Motors and ended up back in Michigan.

I worked a couple of years in Detroit, but then GM transferred me to Sacramento, California. Now I was living out west *and* working for an automobile company! My dream had just come true.

•••

Twenty years later, General Motors got into severe financial trouble. Ever since I had started with them back in 1976, GM's sales had slowly but inexorably declined to an unimaginative low level. Where GM had 47 percent of the market in 1976, it controlled only 22 percent in 2008. To reduce expenses, the company offered early retirement to employees who met certain age and years of service requirements, which I did. I didn't want to leave the company because I loved my work. Besides, I wasn't that far from regular retirement. But the offer was too good to pass up, so I left in December 2008.

And it was a good thing I did, too, because the great General Motors went bankrupt six months later!

The exact thing that Al Thieme had warned against time and time again, and to which everyone else rolled their eyes, had come true!

When that happened, my thoughts immediately went back to Al Thieme's comments.

•••

Over those years, I kept in touch with the Thiemes. When they were in California for business, Al and Beth would stop by and see us. Then, in 2017, Pat and I met them in Cancun, Mexico, to celebrate Al's eightieth birthday. With a full head of hair and perpetual mustache, he looked more like a sixty-year-old than an octogenarian, and he still exhibited that dynamism that attracted me to him some four decades earlier.

My interest in automobiles is what got me into writing. I had already read a number of books about Henry Ford and the Ford Motor Company, and I noticed that there was precious little written about Ford's dealer organization, styling, and Henry Ford's only child, Edsel, who had been the company's president for twenty-five years. So, I concentrated on writing about these overlooked topics.

My first book was a history of the Ford dealer organization, and my second book was a biography of Edsel Ford. It took me twelve years to write Edsel's biography, but it is the only biography written on Henry Ford's son.

My next book, which was an offshoot of the Edsel Ford biography, covered Ford automobile styling from the Model T to the famous 1949 Mercury. For that book, I interviewed a dozen designers who not only designed the beautiful Fords of the 1930s and 1940s but also knew Henry Ford and Edsel Ford. They were all old men, of course, but they could remember the old times just as if they were yesterday.

In 2010, I came up with an idea for another book. Through all my research on the Ford Motor Company and Henry and Edsel Ford, I knew that there was a lot of material available about the death of Henry Ford—newspaper accounts and, more importantly, interviews of people who were not only with Henry Ford during the last day of his life but were there when he died. I took that material and tracked down thirty-six people who had witnessed these events. One of them was Henry Ford's niece, Carol Lemons. When I interviewed her, she was a spry ninety-year-old, and she had been with her uncle Henry on Easter Sunday, the day before he died.

With all this material, I wrote *The Last Days of Henry Ford*.

After Al had read that book, he called me to see if I would write the story of the Amigo Company. It must have been destiny because I had just finished up another book and was looking for a new project.

To start, Al provided me with anything and everything I asked for to put together the Amigo story, from personal anecdotes and company financial information to access to his personal journals—more than fifty years of daily happenings in his personal and business life. There was no topic off-limits, no question he refused to answer.

I also interviewed over fifty other people—friends, family members, and employees—to get their stories about Al Thieme and Amigo Company. Since I worked at the company for quite a few years, I knew many of them, and it was fun catching up after thirty years. It was like old home week.

Like Al and Beth, none of them hesitated to answer my questions and, much to my delight, told me stories that were simply unbelievable! In fact, their stories are what turned this book from a simple narrative to what it takes to run a business.

While I was part of some of the incidents in this story, I wasn't part of the whole story, so that is why I wrote this book in the third person and not as a personal account.

•••

So, it has been a long and circuitous journey for me and my association with Al Thieme. But I'm glad that we had kept in touch over the years and that he asked me to write his story, for it is a story that is not only interesting and quite extraordinary, but it also exemplifies American ingenuity and entrepreneurship.

Henry Dominguez
North Ogden, Utah
2022

CHAPTER 1

Small-Town Boy

"We ate ourselves sick when we first got here."
—Erna Thieme

Nobody wanted to be living in Germany in the years following World War I. Four years of war had drained the country of men, natural resources, and food. More than four million men had lost their lives in the brutal conflict, natural resources had been depleted, and food was in alarmingly short supply. The Treaty of Versailles, which forced the German government to pay reparations to the Allied Powers (most notably France), made these horrific realities even worse. As part of the treaty, the Allied countries confiscated all of Germany's coal- and steel-producing areas, which severely limited its ability to produce income.

Unable to make its war reparation payments and with a major percentage of its population unemployed, Germany began printing volumes of money in an effort to shore up the economy. But that did little good, so as the economy continued to flounder, the government printed more money. That became a vicious cycle of monumental proportions that led to hyperinflation.

In the first half of 1922, for example, the German currency

stabilized at about 320 marks per dollar, but by December hyperinflation had developed, and now it took 7,400 marks to buy one US dollar. The cost-of-living index was 41 in June 1922, but by December it reached 685. In other words, the income of average German workers would have had to increase by 1,571 percent just to maintain their standard of living. Families' savings vanished, retirement accounts were worthless, and it became almost impossible to buy anything, including food.

At that point, most Germans had two choices: starve to death or leave the country. Thirty-three-year-old Frederick Thieme (pronounced TEE-mee) decided to take his family— which included his wife, Ida, their three children, Alfred, Erna, and Elli—and leave their homeland. He had relatives living in Saginaw, Michigan, so he wrote to them, asking if they could help him and his family to immigrate to America.

•••

In 1881, some cousins of Frederick, the Schweinshaupts, had immigrated to Saginaw and become quite successful. By 1916, the Schweinshaupt Brothers Company, located on North Niagara Street along the Saginaw River, was selling coal, coke, and firewood. The brothers also manufactured cement products, with their most popular and profitable item being burial vaults. To show the durability of that product, the company submerged a dozen sealed vaults in the Saginaw River for three weeks, and when they retrieved and opened the vaults, they were, according to a newspaper ad, "dry and dusty inside."

In the last half of the nineteenth century, Saginaw was "the lumber capital of the world." Thousands of acres of white pine (some 25 billion feet) were felled, turned into lumber, and transported all over the country by train and ship. However, just as the lumber supply was petering out, the automobile industry was beginning to blossom, and in 1906, three enterprising Saginawians founded a company to manufacture steering gears. Since Saginaw Steering Gear was an independent company,

Frederick Thieme family, Berlin, 1915, (L-R):
Alfred, Erna, Ida, Frederick

it designed and built steering gears for any and all vehicle manufacturers. After General Motors acquired the plant in 1917, the company built steering gears primarily for GM products.

*The Thieme family sailed from Germany
to America on the* SS Minnekahda

Immigrants from all parts of the world, especially Europe, came to Michigan to work in the automobile factories. Poles, Greeks, and Russians went to Detroit, while Germans and other Poles went to Flint and Saginaw. The Schweinshaupts never entered the automotive field, but with the dynamic Michigan economy, all kinds of products were in demand, including burial vaults.

•••

How Frederick Thieme was able to buy five tickets on the American ship *SS Minnekahda* at astronomically inflated prices is unknown. Either he brought a wheelbarrow full of money to the ticket office, or he brought something of significant value that he bartered for the tickets. Or—and this is most likely— the Schweinshaupts sent him tickets that they had bought with precious American dollars. All we know is that the Thiemes, according to Frederick's daughter, Erna, "sold all their furniture for money" and left Germany almost broke.

The 646-foot *Minnekahda* was operated by the American Line, which used it specifically to transport immigrants from

Thirteen-year-old Alfred Thieme enjoying himself on the deck of the SS Minnekahda *while on his way to America*

Hamburg, Germany, to New York City. Capable of plying 16 knots, it carried well over 2,000 passengers.

When the Thieme family boarded the ship at Hamburg on January 8, 1923, "it was cold and stormy," recalled Erna. The ship sailed up the Elbe River to the North Sea, through the English Channel, and out into the Atlantic Ocean, traveling the same route that the ill-fated *Titanic* had taken eleven years earlier. The voyage took almost two weeks, during which time Frederick spent much of the furniture money on food.

●●●

Although the Thieme family had made it to America, there was no guarantee that the immigration officials would let them in. According to Erna, they faced a "grueling interrogation" at Ellis Island. Primarily, the officials wanted to know how much money they had and the physical condition of each member of the family. On both counts, Frederick's family came up short.

Frederick Thieme at about the time of his arrival in America

The fact that the Thiemes were broke raised one red flag, and the physical conditions of Frederick and his son, Alfred, raised another.

"My father had some heart problems," recalled Erna, "and my brother's right arm was crippled from polio." According to Alfred's daughter, Emeline (also known as Emy), her father's arm "just hung in back, and he usually kept it in his pocket. He would always, of course, shake hands with his left hand."

"In those days," Erna explained about the immigration officials, "they were really strict. Men were supposed to be the family providers, and they thought my father might die, and we would become a burden on the government." Alfred's withered arm didn't help the situation any. "They wanted to send us back to Germany!" Erna exclaimed. "We couldn't speak a word of English. We were really scared. My mother cried and cried."

Through an interpreter, Frederick quickly and cunningly

explained to the officials that he was a professional house painter, that he had work waiting for him in Saginaw, and that his son had already proven that he could paint as well as any man. Alfred would not become a burden to society, he told them.

"After all," Emy said, "you only need one hand to paint!"

But the immigration officials were not convinced. They told Frederick that unless he could come up with somebody who could vouch for his credentials and verify that work was available to him in Saginaw, the entire family would be sent back to Germany. Frederick told them that he could get that information, but it would take some time. It was at that point that the officials separated Frederick and Alfred from Ida, Erna, and Elli. They were not singling them out. Separating the men from the women was standard protocol if a family had to remain on Ellis Island for any length of time while their application was being processed.

Frederick sent a letter to his cousins in Saginaw, telling them of his dire situation at Ellis Island and awaited their reply.

•••

In the meantime, the Thiemes' life inside the dormitory was tantamount to being in a concentration camp. They slept on bedsprings with no mattresses, Erna said, and had to compete with hundreds of other immigrants for food. They picked up scraps of food that others left behind. Occasionally, the commissary would hand out crackers and peanut butter.

"I remember my father telling me," recalled Emy, years later, "that he was so hungry, he'd stuff so much peanut butter in his mouth that he almost choked. I don't think he ever ate peanut butter again after that!"

As the days turned into weeks, Alfred became so despondent that he considered jumping into New York Harbor and swimming to New Jersey.

"My father was a strong swimmer, even with one arm," Emy said.

But Frederick told his son to put such silly notions out of his

Alfred and Emma Thieme on
their wedding day, 1931

mind. Help would be coming soon, he told him, even though he himself was beginning to have doubts. However, on February 12, 1923, a full five weeks after leaving Hamburg, word came that Frederick and his family were free to leave Ellis Island.

The reason it took so long, Frederick discovered later, is that even with the Schweinshaupts vouching for him and his family, the immigration officials still refused to release them. The impasse was finally overcome when US Congressman Joseph Fordney intervened on their behalf.

"We were really lucky to get off the island," Erna said.

•••

It was a two-day train ride from New York City to Saginaw.

Frederick (right) and Alfred Thieme posing next to their
"F.A. Thieme Decorators" Dodge panel truck, ca. 1935

The first leg was an overnight trip on New York Central's *Detroiter* passenger train, which left Grand Central Terminal in Manhattan at 7:00 P.M. and arrived at Detroit's Michigan Central Station twelve hours later. From there, the Thiemes caught a local train from Detroit to Saginaw, a trip that took most of the day because the train stopped at every little town along the 100-mile route.

Although the Thiemes were elated to be in America and heading to their new home, they were famished.

"We had nothing to eat for two days on the train ride from New York to Saginaw," recalled Erna.

It was a long, ravenous journey indeed, but Frederick and his family made it, for which they were forever grateful.

"America was heaven-sent to us," Erna recalled solemnly. "It was liberation, freedom, and food."

•••

The Thiemes stayed with their Schweinhaupt cousins until

Al Thieme's grandparents,
Frederick and Ida Thieme, 1937

they got settled. It was not difficult for Frederick to find work. As his painting skills became well known in the community, he was soon painting the luxurious Victorian homes of the well-to-do on Saginaw's east side, as well as businesses downtown.

When it came time for the three children to be enrolled in school, Frederick and Ida wanted all of them to attend St. Paul's Lutheran School because it taught subjects in both German and English. But Alfred would have none of that. He was so determined to learn English that he talked his parents into sending him to the local public school instead.

"He had to start in the lower grades until he learned the language," explained Emy, but he learned English quickly and he learned it well. "You wouldn't know that he was born in

Alfred Thieme's children (L-R): Emy, Alden, Allan, 1938

Germany," she explained. "He didn't have an accent at all."

Erna and Elli, on the other hand, retained a slight German accent for the rest of their lives. Instead of being immersed in the English language, like their brother, they only learned twenty words at a time, Erna said. Their teachers at St. Paul's would give them a vocabulary list in German and English to practice every night.

•••

In February 1929, Alfred Bringe (pronounced BRING-ee), his wife, Freda, and their two daughters, Lieselotte and Elza, emigrated from Germany to Saginaw. Like all immigrants at the time, they could have settled anywhere in the country, but the reason they chose Saginaw was that they had relatives there. Alfred Bringe was not only a painter, like Frederick, but he was also his brother!

"You see," explained Emy, "our Grandpa Thieme's mother wasn't married when she had Grandpa, so she gave him her maiden name, which was Thieme, and then she married his father, Mr. Bringe. Bringe was Grandpa's father, but Grandpa never changed his name." So, the Thiemes' name should actually be Bringe.

For a while, Frederick Thieme and Alfred Bringe operated a painting and decorating company called "Thieme & Bringe." They lived only block apart.

"I can still see in my mind's eye," recalled Emy, "where they lived. I don't know how that came to be, but that one whole block bordered by Granger Street, Webster Street, Holland Avenue, and Miller Street was Thieme relatives. They were right down the road from the hospital in Saginaw."

●●●

Alfred helped his father to paint when he could, especially during the summers, when he was out of school. Just as his father had told the immigration officers at Ellis Island, Alfred could paint with the best of them.

Alfred enjoyed the work and the money so much that he quit school in the eighth grade and went to work with his father full-time. But it is not known how old he was at that time because, as his daughter has previously intimated, he "started in earlier grades." He could well have been 15 or 16 years old when he quit school, which might have been the other reason he left. He was so much older than the other students in his grade that he probably felt no reason to continue on.

●●●

With Alfred now working full-time, the Thiemes were able to take on more and larger jobs. One of their most ambitious and lucrative projects was painting the interior of the magnificent Temple Theater in downtown Saginaw.

Completed in July 1927, the theater was somewhat staid on the outside, but the inside was spectacular. There were three sweeping arches in front of the large stage, which extended into an expansive vaulted ceiling, and the walls were decorated with intricate cornices and elaborate pilasters.

Standing on scaffolds extending as high as fifty feet into the air, Frederick and Alfred painted the ceiling and applied gold leaf to the ornate moldings, taking months to complete the task.

More than eighty years later, Frederick's great-granddaughter and Alfred's granddaughter, Jennifer Thieme, had her wedding reception in the newly restored Temple Theater. When she looked up at the glorious gilded-domed ceiling, she could hardly believe that her ancestors had done that magnificent work.

"It was very sweet and sentimental that we had our reception in a place that my grandfather and great-grandfather had a hand at decorating, many, many years ago," Jennifer explained. "We had guests all night, and we had people come in from California, Florida, New York …, all over the country. We had my mother's, my mother-in-law's, and my grandmother Loichinger's wedding dresses on display in the lobby."

All three dresses were elegant, but Mrs. Loichinger's wedding dress was unique indeed. Because she was married during World War II, when raw materials were scarce, her dress was made out of silk from a parachute.

•••

Not long after completing the Temple Theater project, Alfred and his father began painting a wealthy home on Washington Avenue in Saginaw. It was there that Alfred met a beautiful young woman by the name of Emma Elizabeth Hoffmann. Like Alfred, she had quit school in eighth grade, and was now working in that home as a live-in maid.

"That's when store owners could afford big homes like that," explained Emy, "and they had young girls come in and work as a cleaning maid or cooking maid."

Emma's parents, Jacob and Lena (née Knoll), owned a farm in Frankenmuth, a predominantly German community southeast of Saginaw. They were both born and raised in Frankenmuth. Although they could both speak English, they spoke German at home. But they didn't speak "regular" German because most of the German families in Frankenmuth had roots in southern Germany, specifically in Bavaria, which has its own dialect. Just as Americans from Texas speak differently than, say, Americans from Boston, Germans from Berlin speak differently than Germans from Munich.

It is not known how long Alfred and Emma courted, but they were married on June 13, 1931, when Alfred was twenty-one, and his new wife was twenty-two.

They moved into a small bungalow at 920 North Granger Street, right in the middle of the so-called Thieme block. Their first child, Emy, was born there in 1933, as was their second child, Alden, in 1935.

This was in the depths of the Great Depression, so Alfred's painting work slowly but inexorably dried up.

"Nobody was hiring painters," explained Emy, "and because there was no work, they lost their home."

Fortunately, Emma's brother, Roy Hoffmann, who, like his parents, was a farmer, gave or sold to his sister and brother-in-law an acre of land on the southeast corner of his property, which was "kind of hilly," explained Emy. With money hard to come by, Alfred built a home "gradually." He built a basement home to begin with, and as he got more money, he built the house a little further, eventually ending up with a handsome white clapboard structure on top of the basement. He never had a mortgage.

Although the lot was not perfectly flat, it was well located. On the west side of the property was Bow Road (later named Airport Road). On the south side of the lot was the Dixie Highway, a major thoroughfare that ran all the way from Sault Ste. Marie, Michigan, to Miami, Florida.

It was here, on April 5, 1937, that Alfred and Emma's third child was born. They named him Allan Roy Thieme, his middle name obviously in honor of Emma's brother. Their fourth and last child, Miriam, was born in 1945, and the family was thrilled that the new baby was another girl.

In a family portrait taken in 1946, the Alfred Thieme clan looked like the quintessential American family: handsome, healthy, and happy. Alfred is dressed in a dark suit and tie; Emma in a dark dress; Emy in a handsome dress suit; Alden and Al in dark pants, white shirts, white sweater vests, and dark ties; and little Miriam in a dainty dress. Normal Rockwell could have used this portrait to paint one of his iconic covers for the *Saturday Evening Post*.

All of the children had their own personalities, of course. According to Al, Emy was "stern like her mother," Alden was "quiet, very serious, and cautious," and Miriam was "sweet and kind." Al, on the other hand, was energetic, gregarious, and rebellious. He wasn't mean or vindictive; he just didn't like people telling him what to do.

Al may have been the wayward child, but it was Miriam who became the most taxing of the Thieme children. Through no fault of her own, she had been born with a rare congenital disease called Friedreich's Ataxia, which is almost always fatal. The disease attacks the nervous system over time, first causing loss of sensation in the arms and legs, then difficulty talking and walking, and ultimately heart failure.

"Mom and Dad took Miriam to Ann Arbor," explained Emy. "That's where she was diagnosed. There isn't any cure for it, and they said that she would probably die when she was about twenty-one."

•••

The Depression was tough to live through; then World War II broke out.

"I remember my dad was so upset when he heard the news about Pearl Harbor," Emy recalled, "that he turned pale."

He had lived through the horrors of World War I and couldn't

Alfred Thieme's family, 1946 (L-R): Alden, Emy,
Al, Alfred, Miriam, and Emma

fathom America going through such misery again.

Frederick was too old to join the military, and Alfred, with his withered arm, got a physical deferment, but they both still

Al Thieme's confirmation portrait, 1951

did what they could to support the war effort. Alfred joined the auxiliary police. With all the young men, including police officers, going off to war, that organization was formed to protect the community. The members would conduct air raid drills, have people turn off their lights at night, and direct traffic.

Alfred also helped German immigrants who were not yet naturalized to become citizens.

"Otherwise," Emy said, "they were looked down upon and criticized. He taught them enough English so that they could write their names and answer the questions they needed to know to become citizens."

But he probably chastised them, too, for not getting their citizenship sooner and not learning English, as he had done years earlier.

"My father was a very patriotic person," Emy explained.

Obviously, there were many families in the area that still spoke German at home, but Alfred would have no part of that.

"We are in America," he told his family. "So we will not speak German!"

Occasionally, however, Emma would slip back into her native tongue, and Alfred would quickly remind her to speak English.

"Your German is more *bayerische*," he would say, referring to her Bavarian dialect. "I learned only High German!"

"My dad was from *Berlin*," Emy said. "We could have learned a second language when we were growing up, but Dad wanted no German spoken at our home."

Frederick went to work at the Saginaw Steering Gear plant, which was now making M1 Carbine rifles and .30 caliber machine guns. Aunt June (Emma's half-sister) also worked at the plant.

"The young women would work seven days a week," explained Emy.

Emma and the children did their part, too. She took nursing classes "in case the killing came to our soil," recalled Emy, "and she rode a bicycle door-to-door to sell war bonds."

Emy, Alden, and Al would pick milkweed pods, which were turned into life jackets. They also collected paper and anything made of metal, even old keys. The paper would be recycled into shipping boxes, shell containers, and even cartridge wads. The metal would be melted down to make guns and ammunition, which saved precious natural resources. In fact, all natural resources were rationed, including food and gasoline, and people did whatever they could to grow their own food and save on fuel.

"My father would pick up a couple of young ladies who worked in town to help pay for gas," recalled Emy. "Then Aunt June lived with us in Bridgeport because it was easier for her to get into Saginaw from our house than from Frankenmuth, where her home was."

Over 300 men from Saginaw County lost their lives during World War II, and while Frederick Thieme was not on the front lines, he found a way to help on the production lines to support the soldiers. Working at a local plant to help the war effort would also mean the first time that he would have a steady paycheck and benefits. Unfortunately, the heart condition that the doctors at Ellis Island had been concerned about finally caught up with him, two decades later.

"Grandpa was just about ready to be covered with insurance," explained Emy, "when he suddenly died of a heart attack! He was only fifty-three years old."

To keep the roof over her head, Ida washed dishes at the hospital in Saginaw.

"She lived about a mile away," Emy said, "and she'd walk to work every day."

Ida died in 1966 at the age of seventy-eight.

•••

Although the piece of land that Roy Hoffmann had given or sold to Alfred and Emma wasn't in the most desirable area for farming, they were able to grow vegetables and raise animals on it, which was a godsend during the desolate years of the Depression and the war. Emma's experience growing up on a farm really came in handy.

"We'd never buy vegetables at the grocery store," recalled Emy. "We grew all our own vegetables and canned them. We planted our own potatoes. We had a potato bin in the basement."

Occasionally, they would raise a cow or a pig, but they always had rabbits and chickens.

"We had our own eggs," Emy said, "and we'd kill a chicken or a rabbit on Sunday for supper."

A wealthy couple, Walter and Severine Kull, lived across the road from the Thiemes. Walter was the manager of one of the General Motors plants in the area. All of the older Thieme children worked for the Kulls at one time or another. Alden and Al would mow their lawn, and Emy would do housework.

"I cleaned house for Mrs. Kull," Emy recalled, "and when she had company, I did the dishes. People didn't have dishwashers back then. Sometimes, when she had company, I would wait on the table. The Kulls had a big, beautiful raspberry patch that was so tall that I couldn't see my mother behind it when we would pick berries together. It was on the piece of property close to the barnyard, so it grew luscious, big raspberries. My mother and I would pick raspberries in the morning, and then she would send me out by the Dixie Highway and set up a little fruit stand, and I'd sell the raspberries in the afternoon."

In fact, about all Emy did was housework. She would sew, iron, do the dishes, and help her mother with the canning.

"I would sometimes get upset," Emy said, "because there were more things for me to do to help around the house than there were for the boys. They fed the chickens and kept the lawn mowed, but there were always more women's tasks to do. One time, I had to clean the boys' bedroom, and I got so upset because it was such a terrible mess! I put everything I found on the floor on top of their bed, and when they got ready to go to bed …, well, they weren't too happy! I don't know if it did any good."

However, Emy loved both of her brothers and helped her parents to watch over them.

"My brothers were afraid of thunder and lightning," she recalled. "Whenever a storm came in, first they'd pin the drapes shut, and if that didn't take care of the lightning, then they'd crawl into bed with me. Apparently, they thought that I'd protect them."

•••

Thanksgiving was Alfred's most beloved holiday because it reminded him of all the blessings that America had given to him. As far as the rest of his family was concerned, however, Christmas was their favorite. But they celebrated it differently than most families. Instead of putting up a Christmas tree after Thanksgiving or in early December, as most of their friends and neighbors did, Alfred and Emma would bring a tree into the house and decorate it themselves on Christmas Eve, after their kids had gone to bed.

"We slept upstairs, my two brothers and I," recalled Emy. "There was a vent in the floor for heat to come to the upstairs. We would listen, and we could hear the Christmas tree coming in. The next morning, the Christmas tree and the presents would be there! Mostly the presents were homemade. My mother would make me new clothes, and Dad would bring things home from wealthy people he painted for. They would give Dad things they didn't want."

One year, when times were better, Emy got a new doll, and Alden and Al got a train set and an airplane.

"The plane wouldn't fly around free," Emy explained. "It was hooked to a metal stand and would just go round and round!"

Those simple toys kept the Thieme children occupied during the long Michigan winters, but as spring turned to summer, they spent most of their time outside. The best way to get out of the stifling heat and humidity was to head to Anderson Pool, the public swimming pool located just south of downtown Saginaw on the Saginaw River.

"You could go in the morning for free," explained Emy. "They gave swimming lessons there. Mom would take us, and that's where we learned how to swim. We would take a lunch along, go swimming in the morning, and then we'd eat lunch on Ojibway Island. That was a big outing."

Al remembered going to Anderson Pool, but he said that he learned to swim by being thrown into the Cass River!

In August every year, the Thieme children would attend "Children's Day" at the Saginaw County Fair. Alfred would take Emy, Alden, and Al to the fairgrounds and drop them off in the morning on his way to work. They would be there all day by themselves.

"We didn't have much money to spend," Emy recalled, "but we would go on a ride or two and have a few Eskimo Pies." (Eskimo pies are chocolate-coated ice cream on a stick.)

•••

World War II had been raging for less than a year when Al started kindergarten at Bridgeport Elementary School in the fall of 1942. Like all kindergarteners, the children went to school in the morning, then had cookies and milk, and finally lay their blankets down on the floor to take a nap. While the other kids quickly fell asleep, Al would stare at the ceiling.

After three or four days of that, he told his mother, "Mom, I'm not going to go to school, eat cookies, drink milk, and take a nap!"

"OK," she said surprisingly, "stay home! You have chores to do, anyway."

Therefore, he didn't go back to kindergarten!

"I almost stayed in kindergarten," Al explained years later, "because Myrtle Mouldenour, the young teacher, was kinda cute."

The following year, Al started first grade at Phelps Elementary, a one-room schoolhouse located on the corner of Roedel and Portsmouth roads in Bridgeport. The school was a mile and a half away from the Thieme home, but Emy, Alden, and Al made the long walk, regardless of the weather. In the summer, they would ride their bikes.

"Everybody laughs," Emy recalled, "when I tell them that even if the snow was up to our hips, we'd walk through it. But that's true!"

Children attended first through sixth grades at Phelps Elementary, all taught by Mrs. Flora Robertson.

"She knew how to teach," recalled Al. "She enjoyed seeing her students learn."

When Al started at Phelps, there were only thirty kids in the entire school, six of whom were in the first grade: Al and five girls!

As in all small schools like Phelps, reading, writing, and arithmetic were taught, over, and over, and over again.

"That's why students of one-room schools were so well educated," the saying goes, "because they learned the same basic things seven or eight times!"

That's what Al experienced. He learned to read well, write well, and do basic math well. To a great extent, the excellent basic education that he had from Mrs. Robertson would be his saving grace in the years to come.

•••

After his precarious start in kindergarten, Al made it through elementary school, and went on to Webber Middle School in Saginaw in the fall of 1950, which was quite a change for him. Unlike his little elementary school, Webber was an expansive, multistory brick building that held well over 200 students. With the school six miles away from Bridgeport, Al would catch the school bus on the Dixie Highway.

It was at Webber that he began palling around with some of the older, more rebellious boys, and quite often would skip school with them.

"Four or five of us at Webber," Al recalled, "found it fun to walk the railroad tracks to downtown Saginaw and spend a few hours at the pool hall."

That was only the beginning of Al's growing waywardness. Some of it was simply trying to show his manhood, as when he climbed Bridgeport's water tower with Jack Fehrenbach, the local plumber's son. Both boys scampered up the ladder to the walkway that went around the tank, but that wasn't far enough for them. They climbed the ladder that went from the walkway to the very top of the tank—some 110 feet above the ground. One misstep could have been disastrous.

As they stood there at the top of the tower, they could see

Al Thieme's high school report card

the expanse of the flat Saginaw Valley and the Cass River meandering off into the distance.

•••

The Saginaw River is formed by the confluence of the Tittabawassee River from the north, the Shiawassee River from the south, and the Cass River from the east. As the Cass River slowly makes its way from the so-called Thumb Region of Michigan to Saginaw, it passes right through Bridgeport. A truss bridge crosses the river on Fort Street, which is where Al said he learned to swim.

"My friends threw me in!" he laughingly recalled. "'We'll help you!' they yelled. Back then, there were no fish in that river, it was so polluted, but us kids swam in it anyway. We'd get on the bridge and jump down into the river."

However, Bob and Jim Ecker would climb to the top of the bridge—some 50 feet above the surface of the water—and dive into the river! Townspeople marveled at the boys' daring, which prompted a reporter from *The Saginaw News* to come out and take their picture.

When they weren't swimming or diving off the bridge, Al and his friends were playing "King of the Icebreaker," a variation of "King of the Hill," except on water. On the upstream side of the bridge's center pier, there was an abutment made of pressure-treated logs that prevented ice from damaging the bridge. It was steep, curved, smooth, and very difficult to stand on.

"One guy would be up there on the peak," Al explained, "and the other guys would try to push him off! You'd get pushed and slide down the abutment into the water. That was a lot of fun! One time, Don Reimer got knocked off the peak, and as he was sliding down, his ring got caught on a nail, which peeled his finger right off. We helped him swim out of the river, keeping his hand out of the water, and took him to Dr. Chisena. He had to cut Don's finger off because only the bone was left."

•••

As Al entered ninth grade, his older friends were now sixteen to eighteen and had their own cars. One of their favorite escapades was to drive through Millington, a little town in the midst of farm country, about twenty miles east of Bridgeport. Ostensibly, they drove out there to go swimming at Murphy Lake, but they couldn't help tearing through town and throwing firecrackers out the car's windows. By the time anyone figured out what was going on or was able to do anything about it, the ruffians were long gone—except for one occasion.

"So, this one time," Al recalled, "when we came through Millington after swimming at Murphy Lake, we got our firecrackers ready, and we threw fireworks out again. Well, there were about four cars of guys waiting for us, and they began chasing us!"

Al and his friends took off in Tom Prunner's V-8-powered Ford, and it looked as though the Bridgeport boys were going to get away. But then one of their tires blew out, and Tom was forced to pull into a farmer's yard. Everybody jumped out of the car, making a mad scramble to change the tire, but they didn't

*Bob Ecker jumping off a bridge
across the Cass River*

have time. Four cars of Millington boys came to a screeching stop behind them.

At that same moment, the farmer, wondering what all the commotion was about, came running out of house, shotgun in hand.

"Take off into the cornfield!" Tom yelled. "If I'm here all alone, they won't want to fight!"

Al and the others took off, leaving Tom behind, making the

twenty-mile trek back to Bridgeport on foot.

"We didn't get home until five in the morning!" Al recalled.

Meanwhile, the farmer had the Millington boys help Tom change the tire.

However, that wasn't the only time that Al and his buddies had a shotgun pulled on them.

•••

Back in those days, outhouses were common, especially out in the country, so one of the favorite "tricks" during Halloween was for kids to knock them over. That is exactly what Al and his friends had in mind for their school bus driver.

"There were the three of us going along his fence line," Al recalled. "We get to his outhouse, and we were just about ready to knock it over, when suddenly the porch light goes on, and he comes out with a shotgun and shoots it up in the air. We didn't turn that outhouse over *that* year!"

With that trick foiled, "we thought it would really be fun," Al said, "to set some corn shocks on fire. We put two corn shocks in front of Bridgeport's fire department and set them on fire. That was kind of fun. Then we went into the field and set another one on fire. Oh, that was not good, because the field was dry, and began to burn. The fire department put it out. But they never caught us."

Al and his buddies were never caught stealing tires, either. Their cars were mostly junkers, whose tires were always going flat. Since they couldn't afford new tires, they resorted to other measures.

"There was this junkyard in Saginaw," Al explained, "that had a lot of old cars and a lot of old tires. We'd jump over the fence and get some of those old tires. They were junk anyway," he rationalized, "so it wasn't too bad."

That was probably the worst mischief that Al got involved in as a teenager, although he continued his reckless behavior for a while. Jim and Bob Ecker, on the other hand, liked the thrill of living on the edge, so they continued, in Al's words, to "steal bigger things." Even after Bob was sent to juvenile boys' school, Jim continued his bad behavior, "breaking into houses and stealing guns."

•••

Why was Al Thieme, a god-fearing young man, traveling down that destructive path? Was it the friends he chose, or was it because his father was living in Babson Park, Florida, 1,200 miles away?

No one could remember exactly when, but around the time that Al entered junior high school, Alfred and Emma Thieme got a divorce, which ended with Alfred moving away.

Emy was completely surprised by her parents' breakup.

"I can't remember that there was discord in the house," she explained. "Mother always seemed joyful."

Her little brother was surprised, too, but years later chalked the divorce up to irreconcilable differences.

"Dad was a people person," Al said. "He liked to work and play hard. Mom was more of a home person."

With Al's independent spirit, in his mind his parents' divorce didn't affect him too much.

"Because my father wasn't around," he explained, "it made me a stronger, more resilient, and independent person."

CHAPTER 2

Courtship and Marriage

♪ "They try to tell us we're too young." ♪
—Nat "King" Cole

Long before Alfred and Emma Thieme were divorced, the family went to church nearly every Sunday at the Christ Lutheran Church in Birch Run, a town ten miles south of Bridgeport on the Dixie Highway. The other Lutheran church that they would occasionally attend was Redeemer Lutheran, north on the Dixie Highway, but they liked Christ Lutheran better because it was smaller.

The Lutherans in Bridgeport wanted to have their own church, so Alfred Thieme, Joe Fehrenbach, and John Dudek decided to establish a church in their community. They bought an old schoolhouse that was out in the country, moved it to Bridgeport, and turned it into Faith Lutheran Church. Its first pastor was the Reverend Clifford Brueggeman, a young minister fresh out of seminary school.

The congregation was small—about ten families—but as time went on, other families from the surrounding area began to attend.

"One Sunday," Al recalled, "two new girls came into church."

Shirley and Marie Scharrer were sisters from Frankenmuth. Marie was six years younger than her sister and the same age as Al.

"Well, I kinda got attracted to Marie," Al said, "because she was an attractive new face in town."

Normally, the Scharrer girls attended St. Lorenz Lutheran Church, about five miles from their home, which had a large congregation. When the little church in Bridgeport opened, they thought they would see what it was like.

Perhaps not much would have developed between Al Thieme and Marie Scharrer, since she lived so far away. But Al's step-grandmother, Katherine Hoffman, lived just a half-mile away from the Scharrers.

●●●

Katherine Hoffman was not Al's real maternal grandmother, and it wasn't because his grandparents had gotten a divorce, but rather through a strange set of events.

"After my mother was born," Al explained, "her mother died a few days later, probably due to complications after childbirth. Back in those days, a nurse or midwife would come to your house when you had a baby. So, while my grandmother was dying, she told the midwife: 'You have to marry my husband and raise the children.'"

It would seem fantastical if it happened exactly that way, but however it happened, Kate Dommer, the 19-year-old midwife, did marry Jacob Hoffmann, and they had five children together: Lee, Floyd, Alvin, June, and Jacob, Jr. And so with Jacob's first three children—Maletta, Roy, and Emma (Al's mother)—his family became a clan of ten, with his new wife thirteen years his junior.

They lived on a farm in Frankenmuth, where they had a team of horses and a few cows and chickens, and they also raised corn and soybeans. Although tractors had been around for a few years, Jacob still worked the land with horses.

Tragically, in the fall of 1944, while Jacob was hitching his horses up to a plow, something spooked them, and they reared up and trampled him to death. The death certificate listed the cause of death as a "fractured skull." He was sixty-eight years old.

•••

As the two Thieme boys were growing up, Al always inherited Alden's hand-me-down bikes, so he made up his mind one day to get a brand new one. For two years, he had earned money by taking care of the Kulls' yard, working on Uncle Roy's farm, and picking up pop bottles along the Dixie Highway. He would get two cents for each small bottle and five cents for each large one. When he had saved enough money, his mother took him to the Western Auto store in Saginaw, where he bought a fire-engine-red Monarch bicycle, replete with rearview mirror and horn.

"My first trip," Al recalled, "was to show it to Grandma Thieme, who lived on Granger Street in Saginaw. My next trip was to show it to Grandma Hoffmann, and then I'd go see Marie."

What started out as a simple friendship slowly turned into a romance. Particularly during the warmer months, Al rode his bike to see Marie quite often. Her parents took a liking to him as well.

Martin and Martha Scharrer owned a large farm and had a cabin in Rose City, a two-hour drive north of Bridgeport, where Martin would take Al and Marie deer hunting in the fall.

"Marie was a tomboy and loved to hunt," Al recalled. "I was fourteen years old when I first went hunting with 'Pa' Scharrer and Marie. That's when I shot my first deer with my 20-gauge shotgun."

As Al began to see Marie more, he hung out less with his

rowdy friends. If there was ever a time when providence was watching out for him, it was then, for if he had gone out with his old friend Jim Ecker when Jim asked him to, that would have changed Al's life forever.

Short on cash, Jim drove to a little grocery store up north one night, walked inside, pulled a gun on the lady behind the counter, and demanded the money in the cash register.

"She wouldn't give it to him," Al said, "so Jim shot her…, dead!"

The incident made the front page of *The Saginaw News*, and fortunately Al was not part of the story.

"He wasn't with him," Emy recalled. "Al was with Marie that evening."

•••

"There was a theater in Frankenmuth called the Ken Theater," recalled Emy. "It was a movie house. When our mother would leave for the evening, we'd go out to the Ken Theater as soon as mother left. Al didn't have a driver's license yet, but I had my boyfriend's car. He left it with me when he was drafted into the Army. I didn't drive it, Al would. We'd take the back roads. We'd take Miriam with us. She was in a wheelchair by then. Back in those days, you could go to any kind of a movie. It was always good, whether it was Gene Autry or Roy Rogers. You didn't have to be careful what was showing."

Sometimes, they would drive all the way into Saginaw to go to the Temple Theater.

"It cost fifty cents to go in," Emy recalled. "It was gorgeous inside, and it was *the* place to go on Saturday night for a teenager."

•••

Al entered Saginaw High School in the fall of 1952, but he didn't last there long.

"I just couldn't adjust to high school," he recalled. "I went to Saginaw High for about a month, and then quit."

He never went back to high school, either to Saginaw High

or any other high school.

But quitting school wasn't that easy.

"In those days," Al explained, "they had truant officers, and if you didn't go to school, a truant officer would take you back!"

Alfred had moved to Babson Park, a citrus-growing area 70 miles east of Tampa bringing Alden down there with him. Like his little brother, Alden didn't care for school, and quit right after eighth grade. He earned his way by painting with his father and working in the orange groves, which allowed him to buy his own car.

When Al contacted his brother and told him about *his* school situation, Alden said, "C'mon down! I'll send you a ticket, so that you can take the Greyhound bus."

•••

In the days before Interstate 75, it would take twenty hours for a bus to go from Saginaw to Miami on the Dixie Highway. Although the road was a four-lane highway, the bus stopped at every major town along the route to let passengers take a restroom break and get something to eat. The first leg of Al's trip was from Saginaw to Detroit, where there was a two-hour layover before he got on the *Sunliner*—Greyhound's Florida special.

As Al was wandering around the bus station, he walked into a small shop and saw a Florida travel display, showing sun-drenched beaches and people swimming in the ocean.

I need a swimsuit! he thought.

So, with the $5 that his mother had given him, he bought a bathing suit. Now he had very little money left to buy food, but he wasn't too concerned.

When the passengers boarded the bus, Al found a seat by himself. After several hours of traveling, the bus stopped to allow the passengers to get off to get something to eat. Since Al was low on money, he stayed in his seat.

When an elderly lady noticed that he wasn't getting off the

bus, she asked him, "Aren't you feeling well?"

"Oh, I feel good!" Al replied.

"Aren't you going to eat?"

"I'm not hungry."

She quickly realized what was happening, for no fifteen-year-old teenager would pass up a meal unless, of course, he didn't have any money.

"You know," she said to Al, "I've never traveled alone like this before, and I'd really like to have somebody to be with me. And if you do that, I'll buy meals for you."

That would not be the last time that Al Thieme would fall into luck at just the right moment.

The bus arrived in Jacksonville, Florida, at 6:00 in the morning the next day. It should only have taken another three hours to get to Babson Park, but Al learned that the bus was going to crisscross the state on its way down to Miami.

"I thought to myself, *I don't want to go back and forth!* So, I told the bus driver I wanted to get off! I got off, and I hitchhiked down to Babson Park."

Some man who was going to Lake Wales picked him up. When they got there, Al asked, "Do you think you could take me a little further to Babson Park?"

"Why, of course!" the man replied.

About an hour later, the man dropped Al off in front of his father's house.

When Al knocked on the door, his father opened it and said, "What are you doing here? You're not supposed to be in until two o'clock!"

"Well, I'm here!"

•••

Al never used the swimsuit that he had bought in Detroit. In the first place, there were no sun-drenched beaches anywhere near Babson Park; and secondly, his father put him to work painting right away.

Al enjoyed being with his dad and big brother, and not having to go to school, but he didn't like painting houses. Working didn't bother him, just not that *kind* of work.

"Al didn't stay down there very long," Emy recalled, "because he had to get back. It was Christmas, and he had to buy something for Marie!"

When Al got back to Bridgeport, he went to Ashworth's Drugstore, where he saw a lovely music box that he wanted to buy for his girlfriend.

"Mr. Ashworth," he said to the storeowner, "I have no money, but I'll pay you something every week."

With Al's reputation in the community as a hard worker, Mr. Ashworth was sure Al would hold to his commitment, so he sold him the jewelry box on credit.

Marie was delighted with the gift.

During the remainder of the winter, Al saw Marie at church or church functions for young people. When spring arrived, he rode his bike over to see her as often as he could. In April, when he turned sixteen, he bought a car and saw Marie more often.

"Marie and I were in love with each other," Al explained, "but I was only sixteen. I thought I'd better go back to Florida for a while."

●●●

Although Al now had his own car, he knew it was not good enough to drive all the way to Florida, so he took the bus once again. Alden helped him to buy a car down there—an old DeSoto coupe. It wasn't as nice as Alden's Plymouth convertible, but it was a car, and the two enjoyed racing them on the newly built expressway toward Lake Wales.

"Well, I blew the motor in my car," Al recalled. "We tore the engine down, put new rings in it, and put it back together. It ran, but it was leaking water. Maybe we didn't put in a new head gasket. In the meantime, I was getting letters from Marie. We were writing back and forth to each other. I told Alden: 'I gotta go home!' I left him with a car that barely ran, so *he* had to finish paying it off!"

•••

While Al was building a relationship with Marie, his mother was also building a new relationship. His name was Clarence Dupuis, a local businessman and a Bridgeport justice of the peace. How the two met is lost to history, but they began dating on a regular basis. After a couple of years, they were married on August 22, 1954.

The day after the wedding, Al went to see Emy to tell her that he and Marie were going to get married.

"When our mother and stepdad came home from their honeymoon," Emy recalled, "I told them that Al and Marie were getting married."

But they weren't too surprised, Emy said. In fact, Al's mother was quite pleased.

According to Al, "Mom knew I was hanging around with a tough bunch, and she knew that if I was married, that would stop. Plus, she liked Marie."

Allan Roy Thieme and Marie Emma Scharrer were married on September 24, 1954.

"We were both seventeen," Al recalled, and Marie's parents had to sign for her because she had not yet reached the age of consent.

The same thing had had to be done when Emy married Max Goodman three years earlier, on May 6, 1951, and Alden married a Florida girl by the name of Larene Crawford, on November 6, 1953. Like Al, Emy was only seventeen years old when she got married, "but in June, I would have been eighteen," she said. Alden had just turned 18 in May, but Larene still had a few months to go.

Al and Marie's wedding was held in the little church that Al's father had started, and only close family members attended. Max Goodman was Al's best man, and Marie's sister, Shirley, was her maid of honor.

Aunt June and her husband, Maurice Finger, were there.

"I was my aunt's favorite nephew," Al recalled. "When her two children were small, I used to ride my bike out to Grandma's, and Aunt June and Uncle Moe lived at Grandma's house. When their son, Henry, was about four years old, I used to hook his little car up behind my bicycle, and I'd pull him up and down the road. For some reason, whenever little Henry said my name, it sounded more like 'Otto' than 'Allan,' so Aunt June began calling me Otto. Aunt June knew the Scharrers, she knew Marie, and she was so happy when we got married. Aunt June always thought the world of me."

So, by the time they were all eighteen, the three elder Thieme children were already married.

"We weren't teens very long!" is the way Emy put it.

•••

Practically penniless, Al borrowed some money from Marie's sister, Shirley, and bought a little house trailer for them to live in, parking it at the back of Pa Scharrer's home. It was so small, in fact, that it didn't even have a toilet! The newlyweds used a pot, which Al would empty in the woods behind the trailer.

"We were married!" he explained. "We were happy!"

Eventually, Joe Fehrenbach, the local plumber, "sold me a little tiny toilet," Al said. "There was a tiny closet in the bedroom of our little trailer, and I put that toilet in there. Eventually, I dug a hole, got some cement blocks, and built my own septic tank."

While Marie never complained about their living conditions, she was glad that she had a functioning toilet by the time their first child, Jill, was born early the following year.

Not long after, Al's stepfather found out that Jack Wander's Sunoco station—a combination gas station and living quarters—was going to be demolished or moved so that a new gas station could be built on that site.

"My stepdad bought that building," Al explained, "and

moved it half a mile to 4312 Williamson Road."

Then he graciously offered it to Al and Marie on a land contract.

"You can pay me over time," his stepdad told him.

"I pulled our trailer out behind that building," Al recalled. "Marie and I lived in the trailer for about three more months while I made the building into a livable home"

•••

During those first years, Al got jobs wherever he could. He worked at O'Dell's grocery store in Bridgeport and at the McIntyre Ice Cream company on Gratiot Street in Saginaw, putting ice cream in different size containers, making fudge bars and popsicles, and cleaning the freezer.

In the meantime, many of Al's friends, who were two or three years older than he was, got jobs at the Saginaw Steering Gear plant. Getting a job there was tantamount to striking gold in Alaska or oil in Texas! Not only did the company pay well, but it provided free health insurance and retirement benefits.

"You need to come and work with us at Saginaw Steering Gear!" his friends said to Al.

So, Al quit his job at the grocery store and applied for work at Saginaw Steering Gear. But to his surprise, they wouldn't hire him.

"I was only seventeen years old," he explained, "and they only hired people who were nineteen or older."

It was one of those times when Al's impulsiveness got the best of him.

As luck would have it, however, Joe Fehrenbach had noticed that Al had not been at the grocery store lately and wondered what had happened to him.

"Joe lived right next to the O'Dells' grocery store," Al explained. "Every afternoon, he'd come in the store and buy two Dutch Master cigars. He'd see me bagging groceries. I was the best bagger there ever was! He saw my work ethic."

One Sunday after church, a little after the Steering Gear debacle, Fehrenbach pulled Al aside.

"Al," he asked, "where you working now?"

"Mr. Fehrenbach," Al said, "I'm just doing a few odd jobs."

Fehrenbach replied in his thick German accent, "You come to work for me Monday morning, and learn to be a plumber. You need to learn a trade."

•••

Over the next five years, Al and Marie had five more children in quick succession, and they gave all of them, as with Jill, names starting with J: Joe, June, John, Jess, and Jack.

"There was no rhyme nor reason for it," Al explained. "Marie and I both liked the name Jill, Joe was named after Joe Fehrenbach, June was named after Aunt June, and we both liked the names John, Jess, and Jack."

The little house that Al had remodeled had three small bedrooms, but he made it work for his large family. Four boys slept in one bedroom, two girls slept in the second bedroom, and Al and Marie slept in the third bedroom. The whole family lived there for twelve years—until 1967.

In the meantime, Emy and Alden were having children of their own.

"I'd have one," Emy recalled. "Then Marie would have one. Then Alden would have one."

Eventually, Emy and Max had four girls: Waneta, Lynne, Mary, and Laura; and Alden and Larene had three boys and a girl: Jim, Elmer, Nancy, and Allen.

"Marie was a good Christian friend," Emy recalled. "She was like a sister. When we started having children, we would call each other every day about the daily little things that happen with mothers."

•••

Joe Fehrenbach was a one-man operation, installing plumbing in new homes all by himself. Occasionally, his son

Jack would help out, but Fehrenbach mostly worked alone.

"I worked for Joe Fehrenbach forty hours per week," Al explained. "We started at eight o'clock in the morning and got off at four-thirty—never any longer. I was bringing home about thirty-eight dollars a week."

That wasn't enough for a young married man with a family to support, so he got a part-time job at a gas station in Bridgeport, working at night.

"I wanted to learn the plumbing trade," he said. "I guess it was because my grandfather and father were tradespeople. When I worked with my dad in Florida, I didn't like painting. But when I worked for Mr. Fehrenbach, I was building something. Installing piping systems in a home is different in each house, and it was a challenge to find the best way to install piping."

Building and creating things is what appealed to Al, so it was fortunate that he didn't get a job at the GM plant, because he probably wouldn't have lasted long there anyway. He couldn't have done the repetitive labor, day in and day out.

•••

After working all day for Fehrenbach, Al would have dinner, then work at the gas station from 6:00 to 10:00 p.m. On Saturdays, he would work there all day. That brought in an additional twenty-eight dollars a week.

"This gas station was only to get gas," Al explained. "There was no service, and a lot of times I just sat there with nothing to do. There were only so many windows you could wash in a gas station. That's when I took a plumbing correspondence course. I'd study while I was waiting for somebody to get gas."

The correspondence course was a professional plumbing program offered by the International Correspondence Course of Scranton, Pennsylvania, and sanctioned by the state of Michigan. While it was too early for Al to be thinking of owning his own plumbing business, he soon realized that in order for him to make more money, he would have to become a master plumber,

Joe Fehrenbach, Al's plumbing mentor, in his later years
(courtesy Faith Luthern Church)

just like Joe Fehrenbach. But that was going to take some time. In order to become a master plumber, an apprentice had to work for a master plumber for three years, then pass the journeyman's test. After that, the journeyman had to work an additional two years in order to be eligible to take the master's test.

Fehrenbach must have expected Al to take that path, so he shouldn't have been too surprised when Al asked him if he had any books that he could borrow to begin studying for his journeyman's license. Nevertheless, Fehrenbach wasn't interested in cooperating.

"That's *my* job," he said. "Your job is to work!"

Fehrenbach's lack of support is what prompted Al to seek out another avenue to get his journeyman's license, and that's when he found out about the correspondence course. Luckily, he was able to study at the gas station at night.

After three years of studying, Al told Fehrenbach that he was ready to take the journeyman's test and asked him to fill out the necessary paperwork.

•••

The journeyman's test consisted of a written part and a hands-on part. For the written test, applicants had to know plumbing: the sizes of pipes, various angles of pipes, types of plumbing fixtures, and the amount of water every plumbing fixture required.

For the hands-on test, Al explained, "you had to 'wipe' a lead joint. We weren't using lead pipe then, but they tested us on that material, anyway. There was an inch-and-a-half lead pipe, you cut it in half, flared one end of one of the pieces, and put it into a stand. You had a pad that you put on your hand, then you'd pour hot, molten lead on the pad, and wipe it around the pipe."

Al practiced "wiping a joint" over and over, and his diligence paid off. The written test was straightforward, and he passed the hands-on test as well.

•••

Just as things were starting to go well, a recession gripped the country in the early part of 1957. While home construction would normally come to a halt in the winter months in Michigan, housing starts did not pick up when spring arrived, so Joe Fehrenbach was not getting any new plumbing jobs. He did his best to keep Al busy by having him rearrange his workshop and storage buildings, hoping that new work would soon come in. But it didn't, and he was forced to lay off Al.

Looking back at that time, Al appreciated what Fehrenbach had done for him.

"Joe was a very good person," he said. "He expected much and didn't believe in ever giving a compliment, but I had great respect for Mr. Fehrenbach."

For the next few years, Al and Alden did many different types of work, including small painting jobs, plumbing jobs, unloading trainloads of lumber in Birch Run, and clearing wooded lots.

•••

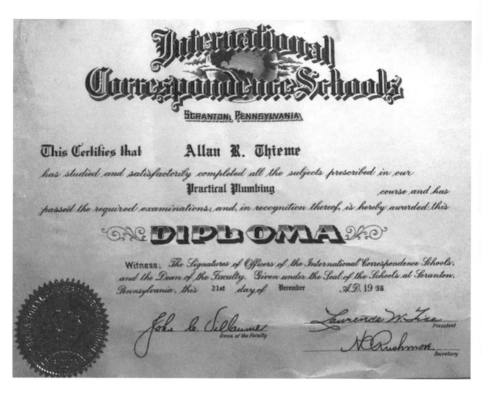

Al's plumbing correspondence school diploma

In December 1960, just as Al's mother was looking forward to a joyous holiday season with her growing family, tragedy struck.

"She was having some health problems," explained Emy. "They thought it was nerves, or something like that. She went to the hospital, the doctor was checking her over, and he noticed some weakness in her arm. 'There's something else going on here besides nerves,' he told her. When they ran more tests, they found that she had a brain tumor. She had surgery to remove it before Christmas, but in January it came back. She died a couple of months later, at the age of fifty-one."

The question was what to do with Miriam, who was now seventeen years old and almost completely helpless.

"We tried taking care of her by having her live with one of us for a while," Emy recalled, "but that didn't work. So, I told

Al's journeyman's license

the court, either you take care of one child, or you take care of fourteen, because by that time, Al had six, Alden had four, and I had four! So, Miriam became a ward of the state until she died," which was six years later at the age of twenty-two, beating the doctors' prediction by one year.

•••

Even though Alden was married and living in an apartment in Babson Park, he missed his little brother, and Al missed him, too.

"Why don't you come home for a couple of weeks?" Al said.

It was going to be just a brief visit, but after being back home among family, Alden decided to move back to Michigan permanently. Now that he and Al were both married and raising families, they had more in common than they ever had before. Not the least of which was that they were both unemployed!

Fortunately, they both got jobs as painters working for Elmer Fähndrich, who was a highly successful painting contractor. Although construction activity was down, Fähndrich was still able to pick up remodeling jobs here and there, both residential and commercial.

Over the next year or so, Al and Alden painted many homes as well as the Morley Building, the Bell Telephone Building, and a number of Marathon gas stations.

Even so, Fähndrich couldn't keep the two Thieme brothers busy all the time, so they picked up odd jobs whenever they could—painting jobs for Alden, and plumbing jobs for Al.

One time, they got a job unloading boxcars full of lumber in Birch Run. And those boxcars were filled up to the roof!

"We'd have to pull that lumber out one board at a time and stack it," Al recalled. "We did that for a few weeks until a boxcar full of twenty-four-foot-long two-by-twelves came in. It was terrible. Alden was good with numbers, and he started figuring what we were getting paid to unload that boxcar, and it came to about twenty cents an hour! So we quit."

They were a little hesitant to quit, since that was not their nature, but in this instance, the pay was just not worth their time.

•••

Whenever Al needed supplies for his sporadic plumbing jobs, he would go to Saginaw Plumbing & Heating Company, and got to know its owners, Mr. and Mrs. Tyner, very well.

"Wonderful people," Al said.

Mrs. Tyner, in particular, liked Al and recommend him to other plumbers or contractors who needed a good worker. One of those plumbers who took her advice was Tom Blower.

"I worked for Tom for a couple of years," Al recalled. "Then his business slowed down, and I was back doing small plumbing jobs with my old blue Ford pickup truck."

One of those jobs was for Herb Bronner, the owner of Bronner Lumber Company in Frankenmuth. While the lumber business was Bronner's primary operation, he also began new home construction. Whenever he built a new house, he would hire Al to do the plumbing work for him.

Unfortunately, Bronner wasn't building enough homes at the time to keep Al working on a regular basis. However, once more, Mrs. Tyner intervened.

Of all the plumbers and contractors who came into her business, she knew that Joe Katz was the busiest.

"You should hire Al Thieme, Joe," she told him.

When the two men met, Al told Katz that he would like to work for him, but he still wanted to do jobs for Herb Bronner.

"That's OK," Katz replied.

That arrangement went on for two years, and Bronner's business continued to grow over that time.

"Al," Bronner said one day, "you need to start your own business."

"But, Herb," Al replied, "I don't have a master's license."

"That's alright. I know a master plumber in Frankenmuth. I'll take out the permits, and you do the work."

"So, I left Joe Katz," Al said.

Al had never taken his eyes off his goal of becoming a master plumber, and six months later, he applied for his master's license.

•••

However, acquiring the master's license didn't go as easily as acquiring the journeyman's license had. Al passed the written part of the test, but failed the hands-on portion. Unlike the journeyman's test, the master's test required the applicant to successfully perform two hot-lead joints: a straight joint and a Y-joint.

"That's what flunked me on the master's test," Al explained. "I couldn't get that Y-joint right."

That was understandable, because the plumbing industry wasn't using those kinds of joints at that time, anyway. For some unknown reason, it was an archaic process that had been carried over from the old days.

"What we were working with then," Al explained, "was cast iron pipe, hub and spigot type pipe, and galvanized pipe. We never worked with lead. In fact, if we worked on a remodeling job, we'd replace any lead pipe."

Al passed the master's test the next time. He received his official Licensed Master Plumber certificate from the State Plumbing Board of Michigan in the summer of 1963. Almost immediately, he founded Thieme Plumbing & Heating.

"The business went well," Al explained. "It grew quickly."

•••

One of the reasons that Al's new company did well from the beginning was that he ran his operation efficiently and was always looking for faster ways to do things.

There must be a better way! he would say to himself.

"I was never satisfied with the normal ways of doing things," he said. "For example, I'd make pipes up ahead of time in my plumbing shop, whereas most plumbers made them up at the job, which was much more difficult. Also, when I got the blueprint of the house, I knew how many bathrooms and how much piping was needed. I had material at the small barn that I had converted to a warehouse in my backyard. We'd load what we needed for the job. We hardly ever had to go to the wholesale house to get material, which saved a lot of time. We would get to work before eight, so our truck would be the closest to the house. That also saved us time walking back and forth to the truck."

Al's penchant for finding ways to improve things not only made his plumbing work more efficient, but it would soon change the course of his life.

•••

"The first complete house plumbing job I did," Al recalled, "was for Mr. and Mrs. Weirauch. They built a big new home on Williamson Road in Bridgeport. I didn't have enough money

Al's master plumber license

to buy the supplies I needed, so Marie's sister loaned me the money."

That's why Al preferred working for contractors, at least in the beginning, since that way he didn't need to come up with his own funds to start a job.

Herb Bronner, of course, was Al's top priority, but he also began doing work for Charles Wellman, an old schoolmate of his, who had started his own construction company, and a couple of other builders in and around Saginaw.

"But never once did I ever go to Joe Fehrenbach's customers," Al said proudly.

It was a quality that he would always cherish: *Never slight someone who helps you.*

●●●

At first, Al was a one-man operation, just like Joe Fehrenbach.

Thieme Plumbing & Heating equipment and crew, 1966
(L-R): John Schultz, Floyd Schmitzer, John Goidosik, Al Thieme

Then he tried to hire apprentices to help him, but young men wanting to enter the plumbing field just didn't have the work ethic that Al had developed.

"I'd hire an apprentice, then he'd leave," Al explained. "Well, I was pretty tough to work with; I worked all the time. There was no such thing as time-and-a-half back then. No such thing as vacations. If we had to work Saturday and Sunday, we worked Saturday and Sunday!"

However, there was one other thing that was probably more disconcerting to new recruits than hard work.

"To get the blood flowing in the morning," as Al put it, he would play John Philip Sousa music. He would bring a record player and a stack of records, and then he and his crew would unload the trucks, run pipe, and install bathtubs and toilets to the sounds of "The Liberty Bell March," "El Capitán," and "The Stars and Stripes Forever"!

Listening to that energetic music first thing in the morning did not sit well with the young crew members.

"So they didn't last long with me," Al admitted.

70

Al Thieme in his plumbing uniform

He wasn't too concerned about losing employees, however, because there were other plumbers in the area who were willing to pitch in when he needed it.

"Two brothers, Tom and John Schulz, were always ready to help me," Al recalled. "They were both journeyman plumbers. Occasionally, Harold McDonald and Dick Letherer would also help whenever I called them."

In fact, when Al had worked for Joe Katz, Letherer was working for the veteran plumber, too. But after work in the afternoon, they would go out together to find side plumbing jobs to earn extra money. Al would have done that on his own, but having Letherer there with him made the work more enjoyable—and on one occasion, lifesaving.

"Dick Letherer and I," Al recalled, "were finishing the plumbing in this new house that had a crawlspace, and there were about three inches of water in the crawl space. We had everything done except connecting a wire to the water pump in the crawl space. The electricians had left a wire hanging there for the pump, and I decided to connect the wire. I went to the fuse box to shut off the wire going to the pump, but I couldn't

Al and Marie's family: Marie, June, John, Joe, Jess, Jill, Al, Jack

find the right switch. No problem. If I just touch one wire at a time, I'll be OK. I had the main wire in one hand, and then I touched one of the two wires. Because I was in water, it got ahold of me. I couldn't do anything! I was trying to talk, but nothing would come out!"

Luckily, Dick saw what was happening and realized that Al was being electrocuted.

"He grabbed a piece of wood" Al explained, "and knocked the wire out of my hand. I had a pocket watch, and that watch never worked again. I learned from that. When you're in water, do not work with electricity unless it is turned off. We did not finish the job that night."

•••

When Emy noticed the trouble her little brother was having recruiting and retaining good help, she made a suggestion.

"You know," she told him, "Floyd Schmitzer is a master plumber. He works for Leslie Hardware in Frankenmuth. He's a good person. You might be able to hire him."

Emy and Floyd knew each other because they had gone to Saginaw's Arthur Hill High School together.

"I didn't know him well," she recalled, "but sometimes the Frankenmuth guys would pick up the Bridgeport girls as they were coming through Bridgeport on the way to school."

Schmitzer was born and raised in Frankenmuth, spoke fluent German, and started working for Leslie Hardware during high school. He learned how to repair appliances, do electrical work and plumbing, and eventually earned his master plumber's license. By the time he went into military service during the Korean War, he was earning one dollar an hour.

When he returned, Mr. Leslie "upped me to a dollar-twenty-five an hour," Schmitzer recalled. "Then, one day, I was in an apartment, working on a boiler in the basement, when Al came along. I didn't know Al. 'How would you like to come to work for me?' he asked."

"Well, I don't know," Schmitzer said. "I have a pretty good job here."

"How would you like to earn four-fifty an hour?"

"When do I quit?" Schmitzer quickly replied.

"Al offered me that much difference! I couldn't afford *not* to leave and work with him."

"Floyd was about three years older than I," Al explained. "We got along together so well. It's amazing how he and I worked together. We just knew what each other would do. He was more mechanical than I was. He was a better plumber. He could do sheet metal work. He could do electrical work. But I was creative. I'd always find a faster, better way of doing things. I developed systems."

They were a perfect combination.

With Al and Floyd as the core of the business, they added

a few more apprentices, which allowed the company to take on bigger projects, which in turn generated more income for everyone. Al seldom had more than five men working for him. He, Floyd, and two apprentices worked on new homes. A third plumber, Chuck Baumer, handled the service work.

•••

Things were going well for Al Thieme. He bought a farm-style house on the Dixie Highway, not far from where he and Marie had been living, and remodeled it. Some of his children were sad when they moved, but once they saw how much more room they would have, they quickly forgot their old house.

For a vacation home, Al and Alden bought a cottage together near Harrison, Michigan, a small rural town in a heavily wooded area, ninety miles northwest of Bridgeport.

Having a cottage "Up North," as Michiganders call the vast area of the state north of Saginaw, was a sign of accomplishment. It signified that Al and Alden were making enough money not only to own a home and a car, but a vacation home as well.

In fact, Al and Alden's "cottage" was a 2,000-square-foot, four-bedroom ranch house, located on the shore of Budd Lake. It had an expansive living room, and a dock ran from the shoreline out into the water, where both of their motorboats were tied up.

Al and Alden went to the cottage only in the summertime. They would go there to work on site and clean the yard. But mostly, Al said, "we went there to drink beer and water ski. Alden had four kids, I had six kids, and we'd go up together. One time, we were pulling eight skiers behind the boat. The kids were all little."

Every once in a while, Al would put one of his kids on his shoulders and ski on *one* ski.

Al also owned a small cabin in the highly forested area of South Branch, Michigan, where he and Alden, along with their close friends Bob Zelle and Dick Vance and their wives, would go deer hunting in the fall and snowmobiling in the winter.

"One day," Zelle recalled, "we were racing across a field in our snowmobiles, and when we got to the end of the field, we looked around, and Marie wasn't behind Al! She had fallen off about halfway back."

Al had met Dick Vance when they were teenagers in Bridgeport. There was a creek that ran through Uncle Roy's farm, and when it froze over in the winter, the local kids would ice-skate on it. That's where the two met. Later on, when Al became a plumber, Dick became a flooring contractor, and they would often meet on construction job sites.

"We just gravitated together," Al said.

Dick and Sue Vance had seven children, so with Al's kids and Alden's kids, when they all went up to the cottage, it made for one lively gathering!

Bob Zelle had not grown up in the area, but ended up in Bridgeport, where his father owned the Case farm equipment dealership, which was just up the Dixie Highway from Al's house. The two men saw each other often at Chamber of Commerce meetings, and eventually became close friends.

"Bob was a good businessman," Al recalled, "and a good salesman. He could sell anything!"

•••

At home, the Thieme family had dinner together every night, went to church together nearly every Sunday, and, in the years before TV and video games, played cards in the evenings and played outdoors in the afternoons and on weekends.

"My main memory of family games," recalled Al's daughter Jill, "was our weekly exercise challenge. We did push-ups, sit-ups, jump rope, and would stand on our heads. We got twenty-five cents for first place, ten cents for second place, and a nickel for third place. The other game was Kick the Can. I remember it well because it was a game that Dad would also play with us. Something very funny I remember was the time I was manning the can and was pretty good at catching everyone. The Zelle family was visiting, and both Dad and Bob Zelle were playing with us. I had pretty much caught everyone, except for Dad and Bob. All of a sudden, I saw a shoulder from behind the house, and I recognized Dad's shirt. I called out, 'One, two, three on Dad behind the house!' Then Bob jumped out with Dad's shirt on! The two guys had switched shirts, and my mistaken identity set everyone free!"

•••

Around that same time, one of Al's schoolboy friends came back into his life. Jim Ecker, the young man who had killed the storekeeper, was getting out of prison. He had been sentenced to life at Ionia State Prison, but since he was so young when he committed the crime and he had exhibited good behavior over the previous ten years, the court was willing to let him out on probation if someone would be responsible for him.

"But nobody would!" Al explained.

Ecker's brother was living in New York somewhere, and his father, who was living in Saginaw, refused to have anything to do with him. That's when a parole officer contacted Al and Marie.

Over the years, Al and Marie had visited Jim to see how he was doing; that's why the prison official contacted them.

"Will you take him in?" the official asked.

At first, they were reluctant, but Al knew that he himself had come precariously close to being in the same situation; so, after talking it over, Al and Marie decided to take Jim in.

We're already caring for six, they thought. *What's one more?*

Jim lived with the Thiemes for about a year.

"We helped him to get a car," Al said. "He ended up getting married, and he stayed on the straight for the rest of his life."

•••

After a full day of cooking, cleaning, doing dishes, and helping with the kids' homework, Marie Thieme was usually exhausted. But after a good night's sleep, she would wake up the next morning fully refreshed.

However, one day in the summer of 1965, Marie became concerned about her health. For a while, she had noticed that she was getting more exhausted than usual. Some feeling of being tired was normal after taking care of a family of eight all day, but she understood *that* kind of exhaustion. *This* exhaustion was different—deeper and more unrelenting. When the fatigue persisted, she made an appointment with Dr. Peter Chisena, the family's physician in Bridgeport—the same doctor who had cut off Don Reimer's finger years before.

"Well, you know," the doctor said, "you've had a lot of children really close together, so your system is just run-down."

But then another unusual symptom appeared.

"We all learned to water ski at our cottage on Budd Lake," Al explained. "But when Marie tried to water ski, she just couldn't balance. Also, that summer, when she would be out on the beach, lying in the sun, she could hardly walk back to the cottage. The sun took all of the energy out of her. We thought, *This is really strange.* Well, we lived with it. Then, that winter, we went to Max and Emy's house to go ice-skating. Max had built an ice-skating rink in his backyard. Marie put on her ice skates, but she couldn't balance, and she had always ice-skated before. We then knew that something had to be wrong. I took her to the Henry Ford Hospital in Detroit, and they said that there was something wrong with her nervous system. It could be multiple sclerosis, they said, but they weren't sure."

Multiple sclerosis is a disease that attacks the protective lining of nerve fibers in the body, which then causes communication problems between the brain and other parts of the body. Symptoms can include weakness, fatigue, and lost control of the arms and legs.

To verify their suspicions, the doctors suggested that the Thiemes visit the renowned Mayo Clinic in Rochester, Minnesota.

"Back in 1966," Al explained, "doctors didn't know much

about multiple sclerosis."

When the Mayo doctors examined Marie, they had the same suspicions as the doctors in Detroit. However, the only way to confirm their diagnosis was to perform a lumbar puncture, more commonly known as a spinal tap. Analysis of the fluid determines if it has certain proteins that are attacking the nervous system rather than defending it.

Unfortunately, the results came back positive. Marie did indeed have multiple sclerosis.

•••

When Al and Marie returned to Bridgeport, they went to see Dr. Chisena to tell him what the doctors at the Mayo Clinic had found.

"What can we expect?" Al asked.

"Well," the doctor explained, "Marie will continue to get weaker, and won't be able to walk, and won't be able to do anything. She could live for two years; she could live for ten or fifteen years. We just don't know enough about multiple sclerosis yet."

"Doctor," Al exclaimed, "you've got to find something to do for her! We've got six kids!"

Dr. Chisena was helpless. All he could suggest was that the Thiemes contact the National Multiple Sclerosis Society in New York for advice and guidance.

Realizing that there was nothing they could do, Al and Marie took it all in stride.

"We said, 'OK, we have MS,'" Al explained. "'We have kids to take care of and a plumbing business to run. We can't let some silly thing like multiple sclerosis stand in our way. Let's get on with life!'"

•••

"I remember the day I heard about it," recalled Emy. "I was outside, hanging up clothes and singing a Christian hymn."

Then she heard the phone ringing in the house and ran in to

answer it. That is when she heard the devastating diagnosis.

"I was shocked," she said.

Emy couldn't remember who called her, but it must have been Marie herself, since they were very close friends.

"It wasn't Al," she said, "because he was always working and too busy to call anyone. We knew of one other person in Bridgeport who had MS, and they were in really bad shape. In other words, we knew the consequences. We prayed and asked for direction."

•••

Al may have been ready to "get on with life," but Marie couldn't get her diagnosis out of her mind. The thought of losing her ability to walk frightened her and losing her ability to use her hands frightened her even more. She asked Al to buy her a piano or an organ, so she could exercise her hands and fingers. Perhaps, she thought, that would ward off any effects of MS. She didn't know how to play either instrument, but she would learn.

Al was sympathetic, but he was in no position financially to buy a piano or an organ, since he was investing all his money at the time in buying trucks, tools, and materials for his business. One morning, as they were getting ready for work, Al mentioned his predicament to Floyd Schmitzer.

Somehow, Al scraped together the funds to buy Marie a small electric organ at Grinnell's Music Store in downtown Saginaw as a Christmas present. It arrived on Christmas Eve day.

That evening, Floyd called.

"Al," he said, "Joan and I want to come over. We have a Christmas present for you and Marie."

Floyd and his wife had also bought an organ for Marie!

Al and Marie were shocked by their kind and generous gesture, but they didn't need two organs.

"What do we do now?" Marie asked.

"We have to keep the one that Floyd and Joan bought you," Al replied. "Let's donate the other one to our church; they've been in need of another organ."

When Al told Pastor Brueggeman, the minister exclaimed, "Oh, this is wonderful! We definitely need it. But we really need a bigger size!"

Al traded the organ in for a bigger one and gave it to the church.

The organ turned out to be exactly what Marie needed to take her mind off her diagnosis.

"She never complained," Al said. "She was a trooper. Hardly ever would she cry about it. When Marie would feel bad during the night, she'd get up and play the organ."

•••

In the meantime, Al studied books about MS, hoping that there was some cure, some remedy that would help Marie. A book by Edgar Cayce—a self-proclaimed clairvoyant, who answered questions on subjects as varied as healing, reincarnation, and the afterlife—stated that eating unprocessed food and raw milk from farms was beneficial, so Marie followed those recommendations.

A doctor in California said that he had had good results with MS by clearing blocked carotid arteries in the neck. But that didn't help.

The couple even flew to Germany to spend four days at a clinic that specialized in treating MS—also to no avail.

Al and Marie soon realized that their efforts were having no positive results.

•••

Marie had always prepared breakfast for Al before he went off to work. But now Al explained, "it was too tough for her to get up early in the morning." So he began going to the local restaurant for breakfast.

One morning in the spring of 1967, Carl DeMaet, who owned an excavating company in Bridgeport, mentioned to Al that a couple who were planning to go to Mexico on vacation with him and his wife, Mary, couldn't make it.

"Marie and I will go with you!" Al said spontaneously.

"I never had any idea of going on vacation, especially to Mexico," Al said. "The only vacation I could think of was taking a long weekend at our cottage."

DeMaet said they would be leaving in two weeks.

●●●

"When we got into Mexico City," Al recalled, "it was quite warm, and the excitement caused Marie's fatigue to get worse, so we rented a wheelchair. We were in Mexico about two weeks: Mexico City, Guadalajara, Guanajuato, and Puerto Vallarta. Marie could walk, but to do anything for any length of time, she had to use the wheelchair."

Pushing Marie around in a wheelchair was quite an eye-opener for Al.

"When we went into a restaurant," he explained, "they wouldn't look at her at all. When they asked for our order, they wouldn't ask her what she wanted, they would ask *me* what she wanted. They'd always seat us by the door because a wheelchair was too wide to fit between the tables. Sitting in that wheelchair, Marie looked weaker than I had ever seen her. I was surprised how people treated her. No one smiled at us."

●●●

As we have seen, anything that was inefficient or ineffective had always been a challenge to Al Thieme, and the wheelchair that he was pushing Marie around in was an example. It was obvious to Al that this type of wheelchair would never give her the freedom and mobility she wanted.

"Marie," Al said, "when we get home, I'll find something for you to use so that no one will have to push you. There must be a better way!"

CHAPTER 3

A Little Machine

"I saw something at the pickle factory!"
—Carl DeMaet

As the Thiemes were flying home from Mexico, Al began to think about a new kind of wheelchair for Marie. It had to be compact, he thought, not bulky like the wheelchair he had been pushing her around in for the past two weeks. It also had to be attractive and battery-powered.

In his office, which was off the living room of their home, he cut off a large piece of paper from a roll of wallpaper, laid it on a table that was next to his desk, and began to sketch on the blank back of it. His drawing of the device had one wheel in front, a T-shaped steering handle, a seat affixed to a vertical post, and two wheels in back, all attached to a flat platform.

"I'm not an artist," Al recalled, "and it wasn't detailed."

Nevertheless, that sketch, which he drew in the summer of 1967, had all the critical elements of a brand-new way for people with walking limitations to move around.

Making a rudimentary sketch is one thing, but getting it made into a three-dimensional form is quite another.

"I needed to find an engineer," Al said.

A friend of Al's recommended an engineering and development company in Saginaw run by two men, Gene Fisher and Gerald "Jerry" McMaster, who had a small office on State Street. But their main development center was in a big building on Lawndale Road on the outskirts of town.

"They would engineer things," Al explained, "and put prototypes together."

Al met with both men, but it was Gene who quickly took over the project.

"I didn't get to know Jerry very well," Al said. "Gene had a brilliant mind. He was quiet, honest, and a very caring and patient man. He had to be patient to work with me. Because of our differences, we complemented each other, which made us a good team."

Gene Fisher had a large family, who lived in a big three-story, white-clapboard house in Freeland, a little town fifteen miles northwest of Bridgeport. For reasons that Al never understood or had long forgotten, Gene had Al meet him at his house; not at his office or development center. Gene had a well-equipped workshop in his basement, and he was going to work on Al's project there—independently from his business.

"He was excited by the concept," Al explained, "probably because we were doing this for handicapped people—people who had trouble walking. That appealed to his nature."

They made an agreement for Al to pay Gene on an hourly basis.

"I tried to convince Gene to take stock in my company, but

he said, 'Al, I can't. I need the money.'"

With all of Gene's kids running around, Al could well understand that.

It took Gene nine months to complete the prototype. He and Al would meet at least every other week. Gene would often drive to Bridgeport to see Al.

"He knew that it was best for him to come to me," Al explained. "That way, I could always keep working to make money in the plumbing business, so that I could pay him!"

•••

The first component that Gene started on was the base or platform. He and Al wanted it to be both strong and lightweight, so he made it out of aluminum. The frame was made out of round aluminum tubing, and welded to it was an aluminum sheet with folded edges. A steel axle was affixed to the rear of the platform, which had hard rubber tires attached at either end.

The next part they designed was the seat assembly, which turned out to be both simple and effective. It consisted of a steel tube, a metal plate, and a fiberglass seat. The beauty of this design was that the seat was not only lightweight, but it was attached to the platform with a hinge, which allowed it to be folded down for easy transport.

The last and most challenging component that they designed was the drive system, which they later called the "drivehead." It was here that Gene's electrical engineering talents came to the fore. The drive had to be compact and lightweight, and swivel with the T-handle controlled by the operator. In other words, the drive needed both to propel the device and to steer it.

Gene designed a drive that consisted of two small 12-volt electric motors, connected by two cog belts through a slip clutch. Switches activated by a shaft that came down through the T-handle controlled the motors.

"To go slow," Al explained, "we would put twelve volts into one motor; to go faster, we would put twelve volts into both motors. It was really clever."

Once the drive had been completed, Gene covered it with an aluminum shroud, from the wheel to just below the crossbar of the T-handle.

The next question was where to put the battery. A conventional automobile battery was too big and too heavy, but Gene found a motorcycle battery that fit perfectly.

When Gene installed the battery and activated the thumb lever switch, the motors turned, and the machine moved! It had two forward speeds, no brakes, and no reverse.

"It didn't need a reverse," Al explained. "How many times do you walk backward?"

Gene was more excited than Al was, "because," as Al said, "*he* was the one who had put this thing together. All the time, I expected it to work, and when it did, I didn't have any emotions—except, 'What took so long?'"

•••

Gene brought the prototype to Bridgeport to show Marie.

"Let me try it!" she exclaimed. "This is really nice!"

"Marie was somewhat mechanical to begin with," Al recalled. "She took right to it."

Al's father happened to be there, too, since he had come up from Florida to work with Alden for the summer.

"What color should we paint it, Dad?" Al asked.

"I think it would look good blue," he said.

•••

Interestingly, Al, Gene, and Marie had never referred to the device as a "wheelchair." In fact, said Al, "we had never referred to it as anything!'"

But just as people name their boats or cars or planes, Al and Marie wanted to call the device something. It was Marie who came up with the perfect name. Since they had been in Mexico when they realized that Marie would need a wheelchair to get around, she said, "Why don't we call it *Amigo*, because that's exactly what it is to me—'a friend.'"

•••

Once the prototype was completed and was operating satisfactorily, Al took it to John Learman, a patent attorney in Saginaw, to have him apply for a patent. After carefully analyzing the device, Learman concluded that the whole machine could not be patented, because it was simply a platform with some wheels. The drive, however, was a different matter. He submitted the paperwork for the drive design on behalf of Gene Fisher and Allan R. Thieme. A patent was issued to them on March 16, 1971.

•••

Although Al came up with the idea that would turn into a revolutionary wheelchair design, he gives full credit to Gene Fisher for its development.

"He was the guy who put this thing together," Al explained. "Gene was helping me end up with what I envisioned. He was able to build what I imagined, and he was excited about the whole concept."

There is no question that both men were delighted with the result, but Al Thieme gave credit where credit was due, which is a testament to his integrity and self-confidence.

•••

As Al looked back on the development of his mobility invention, he became philosophical. Why did it come to him so

The First Amigo designed and built
by Al Thieme and Gene Fisher

easily? Why a front-drive system, and not a rear-drive system? Why did he choose three wheels instead of four?

"As I look at so many things in my life," he explained, "it has made me a very strong believer that there is some Almighty power guiding me. I'm not smart, but I think there was a plan laid out for me in my life. I was always curious, so this Almighty power put this design in my path, knowing that I was curious enough to pick it up and run with it."

The fact that the unique design had a platform on which to sit, a foldable seat, a front-wheel-drive, and three wheels was certainly out of the norm, which may suggest that there was indeed some "force" guiding Al.

"When I was young," he recalled, "I had a two-wheeled scooter, where you stand on it with one foot and pedal with the other. But my device had to be more stable, so I put two wheels where the person sits. Having one wheel in front made the machine very compact and maneuverable, so it could easily get around in a home, even in a bathroom. If you had two wheels out front, it would not have been very functional. It just didn't enter my mind to make it a four-wheeler!"

•••

Marie started using the Amigo immediately—first, just around the house, especially toward the end of the day, when she became fatigued. Then she started taking it to the grocery store, to the mall, to school functions with her children, and to local Multiple Sclerosis Society meetings.

"Her life changed tremendously," Al said.

After returning from Mexico, Marie had joined the Saginaw chapter of the National Multiple Sclerosis Society, just as Dr. Chisena had suggested. Al didn't go to those meetings in the beginning because he was too busy with the plumbing business, and Marie could still drive a car at that time.

At first, Marie didn't know what to expect at those meetings, but it probably wasn't what she had pictured. The group wasn't large—perhaps ten or twelve couples—but half of the people there were using wheelchairs, and the other half were using walkers. With the wheelchairs, either the husband was pushing his wife, or the wife was pushing her husband.

When Al eventually went to a meeting, he found it depressing.

"The subjects they talked about were kind of a downer," he said. "I told Marie, 'I'm not going to any more of those meetings!'"

The meetings were indeed depressing—that is, until Marie finally took her Amigo to one for the first time. Everybody perked up when she came whizzing into the room.

"What is it, Marie?" they asked excitedly. "Where did you

get it?"

"Al made it for me!" she told them proudly.

Whatever topic had been on the agenda that evening was quickly abandoned to talk about Marie's new contrivance. She enthusiastically told the other members how Al had developed it and, more importantly, *why* he had developed it: to give her something that would not only allow her to get around on her own, but would also be pleasing to look at.

The couples could not agree more, and they all began asking her if Al could build one for them.

Marie was so excited when she told Al what had happened at the MS meeting.

"You've got to build more of these!" she exclaimed.

"No way!" he replied. "I'm too busy with the plumbing business."

That probably would have been the end of the story, but then Carl DeMaet called Al.

●●●

Not far up the Dixie Highway from Al's house was the Vlasic pickle factory, an expansive one-story building, where locally grown cucumbers would go in one end, and bottled pickles would come out the other. The plant was so big that the employees used little electric carts to get around, which looked surprisingly like Marie's Amigo!

The little carts were called JETs—an acronym for Jiffy Errand Trucks—and were manufactured by the Kysor Industrial Corporation in Cadillac, Michigan, a mostly tourist town 120 miles northwest of Bridgeport. The JETs, which were painted bright yellow, had three wheels—two in the rear and a powered one in the front. They also had a T-shaped drive handle and a battery right behind the front wheel. The only difference between a JET and Al's machine—except for the color—was that the JET's operator stood up to drive it.

One day, when DeMaet was at the Vlasic factory to do some excavation work, he saw people riding around on JETs and called Al.

"I'm doing some work at the pickle factory," he said excitedly. "You've got to come over and see the stand-up cart they're using. It's similar to what you built for Marie."

Obviously intrigued, Al went right over. He couldn't believe how similar his Amigo was to the little carts running around the factory. They didn't have a seat, but other than that, they were almost identical to the Amigo.

Al called Kysor and made an appointment with its president, Ray Weigel.

Al was excited about the JET because he was thinking that it could be a backup in case Marie's Amigo proved to be unreliable.

"I had no desire to start a company," he said emphatically. "I loved the plumbing business. We were doing very well. I just wanted to keep Marie mobile."

●●●

In April 1968, Al drove up to Kysor's main office in downtown Cadillac. It was not a large building, but it had a pristine setting on the shore of Lake Cadillac.

He met Ray Weigel in his office, which had a nice view of the lake and a number of large photographs hanging on the walls, showing the various Kysor plants that were located throughout the world.

"I thought Kysor was a small company that just made the JET," Al recalled. "But they're a big company. They make radiator shutters, air-conditioning units, fuel tanks, and other parts for large semi-trucks."

When he told Weigel the story about Marie and the little machine that he had built for her, he "was quite intrigued," Al said.

"We have two models," Weigel explained, "a big one and a small one. You can go over to the factory and pick out the one you want to use. We'll sell it to you at cost."

The small model was the one that Al had seen at the pickle factory.

"I liked the small one," he explained, "so I bought it."

Al paid $150 for it.

•••

When Al took the JET over to Gene Fisher's house, he explained what had happened, and asked Gene to revamp Kysor's machine into a backup model for Marie. Gene instantly agreed, so the two men once again worked under the same arrangement that they had had while building the Amigo prototype.

Since the JET and Al's prototype were similar, not much revamping was required. The first and most obvious step was to move the battery from the front of the platform to the rear and add a seat post. When that was done, it left a gaping hole in the front of the platform, exposing the drive mechanism, which needed to be covered to protect the driver's feet.

Gene made a shell out of fiberglass to cover the hole, but Al wasn't happy with its design.

"This looks clunky, Gene," he said bluntly. "It has to look attractive. It has to be pretty."

Gene was a little disappointed, but he understood Al's point.

"We went through five different renditions," Al explained, "until we got the lines of the cowling just right."

All the hard work not only produced an attractive cover but also an unexpected benefit.

"As Gene was working on those molds and forming them," Al said, "he attached a grinding tip to the end of the shaft of a spare JET motor to grind away material. One time, when he reattached the motor to the battery, he accidentally reversed the positive and negative poles, and the motor went in reverse!"

Gene immediately got on the phone.

"Al," he exclaimed, "we can run the motor in reverse!"

At that moment, the two men realized that they could make the new version go forward or backward. No longer would Marie have to push herself backward with her foot. (She still had some strength in her legs at that time.)

After a little more experimenting, Al and Gene discovered that by touching the two wires together, the motor turned into a generator, slowing the JET down while recharging the battery.

That phenomenon, now known as regenerative or dynamic braking, is a feature of all electric vehicles today, but Al and Gene discovered it in the 1960s.

Now the little machine could go forward, backward, and stop! And while it was stopping, it would recharge the battery.

Al was concerned whether this would burn out the motor, so he called an engineer at Kysor.

"Will it hurt the motor if we run it in reverse," Al asked.

"No, probably not," the engineer replied. "But it will have 20 percent less power in reverse, because of the way the magnets are placed around the armature."

"That's good!" Al exclaimed, always looking at the positive. "I want it to go slower in reverse anyway!"

The last improvement that Al and Gene made in converting the JET into an Amigo was to make the seat swivel.

When Al saw people in conventional wheelchairs, they almost always looked miserable. They could get around, but most of the time they would just sit there, slouched down. If they wanted to get out of the chair, that was difficult because the footrests were in the way. And it was almost impossible for them to turn from side to side because the armrests obstructed their movement. They were all but trapped in a device that was supposed to help them. Al wanted more total body movement for Marie.

"With the Amigo," he explained, "I realized that it had to have a swivel seat. That way, Marie could easily move from side to side or turn all the way around with ease. And with her hands up on the T-handlebar, she would sit up straight. Plus, with the swivel seat, she'll be moving all the time, from her toes to her fingertips! That will be very therapeutic for her."

All these innovations turned the Amigo into an even more useful machine. The swivel seat allowed Marie to easily transfer from the Amigo to a car seat or a kitchen chair. More importantly, she could now *back* into a bathroom, swivel the seat, and effortlessly slide onto a toilet seat.

The process of converting the JET into a wheelchair was not as involved as creating the first prototype, so Al and Gene were pleased with the outcome.

The new Amigo weighed 98 pounds and consisted of four major components: the handle, which weighed four pounds; the seat assembly, which weighed eighteen pounds; the battery, which weighed twenty-three pounds; and the platform (which included the drive mechanism), which weighed fifty-three pounds. All of those components could simply and quickly be disassembled without any tools for easy transfer into the trunk of a car for transport. Even so, many Amigo users (including Marie) did not have the strength or physical stability to lift those components into the trunk of their car. So Al developed a trunk-lift, an electric crane of sorts, that was bolted to the trunk floor and could lift the Amigo into the trunk.

Being able to disassemble the Amigo so simply allowed it to be shipped easily as well. The seat assembly was placed in one box, and the platform assembly, battery, and handle were placed in another. Before the platform assembly was placed in the box, it was enveloped in a large clear plastic bag, with the open end twisted and sealed with a red ribbon and bow.

"I want the customer to think they're opening a Christmas present!" Al said.

If customers weren't surprised by that, then they surely must have been surprised when they saw their name affixed to the cowl, right above the serial number.

•••

When Marie used the new and improved Amigo, she was very pleased with it, and so was Al. He wrote a letter to Ray Weigel, informing him of the progress that he had made in just the past few weeks.

"Thank you for all the help on the JET," he wrote. "My wife has found the converted JET a big help in getting around."

•••

While Al had no intention of making a business out of building Amigos, as he had told Marie quite emphatically, something changed his mind. He had seen how much happier Marie was as she scooted around on her Amigo. By now her walking was more limited, and her Amigo gave her independence. It was almost as if she weren't handicapped at all. She could do just about everything a perfectly able-bodied person could do— except climb stairs.

"It was a very unique machine," Al said. "There was nothing like it. It was very similar to when the first cars were built.

Everybody used a horse; then here comes this car. People would look at it, and they'd talk about it. The Amigo was like that."

When Al saw the transformation that had taken place in Marie's disposition, that compelled him to build more Amigos.

"My goal," he said, "was to see other people continue to live their life and go on doing what they had been doing, as Marie did. How nice it was that I didn't have to push Marie around. How nice it was to see that she could take care of the house, fix meals, and do things with the children. At first, I said no, but then I felt a greater purpose calling me, so I might as well form a business. And we had a nice name for the product. We'll call the company Amigo Sales, Inc."

Now there was one more decision for Al to make: he needed to come up with a catchphrase that would tell the public what an Amigo was. Marie quickly came up with the name "Miracle Vehicle," since that was exactly what it was to her. However, Al was reluctant, thinking that was too nebulous. They both thought about it some more and finally came up with the slogan: "The Friendly Wheelchair."

•••

Operating a plumbing business is very different from building a manufacturing, sales, and service company, as Al Thieme was about to find out. There would be many days over the next thirty-five years that caused him much stress, but no one knows what the future will bring, and Al never thought much about it.

"That's both my strength and my weakness," he said. "I just take what comes."

CHAPTER 4

The Amigo Company

"Very busy, very broke."
—Al Thieme's Journal

After Attorney BJ Humphrey drew up the corporate papers, Amigo Sales, Incorporated, informally known as the Amigo Company, officially came into existence on November 12, 1968. Al wasted no time getting to work. He ordered business cards, sold $1,000 worth of Amigo stock to Alden, Bob Zelle, and Dick Vance to raise some cash, and ordered two JETs from Kysor Corporation. Gus Stricker, the manager of the Buena Vista branch of the Frankenmuth Bank, gave Al a loan of $7,500 and a $10,000 line of credit on his signature alone.

•••

When Al ran his own plumbing business, it was pretty straightforward—hire a few workers and go to work. However, by starting a completely new company and building an entirely new product, he was entering unknown waters and had to learn many new skills, such as public speaking, selling, managing, accounting, and marketing. All entrepreneurs have to learn many of those same skills, but since Al was going to be operating both a manufacturing company and a sales company, he had to wear a lot more hats than the typical entrepreneur.

Whatever skills he had to acquire, he learned on his own. For sales, he took Dale Carnegie classes, recommended by his good friend Bob Zelle. To help expand his management skills, he joined the Bridgeport Chamber of Commerce, the Manufacturers Association, and the Manufacturers Core Group. And he joined Toastmasters International to learn public speaking. Every Thursday night, he was at the Saginaw YMCA to attend the weekly Toastmasters meeting. While he was never shy when speaking to people, the skills he learned at Toastmasters would teach him how to speak confidently and clearly.

While the classes and organizations helped, Al knew that he needed to learn more about business, about successful businesspeople, and what it takes to be successful, so he read books and articles every spare moment he had. Ironically, for a man who shunned school, he was now reading three to six books a month.

Along with running two companies, attending classes, organizing meetings, reading books, and helping Marie to raise a family, Al forced himself to write something in his journal every day. Up to the time that he created the Amigo Company, he had never thought of keeping a journal, but something in the back of his mind, perhaps a sense of providence, compelled him to do so now. Even after putting in an exhausting day at work, he made sure that the last thing he did before the day was over was to recap the day's events in his journal.

•••

To transform the JETs into Amigos, Al set up shop in two garages on his property—a two-car garage that was off to the side of the house and a one-car garage behind the house. He completely disassembled and reassembled the JETs in the two-car garage and set up a welding and fabrication shop in the one-car garage. There was also a barn farther down the driveway, which is where Al kept his plumbing supplies and equipment.

During the early years of Amigo Company, Al normally did all of the work transforming the JETs into Amigos.

"Working an average of 55 hours a week at Amigo and 21 hours a week at plumbing," he wrote in his journal.

He had to keep working at the plumbing business because that was where the money was coming in.

Seeing how hard Al was working, Alden, Dick Vance, and Bob Zelle began to help out when they could—usually on nights and weekends. They didn't ask to be paid; they just wanted to help their buddy, so they could all go out and have some fun.

"Let's get these done, so we can go snowmobiling!" Zelle said.

But the work eventually became too much for Al and his part-time helpers. It was time to hire a few employees.

•••

Dick Kern and a man called "Tito" were the first two employees. To modify the platforms, they used a welder, a belt sander, and a drill press to add two braces to hold the seat post (that was made by the Brettrager Machine Company). Then they removed the battery bracket from the front of the platform, ground down the area, and riveted the bracket back onto the platform in front of the seat post.

They next took the revamped platforms over to Alden's house, where Al's brother repainted them the original JET yellow. This would have been the time to paint the soon-to-be Amigo another color, but Al liked the color that Kysor used.

"Yellow is friendly," he explained. "Yellow is a big smile! Yellow is a happy color. We stayed with the yellow."

The color may have been all those things, but the paint he used was not durable. Since Alden was a house painter, he might have used house paint.

"House paint," Al recalled sorrowfully, "is good over wood, over plaster, and on dry wall, but it never holds up well on steel!"

It became one of the Amigo's early product issues.

Ray Pogue and his son, Randy, a neighbor who lived down the street from Al and Marie, took the driveheads apart and installed four more switches, which gave the Amigo forward, reverse, and dynamic braking. Then they wired the driveheads with long lengths of wire similar to what is used in house wiring. However, that caused a second problem. The switches worked fine, but the wiring would eventually break because it could not withstand the back-and-forth motion of the drivehead causing the Amigo to stop in its tracks.

Those two product problems did not become apparent for several months, but they were quickly resolved. The paint was replaced by automotive lacquer, and the house wire was replaced by fine, multi-strand, direct current electrical wire, which allowed it to flex without breaking.

Max Goodman, Emy's husband, worked on the assembly line at Saginaw Steering Gear during the day. In the evenings and on weekends, in his shop at his house, he made armrests, seat locks, and special accessories out of aluminum for the Amigo, utilizing his skills as a welder and machinist. Al, with occasional help from his friends, would then assemble the parts into Amigos.

On the business side, Marie began working on advertising and promotion, and Emy, who was already doing the books for Al's plumbing business, began doing the same work for Amigo Company. In fact, Emy was a godsend. When Marie began having difficulty keeping up with the demands of the household, Emy stepped in and did the grocery shopping and ran other errands for Marie. Also, when Al needed something done that he couldn't do or didn't have time to do, Emy chipped in as best she could.

•••

Based on the excitement generated by the members of the local MS Society when they first saw Marie's Amigo, it seemed to Al and Marie that they would be able to sell all five couples an Amigo as soon as they were built, but their hopes were soon dashed. The members' excitement was one thing; having them part with their money was quite another. When presented with an opportunity to buy, they all declined.

The first individual to voice an interest in the Amigo was a lady who lived in Millington, the little town that Al used to raise havoc in when he was a teenager. Since Bob Zelle was such an experienced salesman, Al asked him if he would take an Amigo to demonstrate and sell to her.

Bob came back with the unsold Amigo, but the lady did eventually buy one.

A short time later, Bob saw a young girl he knew, who had cerebral palsy, pushing her wheelchair backward with her feet on a sidewalk in Bridgeport. People with cerebral palsy often propel themselves that way. Since he knew the girl's family, he took an Amigo over to show them what it could do for their daughter.

"She'll be able to travel forward!" he explained, thinking that would create a slam-dunk sale.

But it didn't, and Bob left their house without an order.

It appeared that people would not accept this new method of mobility.

The third lead that came in was from Rosabell "Rose" Doll, who lived in St. Louis, Michigan, a small town forty miles due west of Bridgeport. The forty-one-year-old woman had severe rheumatoid arthritis, which meant that she couldn't bend her knees all the way back, and she could barely raise her arms. She sat in a wheelchair and had to be pushed around, which was very difficult inside her little house.

When Al helped her onto an Amigo, she could lift her arms just high enough to reach the handlebar. Rose was elated. For the first time in many years, she could get around on her own, and the small, narrow Amigo allowed her to move throughout her tiny house quite easily.

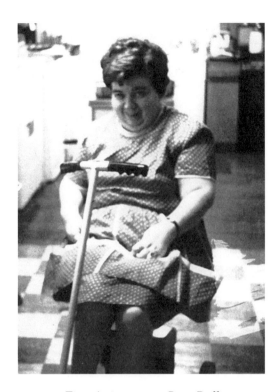

First Amigo owner, Rose Doll

Rose wanted the Amigo, but there was one problem: her outstretched legs were a little too long to allow them to rest on the platform. However, Al wasn't about to let a little obstacle like that prevent a sale.

"If I extend the platform enough so that your legs will fit," he asked, "will you buy it?"

"Of course," Rose replied.

"I came back to my shop with the Amigo," Al recalled. "Dick Kern cut it apart, welded in three inches, and I took it back to Rose. That was the first sale."

Rose purchased that first Amigo on November 19, 1968, and used an Amigo for the next thirty-seven years, until her death in 2005. In 1978, Al traded Rose's Amigo for a new Amigo and put the first one sold on display at the company, where it sits to this day.

Cheryl Highlen, one of the members of the local MS Society, eventually bought one of the very early Amigos. She and her husband, Ernie, were a young couple in their early twenties, who lived in Bay City, twenty-five miles north of Bridgeport. When Al went to their home to sell them an Amigo, he just couldn't get them to buy it.

"I'm going to stay here," he told them, "until you say that you're going to buy it!"

"Well, we're getting ready for dinner," Cheryl replied, hoping that Al would get the hint.

"I'll stay for dinner!" he said.

Then Ernie got serious.

"Al," he said, "Cheryl isn't just going to use this in the house. We may want to take it when we go out, when we go into the city, when we travel and go on vacation, and there's curbs all over!"

"Oh, don't worry about that, Ernie!" Al replied. "This thing can drive right off a curb!"

The sale was made.

But Al was not being completely honest. In fact, he had never tried to ride an Amigo off a curb. When he and Marie came to one, Al would have her get off the Amigo, he would walk it down the curb, Marie would get back on to ride across the street, and they would repeat the process in reverse on the other side.

"I don't know," Al confessed later, "what behooved me to say what I said. I got home late that night, because I had dinner with the Highlens, and I said to Marie, 'In order to make a sale, I told Ernie you could just drive off a curb. I'm going out to the garage to build a curb, and you're going to have to try driving off a curb to see if it really works.'"

It worked great—at least for going *down* a curb. Going *up* took some practice, and a user would need the assistance of another person. Nevertheless, Cheryl used an Amigo for the next 47 years!

"That was a tough sale!" Al recalled. "They were all tough!"

One of the early Amigo sales that was *not* tough was to Colonel David Farr, who lived in New York. He wanted one for his wife, Merry, who had multiple sclerosis.

When Colonel Farr called Amigo Company, Al happened to answer the phone.

"Tell me about her," Al said. "Is she in a wheelchair?"

"Oh, yes," the colonel replied. "She's been in a wheelchair for a long time."

"Can she propel the wheelchair by herself?"

"No, I have to set her in the wheelchair, and that's where she stays all day. When I come home at noon, I feed her and move her a bit."

"I'm sorry, Colonel Farr," Al said. "The Amigo is not for your wife."

But the colonel would not accept that answer.

"No," he replied. "I want her in an Amigo! I don't like her in a wheelchair."

Regardless of Al's protestations, the colonel drove all the way to Bridgeport with his wife to buy her an Amigo.

Just as Al had envisioned, Merry was in bad shape. She could barely talk, and when the colonel set her on the Amigo, she just sat there with a slight smile on her face. But Merry couldn't even lift her hands onto the handlebar.

"This is perfect!" exclaimed the colonel. "I love it!"

Obviously, Al could see the colonel's excitement, but again he tried to dissuade him from buying an Amigo. However, Colonel Farr, used to getting his way in the military, bought an Amigo for Merry anyway. For many months, he would call Al every Friday night to tell him how pleased he was with the Amigo.

"Al, guess what?" he said one night. "Merry sat in the Amigo for two hours today!"

Then, a month later: "Al, I got one of her hands up on the

*Al at the Amigo assembly line located in his home's
two-car garage, ca. 1969*

steering handle!"

Five months after that: "Al, Merry can drive the Amigo by
herself!"

"It was amazing!" Al recalled. "Dave was determined to get
Merry mobile by herself again, and they did it!"

By using the Amigo with her husband's help and
encouragement, Merry continued to get better and stronger.

"It was unbelievable!" Al said. "Then they would travel and
go places they couldn't before."

•••

Over the years, Al has collected file drawers full of letters
from appreciative customers like Rose, Cheryl and Merry.

One customer wrote: "My Amigo gave me my life back after
I lost my ability to walk thirty years ago. I know you all work
every day to make life better for people with mobility problems."

Another customer wrote: "I was born disabled, and I have

The first Amigo, which was sold to Rose Doll—the classic, yellow front-drive

used an Amigo ever since I could operate one. In 1984, I was able to get my first apartment because I had an Amigo. I was also able to go to college and obtain a degree because I had an Amigo."

A third customer wrote: "I got my Amigo when I was in sixth grade, and fell in love with it. It opened my whole world up, and it meant that my mom and dad wouldn't have to carry me anymore."

It was letters like these that kept Al going, even when he was faced with overwhelming challenges.

•••

By the end of 1968, Amigo Company had sold ten Amigos for a grand total of $4,950. While it took a lot of work to sell those machines, Al needed to order more JETs because more sales leads were coming into the office. But he was burning through cash at an alarming rate to pay wages and buy inventory. Al was caught in a proverbial Catch-22: he needed sales to pay for inventory, but he needed inventory to have something to sell!

"You can't sell what you don't have," is the way car dealers explain this predicament. Unlike car dealers, however, who have access to financing from the manufacturer, Al had no such avenue. All he had were banks, and they were becoming reluctant to lend him more money. It wasn't because he wasn't paying them. It was because they didn't understand his business.

"They just couldn't see the benefit that the Amigo gave to people with walking disabilities," he said.

In January 1969, Al ordered ten more JETs to keep up with anticipated sales, and then placed an order with Kysor to ship fifty JETs in June and another fifty in July.

•••

In the meantime, sales were slow and sporadic. Dick Vance was now trying to sell Amigos. But his first prospect, in mid-January 1969, failed to buy. Shortly thereafter, however, three MS people bought Amigos, based on information they had gotten from the MS Society. One of those individuals was a Mrs. Pacey; another was a Mr. Schaumann, who lived in Bridgeport; and the third one was Tom Thomas in Detroit.

"They love them!" Al wrote in his journal.

•••

Tom Thomas, who was a twenty-seven-year-old married man with three children, had multiple sclerosis and lost his job after he became too fatigued at work. Just like Marie Thieme, he could start the day alright, but became fatigued as the hours progressed. Also, like Marie, he could still drive and could walk a little, although he needed a cane to keep his balance.

Tom refused to use a wheelchair because of "the pity they generate," he said. "However, when I'm on an Amigo, everyone thinks it's cool. Children get a real thrill out of it!"

Before getting his Amigo, Tom couldn't keep up with the

family, but now they couldn't keep up with him!

"It puts you back into the stream of things," he said.

Al met Tom at an MS Society meeting in Detroit, noticed how much he loved his Amigo, and found out that he owned and ran his own office supply store. If Tom could sell office supplies, Al thought, he could sell Amigos. And Tom agreed.

Tom Thomas became Amigo Company's first Amigo owner-salesperson. He was paid a 20 percent commission on each Amigo he sold. His sales territory covered the area from Detroit to Flint.

•••

Around this same time, Al asked Clyde Gardner, the owner of Saginaw Medical Supply, if he would sell Amigos at his store. Gardner wasn't interested in buying one to display, so Al let him take one on consignment.

Three months later, Al picked up the Amigo after no sales were made.

•••

By the end of 1969, Al was marketing the Amigo through three fronts: (1) directly to the public; (2) through Amigo owners/salespeople; and (3) through medical supply dealers. The number of sales was in that order, with medical supply dealers in a distant third place.

One might think that dealers would have been a natural fit for Amigos. After all, that's where people bought their medical supplies, whether a pair of crutches, a walker, or a wheelchair. Al thought the same thing. But when he and Marie went to a medical supply dealer show in New York, they had received no interest at all.

"The dealers," Al said, "just laughed at it. They just didn't get it."

However, a few dealers did try to sell it. A large dealer in Chicago sold around three per month. But at the 30 to 40 percent discount that dealers demanded, it was hardly worth the effort to

Al.

If he couldn't develop a more profitable and predictable marketing operation, Al was sure to lose the company.

"I wasn't living on the edge," he explained. "I was living over the edge!"

•••

Although attorney John Learman had told Al and Gene that only the drivehead of their initial three-wheeled machine was patentable, Al nevertheless applied for a design patent on his new JET-based cart on July 28, 1969, and received patent number 220,835 on June 1, 1971.

Ironically, the US Patent Office called Al's new device a "motor scooter," a name he disliked.

"We never called the Amigo a scooter," he explained. "That name was derived as products started coming in from Asia. They used the word *scooter*. They were so strong bringing product in that the name stuck. And the early carts they were bringing in were bigger and had treaded tires, because in Asia and in Europe, people were using them more outdoors. They were probably 80 percent for outdoor use, whereas the Amigo we built was 90 percent for indoor use."

"Al always felt that the word *scooter* made it sound like a toy," explained a long-time Amigo employee. "It is not a toy. It is the most versatile, functional, and fun vehicle for people that need mobility assistance."

"When we started working with the Veterans Administration," Al said, "they called it a POV, a power-operated vehicle. That name stuck with the Veterans Administration, and we used it also."

Actually, Al was hoping that the name "Amigo" would become the generic name for any three-wheeled mobility device, just as "Xerox" had become the generic name for copiers, and "Kleenex" had become the generic name for facial tissues.

•••

Amigo Company sold forty-two Amigos in 1969—a 320 percent increase over the previous year. While that may have looked impressive on paper, Amigo Company's negative income statement told the real story: Al needed more funds to keep the business going, but most banks refused to lend him money. He was able to eke out a loan of $5,000 from the Second National Bank in Saginaw, but when he used that up, the bank refused to lend him any more money. Even Frankenmuth Bank declined to extend any more funds. The bank's president, John Metzger, had known Al for many years as a plumber—and "a darn good plumber," Metzger said. But he refused to lend him any more money for the Amigo business.

"Forget this idea of a battery-powered device," he told Al. "Stay with what you know and are good at."

Perhaps if John Metzger had seen the transformation in Merry Farr, he would have changed his mind.

To raise more money to keep the business afloat, Al called on family members and friends again and sold company stock to them. At a time when a Chevrolet cost $4,000, Bob and Shirley Heckroth (Marie's sister and brother-in-law) lent Al $10,000. Alden bought an additional $4,000 in stock, and Milo Shaner, a local machine shop owner, bought $5,000 in stock. Al even cashed in his life insurance policy, which gave him another $5,000. Needing still more money, Al sold his half of their cottage to Alden, and Bob Zelle agreed to lend him another $4,000.

Those loans and stock sales gave Al a short breather, but he was now heavily in debt. Every month, he had to pay bankers, pay Kysor for JETs, pay for the mortgage on his house, and pay for materials and wages.

"If only we had money," he wrote in his journal, "this sure would be fun!"

•••

Even while he was struggling under a weighty debt, Al went

into hock even more.

Directly across the Dixie Highway from his house, there was a large piece of property with an abandoned building on it. Back when Al was young, there was a restaurant in the front half of that building, and people lived in the back. The building was on ten acres of farmland, and the owner was willing to sell the building and the land for $30,000.

Al really wanted that piece of property because it was conveniently close to his home, and he hoped to expand his business on it. But the owner might just as well have asked for a million dollars for the property, because Al could not afford it at any price. However, the owner was willing to sell it to him on a land contract. Perhaps the owner didn't need the money at the time, or didn't need the land anymore, or just wanted to give Al a helping hand. Whatever the reason, Al was now the owner of a prime piece of real estate.

Al's combined debt came to $1,000 per month, which put him in a serious cash flow crunch. But he wasn't too concerned about that.

"If it needs to be done," he explained, "I just do it!"

It's not exactly clear where he got the time, but Al and Alden began to remodel the old restaurant into an office for the Amigo Company. Eventually, however, Al hired a contractor, who finished the work in a couple of weeks.

Al then hired Gary Dice to work on sales, and Sue Tate as a "Jane-of-all-trades" to answer the phone, reply to mail inquiries, send out brochures, and do general secretarial work. Marie and Emy were now working out of the new office as well.

Emy had to drive three miles from home to work, but Marie only had to cross the street. While that certainly was convenient, it was also daunting. The Dixie Highway is a busy four-lane road, so dashing across could be dangerous. But that didn't deter Marie. She would drive her Amigo up to the edge of the highway, wait for a break in the traffic, and scoot across.

●●●

On September 12, 1970, Al made a note in his journal: "Vance, Thieme, and Thieme out to eat to celebrate 100th Amigo sold."

While the number was certainly something to make a note of and to celebrate, it was less than two Amigos per week since the company had started. No wonder the company was having cash flow problems.

All of Al's money problems were due to poor cash flow and lackluster sales, although that was slowly beginning to change. At the start of 1971, the company was selling about four Amigos a week, but that was still not enough to cover expenses. Even if sales increased significantly, that wouldn't have helped much, because Al was losing $200 per machine!

"That doesn't work too well in business," he said dryly, "but that's the way it was."

Why was Al working so exhaustively to produce and deliver Amigos at a loss?

"Because," he said, "I was changing people's lives! I knew that I could make it a profitable operation ..., eventually."

Eventually would come one day, but it certainly didn't arrive in 1972. Early that year, Al approached the Frankenmuth Bank once again, asking this time for a loan of $50,000.

"Definitely not," was the bank's response, so Al had to tell Sue and Gary not to cash their payroll checks. Fortunately, the Second National Bank came through with a $2,500 loan, which allowed Al to pay his employees and carry the company until more sales came in.

●●●

Al became so desperate for sales that he hired Ray Bauer, a highly successful book salesman, at $30,000 a year to sell Amigos.

Al and Ray were confident that sales would increase rapidly. But Ray soon learned that selling Amigos was not as easy as he

The house/restaurant across the Dixie Highway from Al's home in Bridgeport.
This building became the embryo for The Amigo Company

had thought. After six months, the two parted ways amicably because "Ray just wasn't producing," Al recalled.

A week later, Ray dropped by to see Al to tell him about an idea he had.

"I talked with the manager of Meijer Thrifty Acres in Flint," he said, "and told him that he should have Amigos in his store for handicapped people to use. He's interested. I recommend that you put a big basket on an Amigo and sell it to him."

Founded in 1934 by Hendrik Meijer, a Dutch immigrant, in Greenville, Michigan (a small community not far from Grand Rapids), Meijer's grocery store was one of the first in the country to offer self-service shopping and shopping carts. By the 1960s, the company had over two-dozen grocery stores throughout western Michigan.

First Amigo Company building

In 1962, the company launched its modern format: huge buildings with a grocery store on one side and a department store on the other, which allowed customers to shop for everything they needed in just one trip.

Appropriately, the new stores were called Meijer Thrifty Acres, because they covered four acres of land or a little less than four football fields! They were the first so-called hypermarkets in the country, well before Sam Walton's Walmart chain. No wonder the store's manager was interested in the Amigo. Getting from one end of the store to the other was a feat in and of itself, even for able-bodied customers.

Whether or not Ray Bauer had been working on this idea before leaving Amigo Company is not clear, but it was gracious of him to follow through and let Al know about Meijer's interest.

"I built a large basket," Al recalled, "built a frame for it, and installed it on an Amigo."

It was a little crude, but it worked, so he instructed his daughter, Jill, to take the revamped Amigo, which he called the "Amigo Shopper," to the Meijer store in Flint.

"Don't come back with it!" he told her. "You sell it!"

Jill made the sale.

"We called Amigo owners and people at the National Association for Handicapped People," recalled Al, "and asked them to go to Flint to use the Amigo Shopper. Back then, Amigo owners were like a cult: we were such a family unit. The response was tremendous. The manager was so surprised. That message went to the Meijer corporate office, which picked up that shopping cart and took it to Grand Rapids to see if it would have the same effect there. It did, because we called the Amigo owners again! A member of the Meijer family had arthritis so Fred Meijer had empathy for people who had trouble walking. That helped getting motorized shopping carts in Meijer stores."

•••

Around this time, some of Al's children began to work at the company. Jill joined in the summer of 1971, and Joe started a few months later. Al was elated that they wanted to work with him because he needed their help. Eventually, all of the Thieme children would work for the company in one capacity or another.

Joe Thieme did a commendable job with both building and servicing Amigos, but he also had an innate talent for selling. When he saw his father's need for sales, he took some sales classes at Delta College in Bay City, and became an Amigo salesman. He started out by taking any leads that were outside areas covered by other Amigo sales representatives.

As Joe gained confidence that he could make a living by

The first Amigo Shopper

selling Amigos, he left the security of the home office, and he and his wife, Sheree, moved to Michigan City, Indiana, a bucolic town on the southern shore of Lake Michigan, sixty miles southeast of Chicago. Just as he had done in Bridgeport, he would travel almost anywhere to make a sale.

"He'd drive down to Indianapolis to sell," recalled Al, "and he'd drive to Chicago to sell."

In fact, Joe made most of his sales in those two cities.

Jill Thieme started right out in sales, but not as a sales representative like her brother. On her first day at work, Al gave her a phonebook and told her to start making cold calls.

"But don't start at the beginning of the book," he told her, "because everybody starts there. Start at the middle."

That probably would have been daunting to most people— let alone to an eighteen-year-old—but Jill enjoyed cold-calling. Unfortunately, her efforts weren't quite as successful as she had hoped.

"I was able to get a lead for one out of every ten

Dick Vance (left), Al, Alden, and Bob Zelle, ca. 1980

calls," she said. "But I don't recall one actual sale."

In the meantime, her boyfriend and soon-to-be fiancé, Chuck Priest, had also joined the company as a salesman. Chuck was the quintessential salesman: gregarious, perpetually happy, and eternally optimistic.

"Chuck sold in Michigan," Al said, "but he always wanted to go to Florida, because his dad lived there. Chuck took off for Florida without Jill to try to sell Amigos. After he did that twice, Jill agreed to move down to Florida. That's when they both started making sales."

As sales reps in New Smyrna Beach, on Florida's east coast, just south of Daytona Beach, Chuck and Jill sold their first Amigo in 1974.

•••

Those formative years of Amigo Company were critical, and the help that Al got from Marie, his children, Emy, Alden, Dick Vance, and Bob Zelle was incalculable.

"It's amazing how much they helped me," Al said.

CHAPTER 5

Amigo Owners as Salespeople

"Do you want the sales, or don't you?"
—Donna Layman, Amigo salesperson

Out of the 50 Amigos sold during the first eighteen months of the company's existence, a few were sold by medical equipment dealers, a few by Al's children, and a few by Al himself.

"Whenever a sales lead came into the office," Al recalled, "I'd pack up the car with an Amigo and some accessories, drive to the customer's home, and make the sale."

The rest of the sales, however, had come from Amigo owners themselves, whom Al had set up as salespeople.

"I would use 'be a salesperson' as a closing tool," he explained. "When I couldn't get the person to get their checkbook out, I said, 'You know, when you get this Amigo, you're going to like it so much that you'll want to sell it to others. You can be a salesperson!' 'Oh, really?' they'd respond."

Before he knew it, Al had quite a few Amigo owners selling the Amigo, but they were not organized. He knew that he should have some kind of system in place to manage them, but he didn't have time to put together a formalized sales organization.

"Anyone who said, 'I'll take one, and I'll sell it' was fair game!" explained Beth Loichinger, an early Amigo employee. "Al's not a systems guy. Yet, when it comes to product, he wanted to create systems to make it better, but not so much on people. This is why he hadn't devised a sales system yet. That wasn't part of his nature."

Nevertheless, Al eventually realized that he had stumbled upon a viable sales plan: hire Amigo users to sell Amigos! Who better to sell this unique product than the people who used it?

What he needed now was a way to formalize the sales force and manage it.

•••

Around the time that Al had that insight, two companies were making national headlines about their multilevel marketing techniques. One was the Amway Corporation, in Ada Township, Michigan, near Grand Rapids. The other was the Bestline Corporation in San Jose, California.

A multibillion-dollar company, Amway manufactured a line of eco-friendly detergents and other house cleaning supplies as well as dietary supplements, cosmetics, and water purifying systems, all of which it sold through a multilevel sales force. Instead of manufacturing its products and wholesaling them to supermarkets, as most other consumer goods manufacturers did, Amway set up regional distributors, local distributors, and local salespeople to sell directly to consumers, with each level getting a percentage of the sales. Individuals would start out as salespeople who sold directly to the end users. If the salespeople wanted to grow their business, they could hire other people to work for them and get a percentage of their sales. The advantage of Amway's distribution system was that people could get into business for themselves with very little investment and grow the business as much as they could.

Bestline also manufactured a line of household cleaning supplies and sold them through a multilevel sales organization, which consisted of three levels: local, direct, and general. Individuals started as local salespeople, then moved up to become direct distributors, with one or more local salespeople working for them. Direct distributors could then work themselves up to general distributors, with one or more direct distributors working for them.

Those marketing methods seemed like they might work for Amigo, so Al asked his son Joe, who was seventeen at the time, to help him put together a multilevel marketing plan for the company's growing number of Amigo owner-salespeople.

"I heard," he told Joe, "that Amway has people selling products from their home. Join Amway, find out what they are doing, and put a plan together."

Like a typical teenager, Joe joined Bestline instead.

"He got their entire multilevel selling program," Al recalled. "He had me look at their papers, and for some reason I didn't like what they were doing. I knew that if we didn't implement a multilevel selling process properly, we could get into legal trouble."

Al was right. Bestline not only "looked wrong" to Al, but the Federal Trade Commission thought so, too, and brought suit against Bestline, accusing the company of running a pyramid scheme. According to the FTC, unlike Amway, whose salespeople sold their products directly to consumers, Bestline was "recruiting salesmen who found they had to recruit others to recoup their investment." In other words, "the whole process was aimed at moving products out of the Bestline factory and not really at selling them to the ultimate consumer." And that is illegal.

While Amway had its critics, Al learned that its marketing methods were legal. So Joe set up a multilevel marketing plan for Amigo that was modeled after Amway, with three levels: salespeople, area managers, and distributors.

The individual salespeople (most of whom were Amigo

owners) earned a commission of 15 percent on each Amigo they sold. If they sold six to eleven Amigos in a calendar quarter, they would earn an additional bonus of 3 percent; if they sold twelve or more in a quarter, they would earn an additional bonus of 6 percent.

The area managers received a commission of 24 percent, but were required to sell a minimum of eight Amigos per month and to develop a sales territory by hiring and training additional salespeople.

The distributors operated like independent businesses. They would buy products from Amigo Company at a 30 percent discount, maintain an inventory, and provide service. They also had to order a minimum of fifteen Amigos per month. For that, they were assigned a protected territory, which they could develop by building their own sales force.

Although the area managers and distributors acted like brick-and-mortar businesses, most of them still worked out of their homes.

"They had a little showroom," Al explained, "and a repair shop in their garage."

Still concerned about the legality of the plan, Al presented it to attorney BJ Humphrey for validation.

"This looks fine," BJ told Al. "There's nothing illegal about it."

With his attorney giving him the green light, Al immediately implemented the multilevel marketing plan.

"That's when sales really started to move," Al said.

•••

With that hurdle crossed, the next thing Al had to address was how the company was going to collect the money from the sales representatives when they sold Amigos. After years of struggling with cash flow, Al knew what he didn't want, which was to ship an Amigo to a salesperson on terms and wait for payment.

"When we worked with medical dealers," Al explained, "we shipped the product out, and they'd pay us in thirty days, or maybe sixty days. They actually wanted Amigos on consignment."

That was typical business practice of working with medical dealers, but Al didn't have the money to carry receivables for two months. So he devised a unique system that transformed the company from being a slave of cash flow to being a king of cash flow. It was a clever move and a major turning point in the history of the company.

"The way we set it up," Al explained, "we collected half the money up-front with a customer's order. Then we'd build the Amigo within three days and send it out. When the salesperson delivered the Amigo to the customer, the salesperson would get the other half of the money from the customer and send it to Amigo. Two weeks later, we would send the salesperson a commission check. That really improved our cash flow."

•••

Donna Layman was a typical Amigo user-salesperson, and her story is like that of many others who turned their disability into an opportunity, not only to help others, but to help themselves as well.

Donna Critoph met John Layman in 1969, when they were both attending Parsons College in Fairfield, Iowa. John was studying psychology, and Donna was studying elementary education.

"I was working in the cafeteria," John recalled, "washing dishes to earn money for school. When Donna came by the window to drop off her tray, I intentionally squirted her with a hose. That's how we met."

They started dating, one thing led to another, and they got married that year, right after John graduated. A year later, after Donna graduated, the couple moved to Phoenix, Arizona, where John planned to earn a master's degree in international management. While he was attending graduate school, Donna was a special education teacher at Peoria Elementary School. Eventually, John became a police officer for the city of Phoenix, and the two settled down to an average American life.

But then the unexpected happened.

One Saturday night each month, John and Donna would go out square dancing. It was fun but exhausting, so it wasn't unusual for the couple to sleep in the next morning. But one Sunday morning in 1974, John explained, "Donna got out of bed and fell flat on her face!"

After that, she was able to walk, but not well.

When the Laymans went to a doctor to see what was causing Donna's walking difficulties, they were shocked by the diagnosis. The doctor said that she was in the early stages of multiple sclerosis, and then he gave her the bad news of how the disease would progress in the years to come.

Like many other people with early-stage MS, Donna could still walk with the help of a cane, but after she fell a few more times, she began looking for "alternatives," as John put it. The obvious alternative would have been a wheelchair, but "that was a real turnoff for her," John said.

In the meantime, Donna began to see a doctor who specialized in treating MS. In fact, he had it himself, and while he didn't use an Amigo, he knew about it and gave Donna a brochure, which explained the little three-wheeled device.

"She got all excited when she saw it," John explained, "because she instantly knew that that was the answer to her mobility problem. I was working at the time when she called me and tried to explain it on the phone. I said, 'Just wait till I get home, and we'll talk about it.' Well, we bought her one. There was a gentleman by the name of John Fenn, who was kind of an informal sales rep for Amigo. He had one, but he wasn't doing much with it, so we bought it from him. There were only two or three other Amigos in the entire state. Nobody knew about them, but it was obvious to us from the get-go that the Amigo was the answer to Donna's mobility."

Donna fell in love with the little machine, which gave her the mobility she needed. Just as importantly, it was better by far than a conventional wheelchair. She soon found out that other people felt the same way.

"When she got that little thing," John explained, "people started pursuing her because they wanted to know about it. When we were in a restaurant, they'd follow her into the ladies' room!"

With such strong interest, Donna began talking to John about the possibility of selling Amigos, and he was supportive.

"You know," John explained, "it didn't take a whole lot of abstract thinking to see the advantage of getting into this business, because nobody else was doing it, and nobody else knew about it. It was a ground-floor opportunity."

Taking information from the Amigo brochure that she had gotten at the doctor's office, Donna called Al Thieme.

"I want to sell these things!" she told him.

"No," Al replied. "You've got to use it for a while."

But Donna was adamant.

"I have three prospects right now," she said. "Do you want the sales, or don't you?"

That's how Donna Layman became one of the earliest Amigo salespeople in the country.

While John remained on the police force, Donna ran the business by herself from her kitchen. But as the business grew, John turned the carport into an office. Donna worked there for quite a few years, until the business got too big for that space as well. At that point, they were forced to have a separate building constructed on their five-acre lot. Now Donna had an office, a warehouse, *and* a showroom—all in one building.

The key to Donna's success was not only her sales skills, but her experience as an enthusiastic Amigo user herself.

"That gave her a great deal of credibility when it came to talking about it," John explained, "more so than anybody who

*Donna Layman with her husband, John. She was one
of the first Amigo-owner salespeople* (courtesy John Layman)

isn't walking in those shoes."

Up until that time, John worked with Donna as best he could, but the business was growing to the point where he couldn't help her and be a policeman at the same time.

"I decided that was it," he recalled, "and we went into business together."

Donna started out as a salesperson, and then went on to become an area manager.

"Amigo Company," John explained, "wanted us to take on Arizona, Nevada, and Utah, but that was too much. We tried that for a short time, and then we told them that we would just work

Arizona, specifically the Phoenix area. Eventually, one sale led to another, then to another. It kind of escalated like that."

Beyond word-of-mouth, the Laymans had no idea how or where to advertise.

"There was no advertising medium for handicapped people in those days," John explained. "We did the Yellow Pages for a while, and we did a television ad once, but that didn't work out very well. It was kind of expensive. We had a film made and ran it on TV, but it took too many cha-chings from the cash register. We didn't continue that very long."

In any case, regardless of the cost, the Laymans learned that advertising wasn't the most effective way to promote their business. They got far better results by participating in home health care conventions, setting up a booth at state fairs, and going to MS Society meetings.

"The only way to deal with MS," John said, "is to work, pray, stay busy, live your life, and don't think about pills or shots or whatever. That's what got Donna as far as it did. She was in this business from 1975 until six months before she passed away in 2018, just before Christmas. I credit the Amigo and the Amigo business as the main reasons that got her that far, plus her attitude toward life and business. She didn't sit at home and feel sorry for herself. We ran into some customers who did just that. When we went into the home of one of our customers, she was sitting in the living room, all negative, with the shades drawn. Somehow or other, we managed to convince her to get an Amigo. When we went back a few months later, she didn't look like the same person. She was out doing stuff! That's how it worked."

Of course, not every story was like that, but, as John explained, "the Amigo made a positive effect in almost everyone's life that we convinced to try it."

•••

Another example of an Amigo owner who became a successful salesperson was Jean Lodes of Clearwater, Florida.

Like Donna Layman, Jean had been an active woman, dancing with her husband, Pete, on the weekends, and playing golf whenever they both got a chance. Then she contracted multiple sclerosis, which devastated her.

"She didn't care if she woke up each morning," wrote a reporter for the *Clearwater Sun*. "She was scared, depressed, and had simply given up on life. The pain, the fatigue, and the inability to lead a normal life had gotten to be too much. She couldn't cope."

But eventually, to help herself deal with her MS, Jean joined the local MS Society chapter, and that is where she heard about the Amigo. When Pete bought her one, that changed her life. While she couldn't go out dancing or golfing any longer, she could now get around pretty much on her own.

"She is a different woman," continued the reporter.

"The Amigo is my legs!" Jean exclaimed.

Like Donna Layman, Jean was so enthralled with what the Amigo did for her that she called Al Thieme, asking him to make her a salesperson.

"I want to sell this!" she told him. "I can sell a ton of these!"

Al could hardly pass up hiring such an enthusiastic person as Jean, so he made her an Amigo sales representative for the Clearwater area. She did the selling, and Pete helped her with deliveries and repairs.

"At first," Jean said, "it was fun earning a little extra money."

But soon she realized that she had discovered her niche in life.

"I found people who needed me," she said. "I call my customers '*my* people.' I'm genuinely interested in their welfare."

Along with the MS Society, Jean also became a member of Wheelchair Awareness, an organization designed to help people in wheelchairs to make the public aware of their needs. Through that organization, she was instrumental in removing architectural barriers in the county.

"Every time I see something that isn't accessible to a person in a wheelchair," she said, "I contact the store manager."

She told all of her Amigo owners to do the same thing.

"I'm only trying to pull my share," Jean explained humbly. "I know so many people in much worse condition than I am."

Eventually, Jean worked her way up to a distributor for Northern Florida, with several salespeople working for her, and Pete quit his job as a stockbroker to join her. With the Amigo business now in full operation, they relocated their business from their home to a small retail space in a strip mall.

With her business thriving and barely a spare minute to relax, Jean had overcome her depression years earlier. Thanks to the Amigo, she no longer considered herself handicapped, but just as able and productive as anybody else in society.

"Today," wrote the Clearwater reporter, "Jean opens her eyes each day with this thought: *There is someone who needs my help!*"

"Jean and Pete," Al recalled, "were usually among our top five salespeople until they retired in 1983."

•••

In addition to Joe and Sheree Thieme, Chuck and Jill Priest, the Laymans, and the Lodes, Al soon had distributors throughout the country: John Todd in New Jersey; Brent and Sharon Davis in Georgia; Ray Hamilton in Ohio; Jack McConnell in Michigan; Gene Bauer in Wisconsin; and Earl Gottfried in Southern California, among others.

"Earl Gottfried," Beth Loichinger recalled, "would not accept the fact that he had to start as a sales rep. He convinced us that he could start as a distributor. He said, 'Look, I will buy the equipment, I will have inventory and I will set up service.' He became a distributor right off the bat."

While it took time to recruit and train the company's expanding sales force, the sales plan that Al and Joe had devised was beginning to show results. On July 29, 1974, Amigo

Company sold its thousandth Amigo. It had taken the company two and a half years to sell its first hundred units, but just over four years to sell the next nine hundred. Obviously, sales were heading in the right direction.

When Al got the year-end financial statement for 1974, a big smile came over his face.

"Very good," he wrote in his journal. "Business is running well, except we are out of money again."

●●●

The increased sales were a blessing, of course, but ever-increasing sales generated by the company's growing sales force caused the cash flow monster to raise its ugly head again. The commission system had helped a lot and was still beneficial, but more and more sales were coming from distributors who were on a typical ship-now-pay-later system, which is used by most businesses, but slowed down the company's cash flow. With the increased sales, more employees, more building space, and more machinery were needed to build more Amigos, and that took money.

There was little that Al could do about *those* factors that were increasing his cash-flow problems, but another one was self-imposed.

"From day one," he explained, "I always insisted that when an order came in, we would fill it within three days, and that caused us to have a lot of inventory."

That was indeed true, but the single most contributing factor to the company's excessive inventory was the suppliers' lead times. Just to name a few of the 100 manufacturers that supplied parts for the Amigo, the wheel manufacturer had a three-month lead time; the motor manufacturer, three months; and the electrical switch manufacturer, four months. But the longest lead time of all was that of the Herman Miller company, Amigo's seat supplier, whose lead time was six months. In other words, if Amigo ran out of seats, it wouldn't be able to get any more for twenty-six weeks! So, in essence, Amigo Company had to stockpile six months' worth of seats to ensure that it would not run out, and that cost money—a lot of money.

The most egregious vendor, however, was Amigo's next-door neighbor, Saginaw Steering Gear, which supplied the gearbox for the power seat lift. It wasn't a specially made part for the Amigo but one of their standard items. Normally, they had crates of them sitting in their warehouse. But getting them *out* of their warehouse was like pulling teeth. Although the parts were sitting there, taking up floor space, it would take the GM plant weeks to deliver a quantity of them to Amigo, which was only six miles away.

"Cash flow is the toughest thing in growing a business," Al explained, "because in building a business, you have to grow. Growth needs cash because you need more inventory, you have more receivables, you have to expand your building, you need more equipment. You can be profitable, you can be making 10 percent profit on revenue, but if you don't control the receivables, if you don't have a system together to finance this, you're out of business!"

Al was doing everything he could to raise money, including mortgaging his family home and borrowing against life insurance policies.

CHAPTER 6

The Whiz Kids

"I think we need to divide and conquer."
—Beth Loichinger

Although sales were now going in the right direction, thanks to the company's new marketing plan, every other aspect of the company needed Al's attention. By the start of 1975, the company had fifteen employees and five departments: Sales, International Sales, Administration, Production, and Service. When Al wasn't helping to assemble Amigos, he was taking service calls in the office, or working with vendors to deliver parts in a timely manner. And all that was on top of running his plumbing business, which he had continued all along!

•••

"It was always very difficult to get people to work in the garage," Al recalled. "We were building Amigos in my garage while I was a plumbing and heating contractor, and people were wondering what was going on, building these machines for people that had trouble walking, so it was very difficult to hire people. I worked with vocational rehabilitation centers, an active group run by the government, where disabled and handicapped people had workshops doing odd jobs. There were probably four of those workshops—one each in Saginaw, Grand Rapids, Lansing, and Traverse City. I got to know these managers because I would sell Amigos to their handicapped people."

One time, when Al visited the Traverse City facility, he didn't sell any Amigos, but he came away with a potentially good employee, forty-five-year-old "Dutch Kadrovach," who was "very mechanical" and, in fact, had been a machinist.

"He could do almost anything," Al recalled.

Dutch was in the rehabilitation center, the director told Al, because he had a "terrible drinking habit, and we're trying to rehabilitate him. He's been off drinking for a year now."

Al hired Dutch, and persuaded Marie's parents to put him up in their home. Al couldn't pay him much, but Dutch appreciated the opportunity.

"He did a great job for me," Al recalled.

Dutch had a dilapidated car that he would drive back and forth to Traverse City on weekends to visit relatives. When it broke down, Al let him use his own car as part of Dutch's wages. Then Al had to use one of his plumbing trucks to go to work and get his family around.

When Bob Zelle found out what Al had done, he decided to help his friend.

"Where's your car, Al?" Zelle asked innocently.

When Al told him, Zelle threw Al the keys to his car.

"Pay me when you can," Zelle said.

That car was a two-year-old Oldsmobile Toronado, which cost about $7,000.

But Al didn't need Zelle's Toronado very long. After working for only three months, Dutch went back to his usual ways and Al had to let him go.

Although things didn't go as Al had planned for Dutch, that's how Al got into liking Toronados. He would purchase quite a few over the years, until General Motors shut down the

Oldsmobile Division in 2004.

•••

The long hours of running two companies began to aggravate back problems that Al had had for quite some time. Apparently, the years of bending down into tight spaces and lifting heavy toilets and bathtubs had taken their toll. Looking for relief, he went to see Dr. David Blossom, a highly regarded chiropractor in Vassar, Michigan, whom Al had met when he installed the plumbing in the doctor's new office building.

Al told Blossom about the Amigo Company and how difficult it was to find good people to work with him.

"I really need somebody who is mechanical to help me run the production department," he said.

"My nephew just got out of the Air Force," Blossom replied. "He's very mechanical. I'll send him over."

Tall, handsome, and energetic, Mel Shepard had repaired teletype equipment in the military, and so was accustomed to taking orders and following through on directives. He was indeed looking for a job, but only temporarily.

"I was expecting to go to work with my dad," he said, "who had a heating and air conditioning business. But he had not been in business for himself very long, and the business wasn't big enough to support both of us yet."

On January 14, 1975, Mel met with Al, who put him to work that very day.

"Al had me build and repair driveheads," Mel recalled. "I did service orders. I'd box them up and get them ready to go."

The work was challenging, but Mel was good at it. Al was pleased that he finally had someone whom he could rely on.

Nevertheless, Mel still hoped to join his father. However, the air conditioning business was taking longer than he thought it would to grow, so as one month turned into two, and two turned into three, Mel decided to stay at Amigo.

"The biggest thing," Mel said, "was I found something I

liked. I could see the opportunity for the company's growth and things to develop in the future."

As time went on, Al gave Mel more and more responsibility, which the young man readily accepted.

"When I first went to work with Al," Mel recalled, "for the first two or three years, he was very generous, but very frustrating because he would be unreasonable on some of the things that he wanted. I remember, I'd come home and just grumble about his demands. 'He makes me so mad!' I'd say. Sixty percent of the time I was really happy, and 40 percent of the time I was mad at him. But he gave me an hourly raise of twenty-five cents every one and a half months, and he praised my work."

Over time, Al began to understand Mel, and Mel began to understand Al. Eventually, the two men "just clicked," Al said. "Just like I did with Floyd Schmitzer. We were just a beautiful mix. Anything technical, Mel was smarter, faster, and more precise than me."

Mel was right in his assessment of the growth of Amigo Company, and as the company grew, so did his responsibilities. Within a few years, he was not only in charge of inventory and service, but also of purchasing, manufacturing, production, and eventually engineering. He managed the machine shop, set up an assembly line, worked with parts suppliers, and developed many accessories for the original front-drive Amigo. While it was Al who came up with product ideas, Mel brought them to fruition.

"Al and I agreed on almost everything," Mel explained. "Whenever there was a decision that needed to be made, we'd make it together. There was never any study or much research for anything. Al liked how I thought and made decisions. Over the years, he was generous, very appreciative, and positive—I was less frustrated and angry about things. I always thought he paid me too much money."

•••

Several months after Mel started with the company, Al and Marie attended a convention of the National Association of the Physically Handicapped (NAPH) at the Holiday Inn in Saginaw, a three-day event that started on a Friday night and ended that Sunday afternoon.

"Clarence Averill, from Saginaw," Al said, "started the NAPH. He had polio. He built up that organization with chapters all over the United States."

Such a large event should have been well planned, but for whatever reason, Kay Batterson, the hotel's sales manager, had forgotten about it—that is, until people started showing up for the first event of the convention—a wine-tasting party.

Batterson rushed into the dining room, grabbed a busboy and two waitresses, and led them into the banquet room.

"We need to get this room set up immediately!" she exclaimed. "We need tables, chairs, linen, and wine glasses! Hurry! People are waiting in the lobby!"

One of those waitresses was Beth Loichinger, an attractive, confident, 19-year-old nursing student, who was working at the Holiday Inn to earn money for college.

"I remember," Beth said, "standing there, and the doors opened; about a hundred people are arriving. I had never in my life seen so many disabled people. Some had cerebral palsy, some had multiple sclerosis—every kind of disability. One guy had no arms. He was holding a fork with his feet to eat. I had never been exposed to so many disabled people all at once. It was a little overwhelming. When everybody sat down, we started pouring wine. I got a little teary-eyed, seeing all those people. I went to the back and had a little glass of wine myself!"

Probably any other teenager would have dreaded such an event, but Beth, being a nursing student, was empathetic toward her guests, and made the most of it.

"I thought, *OK, if they can do this, so can I! I'm going out there, and I'm going to make it a fun night for these people.*

We're going to have a good time!"

When she learned that it was the birthday of one of the guests, Beth got everybody to sing "Happy Birthday!" Later, she did her best to talk to a man who had cerebral palsy, although she couldn't understand a thing he was saying. Nevertheless, she tried to make him feel welcome.

"I really tried to put my heart and soul into it," she said, "and make it a memorable, fun evening for everybody."

Al took notice of this vivacious young lady and asked Kay Batterson to introduce her to him.

"Kay introduced me to Al," Beth recalled. "It was a brief meeting."

Al asked her if she would be interested in working at Amigo Company.

"Mr. Thieme," she replied, "you couldn't pay me enough!"

Al wasn't too surprised by Beth's audacity. He simply said, "Fine."

"I didn't mean it *that* way," Beth recalled. "What I meant was that I earned so much money as a waitress—I was making fifty dollars a night waitressing, which was a lot of money at that time. I needed to pay for my schooling. It wasn't about money, but it didn't come out like that."

As Al was leaving that evening, Beth caught up with him.

"Mr. Thieme," she said, "yes, I'll come interview."

Although Beth was going back to school in January, Al hired her anyway. He desperately needed assistance and, while Beth would probably not be around for long, she could be of great help at the company from what he had seen of her performance at the NAPH convention.

Al needed assistance in every department, but most critically in purchasing, so he started Beth there. That was most certainly a baptism by fire, for the department was poorly organized, and the entire production department depended on the purchasing department getting the materials needed to build Amigos.

"We are forever running out of material," Al wrote in one of his journal entries.

Nearly every part of an Amigo was unique, and therefore not readily available. Plus, as we have seen, the lead times could be horrendous. There's no doubt that Mel and Beth had some very intense discussions about how to keep production going.

•••

That fall, Beth met with a guidance counselor at the Hurley School of Nursing in Flint, just south of Bridgeport.

"When I met with him," Beth recalled, "he went through all my papers and transcripts to make sure I had all my ducks in a row for school. He picked up a red pencil and wrote, '*OKAY.*' Then he said, 'You're all set.'"

After Al congratulated Beth on being accepted to nursing school, he hired a young man to take her place, whom she trained before she left.

At that point, Beth was elated.

"I had my bandage scissors engraved and my books bought for the program," she said. "I was ready to go to Hurley."

But her high hopes and expectations were soon dashed.

Right after New Year's Day in 1975, Beth's parents helped her to move into the dormitory at Hurley. The next morning, when she went to the registration desk, there was a message waiting for her that she was to contact the director of nursing right away. The message seemed ominous to Beth, and she was right.

"Your credits didn't transfer," the director told Beth. "You can't stay. You can look at coming back next semester, but you have to pack up and leave now."

Beth looked at the director in disbelief.

"But I met with the guidance counselor," she said to the director. "He took a red pencil and marked it OKAY. Please open up my file, and I'll show you exactly where it is."

"I'm not opening your file," the director replied emphatically.

"You have to pack up and leave."

Beth was in tears, but there was nothing she could do or say to change the director's mind.

"So I went back to my room, called my parents, and packed up. They picked me up and drove me home. As I was walking out past the guidance counselor's office, I looked in and made eye contact with him. He just shook his head and said, 'I'm so sorry.'"

Beth never found out why Hurley rejected her after she had been accepted, but she had her suspicions.

"They only accepted a hundred students out of twelve hundred applicants," she explained. "So maybe someone needed a favor to get somebody in. It was heartbreaking. I cried for a solid week. I still have that envelope. I haven't touched it since my early twenties."

Beth moped around the house for a week, feeling "bluer than blue." She needed to get moving again, so she called Al Thieme, told him what had happened, and asked if she could come talk to him.

Beth had shown her mettle during the few months that she had worked at the company, so Al was more than happy to have her come back.

As the two of them sat across the desk from each other, Al said, "I always thought you belonged in sales. You can be in sales and service with me."

Beth agreed, even though it was against her best judgment.

"I never wanted to be a salesperson," she said. "That was not my interest in life, but I needed a job."

She started on August 29, 1975.

•••

Also in the office at that time were Emy and another new recruit, Don Marquis, who had just retired from Saginaw Steering Gear, where he had been the company's assistant chief engineer. Now he was Al's engineering consultant.

In the early years of his business, Al called on the local office of SCORE (Service Corps of Retired Executives) for advice, and they would send highly experienced businesspeople to help him out. One of those retired executives was Don Marquis.

•••

The office was so small that Al and Beth had to share a desk, sitting across from each other, taking turns answering the phone.

"The phone would ring," recalled Beth, "and it would be somebody who was saying, 'My Amigo is going forward, but not reverse.' I'd look at Al, and I'd mouth the words *Going forward but no reverse. What do I tell them?* Then, another time, he'd pick up the phone, and there was someone who wanted to be a salesperson in Kalamazoo. He'd say, 'Great!' And I'm standing there waving, 'Stop! We already have salespeople there!'"

It was obvious, to Beth at least, that this arrangement was not going to work very well. She was too unmechanical to take service calls, and Al was too impulsive to hire people.

After several days of that, Beth looked at Al and said, "I think we need to divide and conquer. I'm not that good in service, and you just set up whoever comes along as a salesperson. I think we should have it more organized."

Al agreed. So, he took service calls, and Beth took sales calls.

•••

Charlene Frank was a recent graduate of Northwood Institute, a business college in Midland, Michigan, just a short distance from Bridgeport. Catering primarily to students interested in pursuing careers at automobile dealerships, the college could be attended by anyone who was interested in learning all aspects of business. Charlene majored in business administration and minored in accounting.

Al wasn't advertising for help, but many local people knew that he was looking for good employees. It was the Reverend Al Stebbins, a local minister, who told him about Charlene.

Al put her in charge of administration. And like both Mel and Beth, Charlene took control of her department like a seasoned pro.

•••

Mel, Beth, and Charlene became Al's "Whiz Kids." Prior to their arrival, Al had always said, "something will come up." What came up—or through the door, in this case—were these three energetic, confident, and indefatigable young people. And they came none too soon.

"Everyone is coming to me for minor problems," Al wrote in his journal.

With sales increasing and money coming in, he would be able to afford many more well-qualified people in the coming years, but the three Whiz Kids would stick with him through the good times and the tough, and would become instrumental in the success of Amigo Company.

To show his appreciation, Al bought the three of them brand new Oldsmobile Toronados. The company paid $33,000 in cash for the three cars, but with a year-end profit of over $300,000, Al felt the company could well afford it.

•••

During these early years, Marie was just as busy as Al. Along with her responsibilities to raise six children and take care of the home, she also put in half a day each week at Amigo Company, doing almost anything that was required. One of her main responsibilities was writing and editing the company's newsletter, *Friendly Wheels*. The multi-page circular highlighted Amigo owners and "emphasized positivity and possibility through mobility." The first issue was mailed out in December 1972.

Marie also helped to develop advertising, answered the phones, replied to letters, and worked on promotional ideas.

"Have had numerous articles written on Amigo," Al wrote in his journal.

Al Thieme with "The Whiz Kids"
(L-R): Charlene Frank, Beth Loichinger, and Mel Shepard, 1977

•••

All of these avenues helped sales in one way or another, but none were quite so unusual as "Buggy Ball."

A popular school fundraising event that was started back in the 1930s was Donkey Basketball. As the name implies, it's a basketball game in which the players ride donkeys! The local fire department or service club would play against the schoolteachers. Usually, commercial farms provided the donkeys and equipment, splitting the proceeds with the school.

As a member of the Lions Club, Al got involved in these donkey basketball games, competing against the staff of Bridgeport High School.

"A guy named Baker," Al explained, "who lived in Lansing,

would bring in floor coverings, and we'd play basketball on those donkeys!"

It was all great fun, and everyone had a good time. But Al thought it was "ridiculous," because the donkeys had to be taken care of, were messy, and were expensive to transport.

"Why don't we do this same thing," Al told Baker, "only on Amigos?"

Baker got all excited about that, and told Al that if he would put together ten Amigos (enough for two basketball teams), plus a trailer to haul them on, he would promote the new game, which Al called "Buggy Ball."

For the next year or so, Al and Dick Vance traveled from school to school all over eastern Michigan with an Amigo-stocked trailer. Al would get up in front of the crowd and talk about the Amigo—how it worked, why it was developed, and how strong and versatile it was—and ended by saying, "Today, we're going to use Amigos instead of donkeys!"

Audiences loved the Buggy Ball games, as did Al and the schools, since they both made a little money off the events. And because the events were so unique, the local newspapers would run an article about the basketball game played on Amigos.

"We got a lot of exposure from that," Al said.

Although the Buggy Ball games were successful, they required a lot of work to put on. Normally, they were held on Friday nights, and the last thing that Al and Dick wanted to do after a long week of work was pack up a trailer full of Amigos and travel two or three hours to some town to put on a Buggy Ball game.

Eventually, Baker bought the Amigos and trailer from Al; after that, Buggy Ball was his "baby."

•••

Another unusual activity that Al developed not only promoted Amigos, it encouraged his new customers to get out and use them.

"After a person bought an Amigo," Al recalled, "I'd call them up: 'How's it working?' And they'd say, 'Well, we use it mostly in the house. We don't go out with it because we feel awkward and out of place.' I kept hearing people say that they weren't taking their Amigos out to the store, out to church. 'Why not?' I asked them. 'Because we don't feel right. Nobody is using anything like this.'"

To help customers get over that feeling, Al developed an event called the Amigo Round-Up. Al's sister, Emy, usually planned the whole event.

The first Round-Up was held in Frankenmuth for three days between August 20 and August 22, 1973. The event started with an arrival party, then sightseeing, and ended with a departure party. Everybody had such a good time riding together on their Amigos that another Round-Up was planned for the following year.

For the next eighteen years, Round-Ups were held all across the country, and the number of Amigo owners who attended constantly grew. It wasn't unusual for a hundred people to show up—fifty Amigo users with their spouses or friends.

"For some of these people," Beth recalled, "that was their annual trip! They looked forward to it."

The last Round-Up was held in Las Vegas in 1991.

•••

Whatever stigma the Amigo Round-Ups did not erase, the use of the Amigo by celebrities eliminated the rest. Comedienne Totie Fields began using an Amigo after having her left leg amputated due to diabetes. She enjoyed scooting around on stage during her performances.

Legendary jazz pianist William James Basie, better known as Count Basie, used an Amigo during the latter part of his life, and unashamedly drove it wherever he went—even on stage.

But no celebrity relishes his Amigo more than violin virtuoso, Itzhak Perlman, who contracted polio when he was four years

Lively scene at a typical Amigo Round-Up, *where Amigo owners gathered to celebrate their new-found mobility*

old. He is able to walk with crutches, but the Amigo makes his getting around so much easier.

"I first saw an Amigo in Washington D.C.," Mr. Perlman recalled. "I saw somebody on one and thought it was pretty neat. So, I bought one."

That was back in the late 1970s, and Mr. Perlman has used an Amigo ever since.

"The Amigo allows me to get around," he said during a telephone interview. "I have five or six Amigos today. I have one everywhere I go! Right now, I'm 'pacing' in my apartment while I'm talking to you. You know how people walk around while they're talking on the phone? Well, I do that too, only on my Amigo!"

•••

With a top-notch office staff in place, Al could finally take the time to think strategically about the future of the company. The first thing he decided to do was to get out of the plumbing business. Amigo Company was growing, but not making the profit needed to handle the growth, and he just couldn't continue

World-famous violin virtuoso, Itzhak Perlman
(courtesy Itzhak Perlman)

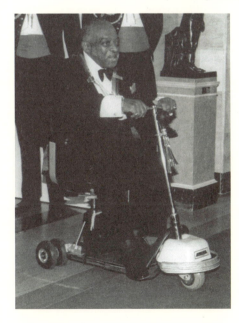

*Legendary American jazz pianist,
William James "Count" Basie*

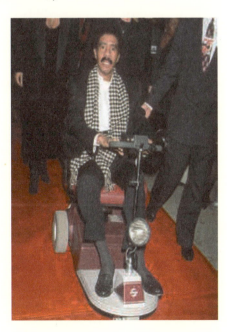

Comedian Richard Pryor

to run two companies. He hated to do it, for he loved the plumbing business, but if he didn't give up one company, he risked losing both.

Al talked to Floyd Schmitzer about taking over the plumbing business, and after thinking about it for a couple of weeks, he told Al that he would do it.

Floyd would not be taking an overwhelming risk; after all, he had been working with Al for many years, and the price was right.

"Just pay me for the trucks, tools, and inventory," Al told him, "and the business is yours."

Floyd took over Al's plumbing company on January 1, 1976, and changed the name to Schmitzer & Sons Plumbing & Heating. Floyd ran it for the next thirty-seven years, until he retired at the age of eighty.

•••

Over time, Al and Beth built up a nationwide sales force with ten distributors, sixteen area managers, and more than a hundred salespeople, who sold some 500 Amigos per month.

"Today was one of the most rewarding days in my life," Al wrote in his journal on June 30, 1978. "We ended the month above projections."

To share the accomplishment, Al gave everybody July 3rd off, which gave them a long four-day weekend. Everyone was shocked, for normally Al wanted all of his employees at work *all the time.*

•••

If June 30th, was one of Al's best days, August 10th was surely one of his worst.

During the week of August 6, 1978, Al and Marie went to Chicago to attend a health care show. Their son, Joe, and his wife Sheree, met them there for the three-day event.

On Monday, August 7th, Al and Marie met with vendors, distributors, and Amigo representatives. On Thursday, August

10th, they planned to have dinner with Charlie and Dorothy Cardan, the company's representatives in Canada. Joe and Sheree left to get back home to their children.

The foursome had barely ordered drinks, when Joe rushed back in. Al and Marie were surprised, since he had just left, but the expression on his face told them that something was horribly wrong.

Al got up and intercepted Joe before he had a chance to make it to the table.

"What's wrong, Joe?" he asked.

"John's been in a terrible car accident," Joe replied, trying his best to hold back his tears over his brother.

"Is he OK?"

"I don't know. Uncle Alden wants you to call him right away."

Al rushed to the nearest phone to call his brother, who had terrible news.

"I'm sorry, Al. John's been killed in a car accident."

John had just graduated from high school a few months earlier. On this night, he and two friends were in a car, with John driving. At some point, he took a corner too fast, and the car hit a patch of gravel, which sent it sliding into an irrigation ditch, where it landed on the driver's side, pinning John underneath. His two friends were able to escape, but John was trapped.

Since it would take several hours for Al and Marie to get back to Bridgeport from Chicago, Emy and Max went to the hospital, where Max identified John, and Emy signed the death certificate.

"It was hard," she said. "I still remember standing there, holding a pen in my hand. 'Just sign your name,' someone said."

Nearly all of Bridgeport went to John's funeral. Al purchased a large plot in the Oak Grove Cemetery in Bridgeport and had his son buried there.

Al had had many challenges in his life up to that point, but nothing as devastating as losing his son.

"People ask how you recover from the loss of a child," he said. "You don't. It changes you forever."

CHAPTER 7

Medicare: Boon or Bust?

"We didn't realize what we had done."
—Al Thieme

A lot of the company's salespeople, with Joe Thieme as the most vocal, began to tell Al that the Amigo should be treated as a medical device, not a consumer product like a refrigerator. If that were done, they said, the government would help customers to pay for it under Medicare. And potential Amigo owners were saying that as well.

As one of them said, "If I needed a wheelchair, insurance would pay for part of it."

The suggestion seemed logical enough, so Al asked Beth to research what it would take for the government to put the Amigo on its approval list. She learned that the decision maker in this matter was Thomas Tierney, director of the Bureau of Health Insurance, which was part of the Department of Health, Education, and Welfare (HEW).

When Beth called him, Tierney listened politely to her argument for listing the Amigo as a medical device, but was reluctant to change his bureau's policy that all devices covered by Medicare had to be exclusively used by ill or disabled individuals. He had the power to make the change himself, but he just kept putting Beth off, apparently hoping that she would give up.

"I guess he was a busy guy," Beth explained. "Here's this young, twenty-two-year-old girl in Bridgeport, Michigan, calling him. I don't think I showed up on his radar as important."

Over the next weeks and months, Beth called Tierney many times, trying to convince him to add the Amigo to Medicare's approval list.

"Nothing was happening," she said.

Finally, tired of the back-and-forth, Tierney wrote Beth a two-page letter, stating HEW's formal position, clearly hoping that it would put an end to the discussions once and for all. The letter was cordial, but to the point. The reason that HEW would not consider the Amigo as "durable medical equipment" was that it could be used *by anyone*, just like, he said, "air-conditioners, stairway elevators, and even bathtubs." In other words, Tierney said, "the Amigo can be of value to ill or injured persons, but it also has a high degree of usefulness to other persons." Therefore, the letter concluded, "The broad and general attractiveness of the item would make its Medicare coverage contrary to the principle that Medicare's coverage of equipment used in the home be limited to items customarily neither wanted nor needed, except by ill or injured persons with specific medical requirements."

•••

In essence, Tierney's argument punished disabled people because some able-bodied individuals might abuse the system.

"It wasn't right," Al said. "I thought about Marie and the drastic change the Amigo made in her life. It helped her so much. Although I didn't realize it at the time, it helped me, too. With the Amigo, we were side-by-side. We traveled with a smile. If the medical community wanted to ignore the Amigo, OK, we could handle that. But what wasn't fine was the government confining everyone with mobility issues to a wheelchair, regardless of their condition. Even more outrageous was the fact that conventional power wheelchairs cost hundreds of dollars more than an Amigo. People deserved to have a choice."

The fight was on.

●●●

Beth called Tierney one more time—not to ask him to change his mind, but to get some information.

"I knew he didn't want to talk to me," she recalled, "so I used a different name, and they put me through."

"Mr. Tierney," I said, "this is Beth Loichinger. Please don't hang up. I just have one question for you."

"What's that?" he replied unenthusiastically.

"Why won't you consider the Amigo as a medical device?"

"Because I don't see them in hospitals."

"Then, what do I do?"

"Change the law!" Tierney replied forcefully, certain that that would be the end of it.

"Thank you!" Beth replied. "That's all I needed."

She hung up the phone and very matter-of-factly said, "Al, we've got to change the law!"

●●●

Robert P. Griffin, who was one of the two senators for Michigan at the time, was very sympathetic to Amigo Company's cause. He lived in Frankenmuth and was well aware of the company. However, more than that, he had seen two of his colleagues, Senator Margaret Chase Smith and Senator Charles Potter, tooling around the halls of Congress on Amigos. Senator Smith wasn't handicapped, but she had had surgery that required her to use a wheelchair until she recuperated. Senator Potter had lost both legs in World War II and therefore needed a wheelchair all the time. Both of them chose Amigos to get around.

So Senator Griffin went down the same road that Beth had

Thomas Tierney,
Director of Medicare, 1967-1978 (courtesy CMS)

taken in trying to persuade Tierney to approve the Amigo as a medical device. However, he got the same negative response, except with different language. Tierney wrote to Senator Griffin that he would not accept the Amigo because it was "a golf-cart-type vehicle, which could be used by those who are not sick or injured."

The senator was not too surprised by Tierney's response, after what Beth had told him earlier, but he was outraged when he discovered that, up until 1976, HEW *had* allowed the Amigo to be covered by Medicare!

"However, in that same year," the senator said, "for no good reason, the regulations were 'revised' to preclude the Amigo from Medicare coverage." And that "no good reason" was because the Amigo was too pretty! To the bureaucrats at HEW, durable medical equipment, in their perception at least, was supposed to look sterile and utilitarian. It's likely that when someone at HEW, probably Tierney himself, saw how attractive and lively the Amigo was, it was immediately struck from HEW's "approved" list.

Senator Griffin considered that decision not only arbitrary, but also "bizarre and ridiculous." He was now more determined than ever to get the law changed.

•••

Since Senator Griffin's simple request had been quashed, he asked Beth to have Amigo owners write to their congressmen to ask that the law be changed. If they could drum up enough support, he would arrange a congressional subcommittee hearing, so that Amigo owners could state their opinions in person.

Utilizing the company's *Friendly Wheels* newsletter (written for the owners) and its *Activator* newsletter (written for the salespeople), Beth sent out a call to action, urging the owners and salespeople to write to their congressional representatives.

Beth was confident that the owners and representatives would respond, but, she recalled, "They were unbelievable! Our senators had never seen so much activity on something like this."

Senator Griffin was surprised, too—so much so, in fact, that he bypassed the subcommittee hearing by drafting a bill directly and taking it to the Senate floor.

"Mr. President," he said, "I send an amendment to the desk and ask for its immediate consideration."

"The amendment will be stated," declared the Presiding Officer.

"The senator from Michigan," read a clerk, "proposes an unprinted amendment numbered 1070. At the appropriate place in the Social Security Act, insert the following new section: 'Coverage under Medicare of certain devices serving the same similar purpose as that performed by a wheelchair.'"

Senator Griffin then proceeded to explain to the other senators why he wanted the Act changed, which was a direct affront to Tom Tierney.

"This amendment," he said, "is offered primarily because the bureaucracy in HEW has taken a very arbitrary view of interpreting the word 'wheelchair' in the Social Security Act as it applies to Medicare, and has precluded the coverage of a very fine electric-powered vehicle that is produced in my state specifically for handicapped or invalid people."

He went on to explain in great detail the advantages of the Amigo over conventional wheelchairs: how it was lightweight, narrow, and very maneuverable, especially inside the home. And then he came to the point.

"Mr. President, this amendment should make it clear, once and for all, that the Amigo is a wheelchair within the meaning of the statute."

After a few questions from fellow senators, Senator Griffin's amendment was voted upon and passed. So, on November 4, 1977, the Amigo became a bona fide piece of medical equipment.

"It was a huge victory," Al said. "A victory for anyone with a physical disability or with limited mobility, and a victory for Amigo Company."

•••

The amount that Medicare would pay for the Amigo was based on 80 percent of the retail price of an Amigo Basic in 1977 ($1,200)—namely, $960. This was called the "allowable" amount, and it would remain $960 for many years.

Once the Amigo was approved for Medicare reimbursement, private insurance companies such as Blue Cross and Blue Shield, Kaiser Permanente, and United Health began to recognize the Amigo as a wheelchair, and also paid 80 percent of the cost. If buyers had supplemental insurance, they could get the Amigo paid in full.

Without supplemental insurance, the only organizations that paid 100 percent of an Amigo's cost were the Veterans Administration and some state vocational rehabilitation centers.

"The only requirement the VA had," Al said, "was that the Amigo needed two rear-wheel brake locks because a conventional wheelchair had two brake locks, one on each large wheel."

•••

Like most things that the government gets involved with, however, there are often unintended consequences, and Medicare's approval of the Amigo as a piece of durable medical equipment was no different. The first consequence, while difficult to believe, was that it was now more difficult to sell the Amigo.

Before Medicare got involved, Amigos were sold like vacuum cleaners, refrigerators, automobiles, or any other consumer products.

"If you needed an Amigo," Beth said, "you bought it!"

Buyers probably didn't even consider the Amigo a wheelchair; they just saw that it was a cute little machine that could help them to get around. For example, when Jean Csaposs, a polio victim, first saw the Amigo, she said, "I gotta have one of these things!" She didn't ask if her health insurance would pay for it or if the government would pay for it. She gave the Amigo salesperson a personal check!

After Medicare got involved, however, the program would only help to pay for an Amigo if the customer had a prescription from a neurologist, a physiatrist, or an orthopedic physician.

"If you had polio," Beth explained, "you weren't seeing a neurologist. So it wasn't that easy for people to get a prescription."

Also, the paperwork required to apply for Medicare reimbursement could be overwhelming.

Regardless of which type of doctor issued the prescription, or what the patient's malady was, the overriding factor in Medicare's decision to pay or not pay for an Amigo was—according to the agency's guidelines—"you have a medical need for a wheelchair for use in your home."

•••

"Medicare," John Layman explained, "just made it untenable as far as trying to get anything done. We had to do a lot of work, a lot of documentation."

Even when all of the *i*'s were dotted and the *t*'s crossed, it could still take months for buyers to get their checks from the government. Amigo salespersons would explain that to customers, but since they were getting the Amigo practically free, they were willing to wait—or at least they thought they were.

"Sometimes," Layman explained, "they'd come back and say, 'Just give me an Amigo, I'm tired of all the runaround.'"

"The whole process got delayed," Beth lamented. "It became more difficult, more cumbersome, to sell an Amigo. It was a lot more fun selling Amigos *before* Medicare, because if people wanted an Amigo, they'd buy it. Maybe they had to get a loan, maybe they had to take money out of their savings, but the Amigo was meeting people's needs, so they bought it."

•••

There was one method that combined filling out the paperwork for Medicare reimbursement and getting the Amigo immediately, and that method was called "assignment." If the Amigo salesperson were willing to wait months for payment, the customer could fill out the Medicare paperwork and assign payment directly to the salesperson's company. That way, the customer could take possession of an Amigo immediately, as if paying with cash. While this process appears innocuous, sometimes Medicare would deny a claim, and if that happened, the salesperson would have no recourse to be paid; he or she simply lost the money. That's why few salespeople accepted assignment; the majority did not. With Al's yearslong struggle over cash flow, Amigo Company did not accept assignment.

•••

To help people who were not on Medicare or did not have the immediate means to buy an Amigo, Al established the Amigo Leasing Company, a separate and independent company to finance Amigos for customers. The company was created in the early part of 1976 and had only three stockholders: Bob Zelle, who invested $17,000 in the enterprise, and Al and Marie. Initially, Al ran the leasing operation, but soon he hired people to run it for him.

"Amigo Leasing worked really well," Al said. "The person would pay the first two months of the lease as a deposit, then make monthly lease payments. They could purchase the Amigo at any time by paying the remainder due, and 50 percent of the lease payments would be credited to the remainder due. It was a good business."

An Amigo salesperson would have the customer fill out a simple one-page application form, then fax it to Amigo Leasing for approval. If the application were approved, the customer would have a brand-new Amigo to use for three years. Once the lease was up, the customer could (a) buy the Amigo, (b) return it, or (c) start a new lease on a brand-new Amigo.

●●●

Joe Thieme began using the leasing option immediately, but Al rejected 80 percent of the leases Joe sent in.

"Dad," Joe asked, "why are you turning all these leases down?"

"Because the people aren't working," Al replied. "Where's their income?"

"You gotta accept more."

"Oh, you want *me* to accept the risk? Why don't *you* accept the risk?" Al countered, thinking that that would end the conversation. But Joe quickly took him up on the challenge.

"Alright," Joe replied. "I'll guarantee every one I submit. If the people don't pay you, and after you have tried three times to get payment from them, I will take over the payments!"

That was an offer too good to pass up, so Al agreed. And it worked out.

"Joe leased a lot of Amigos," Al recalled. "There were very few that he ended up paying for."

●●●

There was a second unintended consequence of Medicare approval. Up to the time that Medicare approved the Amigo, the

The Lem
$700.00

Port-A-Scoot
$500.00

Tri-Wheeler
$650.00

Commutor
$650.00

Chair-E-Yacht
$600.00

Outside
Amigo Carrier
$500.00

Early copycats of the Amigo

company had little competition. There were a few companies that tried to compete, but they were having a hard time. However, when both wheelchair manufacturers and non–wheelchair manufacturers alike discovered that Medicare was now paying for Amigos, they entered the marketplace with a vengeance.

"That's when competition came on strong," Al explained. "We didn't realize what we had done. We had just opened up the floodgates to competition."

CHAPTER 8

Amigos to the World

"I never saw Paris."
—Beth Loichinger

In February 1970, Al received four Amigo fliers written in three different languages (French, German, and Swedish) from the Swedish Institute in Stockholm. He had been thinking about selling Amigos in other countries for a while, but he was too busy trying to build sales in the United States. The brochures, however, got him thinking about export sales again.

"I read somewhere," Al recalled, "that in Europe the government paid for wheelchairs. I do remember thinking, *Wow, we should really find out more about that*."

Then, right after the first of the year in 1972, an order for an Amigo came in from Australia, and the company didn't know how to process it. What paperwork was required? How would they get paid? How would it be shipped?

"We never thought about the details," Al explained. "It didn't matter if an order came from Russia or Japan or South America. They want an Amigo. OK! We'd get it out! We had people in the company, who, if something came up, they just knew that they had to get it done. I don't think I got too involved in it."

•••

Al knew that in order to begin "international sales," as he called it, the company would need to get some professional advice about how to export Amigos and set up a separate department for that purpose.

"We had people from the Service Corps of Retired Executives come up from Detroit," Al explained, "and they advised us on exporting. We got a lot of information from them."

"I'm pretty sure," Beth added, "that international awareness started with the Multiple Sclerosis Society. Sylvia Lawry not only started the MS Society here in the US, but she started the Multiple Sclerosis International Federation as well. She was a very strong lady. She would reach out to other countries to learn more about MS. I'm confident that it was through her international organization that the Amigo got known. The magazine that they put out with Marie on the front page didn't just go to the US. It went to other countries, too."

Another way that people from other countries found out about the Amigo was at the annual President's Committee on Employment of the Handicapped Convention, held in Washington, D.C. Along with speeches from the Vice President of the United States and other dignitaries, the convention was also a tradeshow, allowing medical equipment companies to showcase their products.

"It attracted an international audience," Beth said.

•••

Amigo Company's first director of international sales was William "Bill" Brown, and his assistant was Fran Neville. Bill had recently retired from the Baker-Perkins Corporation, one of the world's largest manufacturers of food-processing equipment, such as dough mixers and bread ovens. While he had worked in various capacities, Bill spent many years in international sales.

When Fran Neville left Amigo, Martha "Marty" Rottiers took her place. She was the complete opposite of Bill Brown, who was more laid-back and demure, but they made a great team.

The international department's responsibility during those early years was not so much to recruit salespeople in other parts of the world as to process foreign orders that came in.

"We more often waited for people to contact us," Marty recalled.

People throughout the world did contact Amigo, once they found out about the unique cart. Over time, the international department did enlist sales representatives in almost every corner of the globe: Aggie Taylor in Argentina; Alrabah, Ltd., in Kuwait, Saudi Arabia, and the United Arab Emirates; Anax Company in Australia; Lubar, Ltd., in Israel; Mobilité-Plus in Montréal, Canada; and Preston, Ltd., in India.

"Preston," Al said, "was a large company in India. They sold mainly through a catalog of medical and rehab equipment. In fact, other countries would order through Preston."

"During the first quarter of 1979," announced *The Exporter*, the international department's newsletter, "we sent Amigos to Australia, the United Kingdom, Denmark, Sweden, Belgium, Colombia, Holland, Japan, Switzerland, Puerto Rico, and Canada."

No Amigos were ever sold in Russia, but at least one did end up there for a while. In May 1979, Robert Arthur Douglas Ford, Canada's ambassador to Russia, ordered one to be shipped to him in Moscow.

•••

Of all the countries that Amigo Company was now selling to, only Japan had any special requirements or stipulations for the Amigo. In the spring of 1979, the Japan Controls Company ordered five Amigos. Everyone in Amigo's international sales department was excited, not only over that order, but also over

162

the prospect of many more. However, none came, at least not for a year.

It turned out that the Japanese company was evaluating the Amigo during that time and had come up with changes that it wanted made to the Amigo in order to sell it in Japan. It is not clear if those requirements were of the company's making or were somehow required by the government.

Amigo Company agreed to make the modifications, so long as Japan Controls ordered a large quantity. Otherwise, it wouldn't be cost-effective.

Japan Controls placed an order for 800 Amigos, 50 per month, built to its specifications. Everyone at Amigo was excited about the order, but then something went horribly wrong.

After accepting only fifty Amigos, Japan Controls refused to accept any more.

"Apparently," Al explained, "we didn't have a tight agreement with them to say that they had to take them, so we were left sitting with many special, unusable parts That was a tough one."

•••

The first people in Europe to contact Amigo Company, asking to become sales representatives, were John and Lene Saunders of Ishoj, Denmark. Like so many of Amigo's salespeople in the United States, Lene had multiple sclerosis. She had undoubtedly found out about the Amigo from one of those Swedish MS fliers. The couple joined Amigo's sales force early in 1978 as Amigo-Denmark.

A few months later, a second Amigo distributorship was established in Europe, but neither of the owners, Ray Hodgkinson and Martin Corby, had a disability. In the late 1970s, they formed the Raymar Company when they became the UK's distributors for ROHO cushions and American Stair Glide, both American companies. The ROHO cushion is a so-called "dry flotation" pad that helps to prevent pressure ulcers in people who sit in wheelchairs day in and day out. The Stair Glide is a seat that lifts a person from one floor to the next.

"Martin met a physical therapist named Alison Wisbech," recalled Hodgkinson. "She was working for the Wolfson Center in London, which specialized in pediatric disabilities. Martin met with her regarding the ROHO cushion, and she mentioned this particular wheelchair, that a doctor from the United States brought with him to use in the UK. After looking at it, Martin asked me if I would like to see it. We both agreed that we ought to have a look at it."

After seeing the Amigo, they called Al, told him that they were in the health care business, and that they were interested in representing Amigo. Al gave them the distribution rights for the entire United Kingdom—England, Scotland, Wales, and Northern Ireland. As Al was used to doing, there was no formal contract drawn up between Amigo Company and Raymar stipulating mutual obligations, just a "letter of understanding," which stated simply that Amigo Company would supply Amigos to Raymar.

Raymar was located in a warehouse in Henley-on-Thames, a small town 40 miles west of London. The company's service department got the Amigos ready for delivery and did all the repairs.

"The Amigos didn't break down very often," explained Hodgkinson. "They were very well made and extremely reliable."

For their large territory, Hodgkinson and Corby did most of the sales themselves. They did appoint an agent in Northern Ireland and one in Scotland, but most of their sales were "direct."

"We managed to get a lot of interest," Hodgkinson explained, "and the Amigo began to sell quite well because it was so new, so unique. It was well made. It looked good. It certainly looked different from a regular wheelchair. The Amigo didn't make a person look disabled in the sense of the word, and people didn't

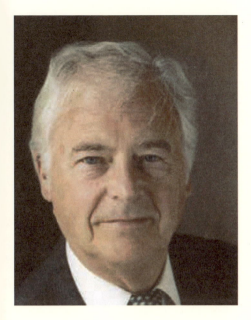

Ray Hodgkinson (left) and Martin Corby, partners in RAYMAR
(courtesy Ray Hodgkinson)

want to look disabled. There's no question that when the person got on the Amigo, their whole mindset changed. It's dramatic! Other people's attitudes change as well. They don't feel sorry for you! It took a bit of time to get it going, but we stuck with it. I suppose we were selling 600 to 700 Amigos a year at one stage."

That kind of volume was about all Hodgkinson and Corby could manage in their small organization.

"We would have conversations with Al about sales," Hodgkinson said, "but there was no pressure. It was pretty comfortable is how I'd describe it. We just got on with the job and did what we could. Nobody talked to us about setting any targets or saying we need so many a year. We'd talk about how many we thought we could sell per year. There was no businesslike approach to it in that respect. We were very much left to ourselves."

Looking back over the years, Hodgkinson said that there

wasn't much that his company could have done to increase sales significantly because he and Corby had the same restraint as their parent company in Bridgeport: lack of cash.

"We didn't have large sums of money to spend on marketing," Hodgkinson explained. "We were in three major product lines: Amigo, ROHO, and The Stair Glide. We did rather well with the ROHO cushion, which took quite a bit of our effort."

Hodgkinson and Corby were fortunate to tie up the entire UK when they did, because they could have easily been relegated to mere sales representatives if a young man from Brussels, Belgium, had acted more quickly.

•••

Tall and thin with a full head of blond hair and a bushy beard, Georges De Coster was paralyzed from the waist down. Georges didn't have any medical malady, such as MS or polio; he had lost his ability to walk in a dreadful automobile accident when he was eighteen. He lived in Waterloo, a small town south of Brussels, where he and his nephew, Luc Magnus, owned and operated a hi-fi shop beneath their apartment.

"Luc had curly hair and could speak five languages fluently," Beth recalled. "You talk about something in Germany, he'd switch to German, then to English, Italian, Spanish, and Flemish. He was unbelievable."

While attending the Consumer Electronics Show at the expansive Chicago Hilton Hotel in 1974, Luc saw Gene Bauer, an early Amigo owner, scooting around the convention center on his Amigo.

What a great and good-looking solution for Georges, Luc thought.

Bauer owned a hi-fi shop in Sheboygan, Wisconsin, but he was also Amigo's area manager in that territory. Luc took him over to see Georges.

"I've got to go home with that!" Georges told Bauer and bought the Amigo right out from under him!

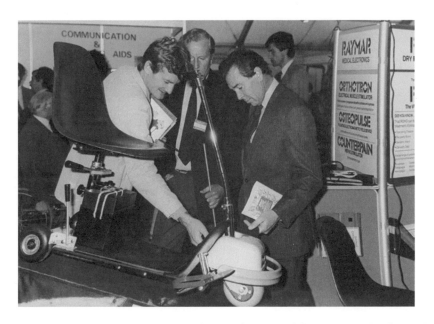

Inventor James Dyson (L) explaining features of the Amigo to Lord
Snowdon, who was an advocate for people with disabilities

Bauer wasn't expecting that, but he was happy to comply, since he didn't need his Amigo all the time anyway; he could still walk with a cane.

Georges thoroughly enjoyed his Amigo, but had no intention of selling them.

"We had a very good hi-fi business," explained Luc, "and we were not interested in getting involved in the disabled world."

That is, not until they visited Amigo Company a year later.

While on a business trip to the States in 1975, they dropped by the Bridgeport plant because Georges needed a new front wheel and some other maintenance done on his Amigo. That's when Georges and Luc met Al. Before long, Al had convinced the two businessmen to sell Amigos in Belgium.

"As businessmen," Luc recalled, "we calculated very quickly that importing a few Amigos at a discounted price could be positive. Amazingly, I sold three Amigos very quickly, so we ordered some more. Some more became a forty-foot container, then a second and a third . . . ." (A container could hold over thirty Amigos.)

Business became so good, in fact, that the two stereo aficionados sold their hi-fi shop and started selling Amigos full-time from a new location in Zaventem with two new employees.

"In no time," recalled Luc, "we had three salesmen, two technicians, and we started to get contacts in Germany, the Netherlands, and France."

Initially, Georges and Luc sold Amigos only in Belgium, but they were doing so well that Bill Brown also assigned them Luxembourg and the Netherlands in 1979. Shortly thereafter, they formed Amigo-Benelux, an acronym for the three countries they covered: BElgium, NEtherlands, and LUXembourg.

"Georges' operation grew very fast," Al explained.

•••

Al visited Amigo-Benelux less than a year after Georges and Luc had formed it, but he didn't return to Europe until the end of 1983. By then, he hadn't seen Georges and Luc in almost four years. Al not only wanted to see their new facility, but also to meet their employees and congratulate the Belgian team for selling over 800 Amigos.

Beth was on this trip. She wanted to analyze the sales processes that Amigo-Benelux was using that was generating such laudable sales.

Georges and Luc were overjoyed that Al and Beth were taking the time and effort to come all the way to Europe to visit them. They cleaned the warehouse, tidied up the office, and developed a complete itinerary for their three-day visit.

"I always called Georges the European Al Thieme," Beth said. "They were both born in April. Georges was very entrepreneurial, and his wife, Yvonne, worked with him. We were so much alike. We truly bonded with them."

The one thing that Georges did, however, that Al didn't do was live at his company—he and Yvonne lived upstairs.

•••

Georges De Coster of Amigo Benelux

After Al and Beth had spent two days in Brussels, Georges insisted on taking them to Paris. Luc would drive them there, he said. It wasn't that far, about 200 miles—a short distance for Americans.

Not that Georges couldn't drive. With his car equipped with hand controls, he could drive just fine. Maybe too fine, Al and Beth found out later on another trip. "He drove a hundred miles an hour!" Beth recalled.

"Maybe more than that!" Al said.

"Yeah, probably," Beth added. "Nothing held Georges back!"

With Luc driving, however, the four of them arrived in Paris no worse for wear.

"We stayed at a beautiful hotel," Beth said, "I thought, *Good, we need to just sleep*. Then Georges said, 'We'll pick you up in an hour. We're taking you to dinner and the theater.'"

All Beth wanted to do was sleep, but she somehow made it through the evening. However, as she and Al were about to head to their room, Georges told them that he would pick them up early in the morning.

"We're taking you on a bus tour of Paris: the Eiffel Tower…, the Louvre…, Notre-Dame!"

"I remember getting on that bus," Beth recalled. "I slept the whole way! I never saw Paris."

After visiting Georges, Al and Beth went on to London to meet with Ray Hodgkinson and Martin Corby, who also entertained the Thiemes, but not so insistently. They all went to see Big Ben and Buckingham Palace and then took a boat ride on the River Thames.

Al and Beth found Ray and Martin just as gracious as Georges and Luc, and the admiration went both ways.

"A more sincere man, you couldn't find," recalled Hodgkinson about Al. "Straight as a guy-wire, I always thought."

•••

With the efforts of Amigo-Denmark, Raymar, Amigo-Benelux, and other Amigo distributors throughout the world, international sales were 10 percent of Amigo's business by the early 1980s, and they were growing exponentially. While that didn't translate into a significant volume in terms of sheer numbers, Amigo's exports expanded 76 percent between 1979 and 1980; and between 1980 and 1981, they expanded 108 percent. It was those stunning export sales that caught the attention of the US Department of Commerce, which gave Amigo Company the prestigious "E" Award for Exports.

During World War II, the "E" Award represented excellence in producing ordnance. In 1961, President Kennedy revived the "E" Award to present to people or companies who "make significant contributions to the expansion of the export trade of the United States."

More than 200 people attended the awards ceremony,

which was held at the Bridgeport facility. All of the company's employees were there, as well as local and state officials. Raymond Riesgo, the Michigan Director of the US Department of Commerce, presented the award plaque to Al.

"With foreign firms selling in our backyards," Riesgo said, "we'd better be selling in *their* backyards! We need a thousand more Amigo Companies, and our problems would be solved!"

After receiving the award, Al proceeded to say a few words. But "he faltered," wrote a *Saginaw News* reporter, "apparently overwhelmed as he looked out over the sea of friendly faces and proud smiles."

Nevertheless, Al quickly composed himself and recognized all the "good people" who believed in him. Then he became philosophical, talking about America as "a country where a dream can and will come true with perseverance and hard work."

Everybody applauded.

After the ceremony, lunch was served, and then everyone went outside to the front of the building to watch the "E" Award flag—a white pennant with a large blue *E*—raised on the company's flagpole.

•••

When Bill Brown retired, Amigo Company's chief engineer, Bud Paffrath, asked Al if he could take over international sales. Edgar "Bud" Paffrath was a Valparaiso University graduate engineer, who had been working at General Motors' Saginaw Steering Gear Division. Tall and slender and sporting a bushy mustache, Bud was bright and affable. He and Al had met at church, and almost immediately Al began trying to recruit Bud to join his company.

"You know, Bud," Al said, "working at a small start-up company, you can make a big difference. It's a lot more fun than being lost in a big corporation."

Bud didn't quit General Motors immediately, but instead worked for Al part-time for a couple of years. Eventually, however, he decided that Al was right—it *would* be more fun working at a small company. So he left the giant corporation and joined Amigo Company on March 1, 1978.

After holding various positions within the company for more than three years, most notably the head of engineering, Paffrath wanted to widen his horizons, and Al thought that was a good idea. Directing international sales would give Bud the necessary experience that he needed to become a better-rounded executive.

Paffrath became the director of international sales on February 1, 1981. Marty Rottiers stayed on, as did Jan Campbell and Debbie Mills.

•••

As sales to Belgium began to increase, Amigo-Benelux started importing Amigos in parts "and assembling them," Luc explained, according to what customers ordered: "different motors, seats, steering handles, arm rests and footrests, etc. Importing assembled Amigos in advance was a difficult task. You never knew what you would need next. I always had to modify Amigos in stock to the needs of the users."

Although Amigo-Benelux was receiving Amigos by the container load, that system wasn't especially efficient.

That's when the idea of importing Amigos in parts instead of complete units was developed.

"Bud and I visualized a small but very efficient assembly line," Luc said.

•••

Amigo-Europe, Ltd., was formed in January 1983, between Amigo Company and Amigo-Benelux, with the former owning 80 percent of the joint venture, and the latter owning the remaining 20 percent. The intent of the new organization was to expand Amigo Company's sales force throughout Europe and to ultimately produce Amigos on the other side of the Atlantic.

"It made sense," Al explained, "because we would be able to sell Amigos to the people in Europe at a lower cost, since the

Amigo would be fabricated and assembled in Europe."

On February 15, 1983, a meeting was held in Bridgeport to elect officers of Amigo-Europe, the new company. Since Al was out of town, Paffrath acted as temporary chairman, and in short order the officers of the company were chosen: Paffrath was elected president; Alden, vice president; and Marty Rottiers, secretary. Georges De Coster, while the minority owner of the joint venture, had no official title.

It made sense to make Paffrath president, because he was an engineer and was intimately acquainted with the Amigo product. There was probably no one in the company other than Paffrath who could quickly find and evaluate new manufacturers in Europe. In order to do that, he preferred to be located there.

But there was another reason why Paffrath should go to Europe.

According to Luc, "Georges did not want to take the risk of losing a part of the Amigo-Benelux market to Amigo-Europe. You know the expression, 'Keep your friends close and your enemies closer'? Georges insisted on starting Amigo-Europe in the same building, and Bud would come to Belgium with his family."

In that way, Georges could keep a close eye on marketing plans and perhaps steer them in a direction that he wanted.

•••

While most of the emphasis on international sales was being focused on Europe at that time, Federico Fleischmann, a businessman in Mexico City, contacted Amigo Company to see if he could sell Amigos in Mexico.

Fleischmann was disabled due to polio, but he could walk with crutches, so long as he didn't have to go too far. For the most part, in fact, he didn't even consider himself handicapped.

It was while he was on vacation in Houston in 1985 that he saw his first Amigo.

"It was one of those black-and-yellow Amigos ..., the front-wheel-drive model," Fleischmann recalled. "There was a big guy riding his Amigo from one point to another, perhaps for me to notice him riding the Amigo!"

Immediately, Fleischmann saw the usefulness of this little machine for people with walking disabilities, but ironically he didn't think of himself. He was thinking about his uncle, Roberto Pla.

"Roberto," he said, "had emphysema, and he couldn't walk very far. It was very difficult for him to take just a few steps. I thought this specific mobility thing would help him a lot. I started talking to the guy I had seen, I bought the Amigo from him. . . . I just paid him cash! It was used, but that was OK."

Fleischmann used that Amigo for the rest of his trip and was anxious to give it to his uncle when he got back to Mexico City. It would be the first in a long time that his uncle would be able to move around. But tragically, Roberto died before having a chance to use the Amigo.

"So, I kept it for myself," Fleischmann said, "and started using it on my trips, or when I went shopping, or when I went somewhere where there were long distances. I fell in love with it."

In fact, Fleischmann fell so much in love with the Amigo that he talked to his brother, Eduardo, about selling Amigos in Mexico.

"There's nothing like it in Mexico!" he said.

Eduardo agreed.

When Federico called the Amigo Company and asked for the owner, Al came to the phone. Within minutes, he invited Federico to Michigan to see the plant and talk business.

"We started an agreement," Federico explained. "Nothing written…, just our word…, and we started trying to sell Amigos in Mexico."

And *trying* is the operative word, because Federico and Eduardo were immediately met with two overwhelming

Federico Fleischmann with his wife and grandson

obstacles.

"Yes," Federico explained, "people became interested. But when they saw the price, they left. Mexico, of course, is much poorer than the United States, so each individual has less money to spend."

But an even bigger problem was that in Mexico, to quote Federico, "There were no ramps ..., no curb cuts! Nowhere! No ramps, no Amigos. Amigos don't work when there are no ramps."

Actually, there were no curb cuts in the United States at that time either, but the street curbs in America were—and still are—only about six inches high, whereas most of the curbs in Mexico were and are twelve inches high. Thus, it was difficult enough for able-bodied pedestrians to negotiate the curbs, let alone people on Amigos.

In the end, Federico and Eduardo sold a grand total of three Amigos. But the entire experience of trying to sell Amigos, meeting people with walking disabilities, and seeing the difficulties they had getting around opened up Federico's eyes.

"Because of that," he explained, "I started a foundation in 1989 that fought for getting access for people with limited mobility. That foundation went very well. We were very lucky. We had a good relationship with three mayors of Mexico City and two presidents of Mexico. I worked with the government in order to make a new construction law. Now, in Mexico City, everything that is built new has to have ramps by law."

For his efforts, Federico Fleischmann was awarded the 2011 Premio Nacional De Derechos Humanos (National Human Rights Award) from then President Felipe Calderón.

"He gave me the prize!" Federico said proudly. "We had a ceremony, and the picture went all the way to the Thiemes because I was sitting on my Amigo!"

●●●

Not long after Amigo-Europe was formed, Al got a call from Alden, saying that Bud Paffrath wanted to manage Amigo-Europe from Belgium. He and his family would move to Brussels, Alden explained, Bud would find suppliers and manufacturers to make Amigo parts over there, hoping to save money not only on shipping costs, but on parts costs and exchange rates as well.

At first, Al said no. He didn't have any problem with Bud being president of Amigo-Europe, but he felt that Bud could run the organization just as well from Bridgeport. However, Alden began to call Al with new reasons why it would be a good idea to send Paffrath to Europe. Not the least of those reasons was that Georges wanted Bud over there.

During the previous year and a half, Georges and Bud had become good friends.

"I don't agree," Al told Alden, "but if that's what we have to do, we have to do it."

Looking back on that capitulation, Al regrets it.

"I should have held my ground," he said. "I should have listened to my gut. But I didn't want to be bothered with it anymore. At that time, I was living in Albuquerque New Mexico. I was too focused on building our Western division."

So, in the spring of 1984, as soon as their adolescent girls got out of school, the Paffraths moved to Belgium. They sold their beautiful custom-made home in Frankenmuth, keeping whatever furniture and household goods they wanted to remain in the United States stored in the basement of Murl Hoppe's home. Luc found them a nice apartment in the quaint Woluwe-Saint-Pierre district in Brussels, and Bud's wife, Mary, enrolled her daughters in the International School, which was only about four miles away.

When Bud arrived at work, everyone at Amigo-Benelux welcomed him with open arms, and Georges showed him to his new office, which already had his name on the door.

Bud was a little overwhelmed by the warm greeting, but he didn't waste any time getting down to work. He helped Luc to set up an assembly line, and he helped Georges to develop inventory and ordering processes. He also began sourcing parts locally, which had always been one of his main objectives.

In fact, Luc recalled, Bud "helped Georges in many tasks. But he did not work in sales. Paffrath had no salesman blood in his veins!"

However, as far as Bud was concerned, that was Georges's responsibility anyway. After years of working with Al, Bud understood perfectly well that while Al supported the whole idea of retaining suppliers in Europe, the primary objective for Amigo-Europe was to sell more Amigos, and that strained the relationship between Bud and Georges.

"Bud pushed Georges too hard to grow sales based purely on numbers," recalled Luc, and eventually the "friendship cord broke."

•••

The Paffraths hadn't been in Belgium six months when signs of trouble began. Al just shook his head when Alden called him in December 1984 to tell him that Amigo-Europe owed Amigo Company $550,000.

"Bud will not send money," Al wrote in his journal.

Al was kicking himself for not following his instincts.

•••

When Bud Paffrath and his family moved to Belgium, the understanding was that he was going to build in Europe what Al had built in the United States.

"It used to be that Georges De Coster and I were very close" Al recalled. "But after Bud went over to Belgium, I didn't hear too much from Georges anymore. I heard that Georges thought that I might have sent Bud over there to take over his business. It was one of Georges' employees who called me and said, 'You know, Bud Paffrath is not even allowed in our building anymore. Georges won't let him into the building.' I couldn't believe it. I was shocked."

Frustrated, Al called Georges to find out what had happened, but Georges was evasive.

Then Al called Paffrath.

"If you and Georges can't work together," Al told him, "you need to find another job. With your education and talents, you'll easily get a job in Belgium."

And just like that, one of Al's longtime employees and friends was gone.

•••

The Paffraths stayed in Belgium for another thirteen months. Then Bud sued both Amigo Company and Amigo-Europe, seeking $138,000 in severance pay, vacation pay, and moving expenses.

Attorneys in Belgium recommended that Al settle the case out of court.

"Settlement negotiations are underway," they said.

However, no records can be found about how the case was settled. Al believes that nothing came of it.

"Bud was president of Amigo-Europe," Al explained. "Who is he going to sue? Himself?"

As for Amigo-Benelux, it went on for five more years until Georges De Coster died on August 14, 1991.

CHAPTER 9

Amigo West

"But that was *his* business."
—Bob Zelle

The year 1980 was very successful for the Amigo Company. The distribution network was producing record sales domestically, Amigo-Benelux was producing laudable sales, and cash flow was good. It was time, Al thought, to open a second facility in the United States.

"By having a plant in the West and one in the East," he explained, "we could service our customers faster, meet with our sales force more often, and maintain a more personal relationship with our employees, as two plants would have fewer employees than having one plant."

He didn't want to have more than 100 employees at any one facility, because he felt that that size was most manageable. In his journal, he wrote that it was time for a plant in Colorado, since he already had eighty employees in Michigan.

The expansion wasn't a complete shock to the employees, for Al had been talking about adding facilities for some time.

But now it was real.

Bob Zelle didn't think it was a good idea for Al to open a western plant.

"But that was *his* business," Zelle explained. "It wasn't mine to tell him this is wrong. I never advised him. He did as he wanted to do, anyway."

•••

Al had started planning for an expansion two years earlier, when he began hiring college-trained professionals to strengthen his management team.

"I read a lot of business books," Al explained, "and the books said that if you really wanted to have a business, you had to have MBAs."

Al didn't hire MBAs, but he did recruit college graduates.

The first of that group had been Bud Paffrath, whom we have already met.

Next to join the company was Murl Hoppe, a certified public accountant who was working for a CPA firm in Bridgeport.

"I saw Al Thieme over the years at lunch and other places," Murl explained, "so he kind of knew who I was."

Al was looking for somebody to take over accounting and oversee the implementation of the company's new computer system. When Al made Murl an offer as comptroller, "I accepted it," Murl said. That was in May 1979.

The third professional to join Amigo was Robert Boes, who had earned a BS degree from Saginaw Valley State University, with a major in marketing and a minor in economics. When he graduated, he became the purchasing manager for the Bridgeport School District, whose offices were on the other side of I-75 from Amigo Company. Disgruntled with the school district and with little chance for advancement because his degree was not in education, he began to look for opportunities in the private sector.

"I knew Marie and Al through the Chamber of Commerce,"

he said. "They were also members of our church. We all lived in Bridgeport and attended Faith Lutheran Church. I looked into his business, and Al made me an offer. I went to Amigo."

Initially, Al put Boes in charge of international marketing, and then assigned him to domestic sales, eventually making him executive vice president.

Another member of the Bridgeport school system whom Al recruited was the superintendent, Marty Atkins. Unlike Boes, however, Marty was not discontented at work, but was getting close to retirement age and thinking about his future.

"I got to know Marty," Al recalled, "during the years that he led our Bridgeport schools to be outstanding, second only to Frankenmuth's schools. I worked with Marty on many community organizations, and started convincing him to work with me five years before he retired."

Energetic and highly personable, Marty became the company's personnel manager in October 1979.

The last person to join this group of managers was Warren Light, who had had many life experiences. For example, during World War II, he flew the famous Curtis P-40 *Warhawk* fighter aircraft. Equipped with a 1,000-horsepower Allison V-12 engine, six .50 caliber machine guns, and four bombs, the aircraft could fly at 300 miles per hour. After the war, Warren joined the A. T. Ferrell Company, a manufacturer of grain-processing machinery, and worked his way up to plant manager. He was a longtime member of the Saginaw Downtown Rotary Club, and a volunteer with the Saginaw County Sheriff Department's Aero Patrol. Before joining Amigo Company, he had been the mayor of Saginaw.

"Warren was hired as my administrative assistant," recalled Boes. "He kind of did troubleshooting where there were special needs areas."

Al's brother Alden began working full-time at Amigo as well.

"The Four Wisemen" (L-R): Don Marquis (engineering),
Bud Thayer (sales) Marty Atkins (personnel),
Bill Schroeder (accounting)

With his new team in place, Al had put the company in a good management position so that he could focus on building sales in the West.

•••

In October 1980, Al went to Colorado with Dick Brookins, the company's production manager, to look for a second plant location.

Why Colorado? Because the company already had a salesperson in Longmont, who had sent Al pictures of the area, and Al figured "that was the place to go."

However, according to Al, Colorado had so many rules and restrictions for setting up a business and constructing a building that he was compelled to look elsewhere.

At the November company meeting, Al told his employees that although he had not found a place in Colorado to establish a western plant, he would be leaving again soon, this time alone, to look for a site in either Arizona or New Mexico.

On his return trip out west, Al visited Tucson and Nogales, Arizona He attended a Christmas party at the Walbro Corporation, a Michigan-based carburetor manufacturer, which had a plant across the border in Nogales, Mexico. Al had met Robert Walpole, the company's owner, through the Chamber of Commerce. When he mentioned that he was looking for a place out west, Walpole suggested that he look at Nogales, Arizona.

"Nogales didn't impress me," Al said.

And neither did Phoenix.

Next, he went to Albuquerque.

"I met Harriet Bolling, a real estate lady, at the airport," Al recalled. "She took me all around Albuquerque. She was a native of the area and loved it. Harriet and her husband took me to the Albuquerque Chamber of Commerce dinner; the people there sold me on the benefits of Albuquerque. The decision was made."

•••

Al didn't waste any time in moving to Albuquerque. He wanted to look for a house for himself and for a commercial property for the business, but was surprised at how expensive the houses were in town and how fast they were selling.

"One for $160,000 just sold," he wrote in his journal, "and another for $186,000." One house he really liked was a Spanish-style ranch house located right on the edge of the West Mesa. From the front porch, he could see 11,000-foot-high Mount Taylor, the highest point in the San Mateo Mountains, and watch the sun set behind it. From the backyard, which had an expansive swimming pool, he could admire the majestic Sandia Mountains and the city of Albuquerque to the east.

Bob and Joyce Jensen, the owners of the home, were there when Al went through it. Bob, Al soon learned, was a highly successful salesman for the Pitney Bowes Company, a manufacturer of postage machines for businesses.

Al loved the house, but after thinking about it, decided not to buy it.

"I didn't need that size of house," he said.

In fact, he didn't need a house at all. Instead, he settled on an apartment at the Paradise Hills Golf & Country Club. Al wasn't a golfer, but the apartments were new, and there was a good restaurant on the premises.

For the business, Al rented office space in the Albuquerque National Bank building, located on the corner of Coors Boulevard and Bluewater Road, which was ten miles south of the country club. A little way up Bluewater Road, he leased 25,000 square feet in a commercial building, which he turned into production and service areas with a showroom.

All three sites were on Albuquerque's West Mesa, the expansive area located on a bluff west of the Rio Grande River. At that time, there was not much going on in that part of town, aside from a few restaurants, gas stations, and convenience stores. But Amigo West, as Al called the new facility, was located close to the freeway interchange of I-25 and I-40. Soon, Amigos would be heading by the truckload everywhere west of the Rocky Mountains.

•••

With the plant location leased and an apartment rented, Al returned to Michigan. At 8:00 a.m. on the morning of December 29, 1980, he met with his management team.

"You've been working in your positions for quite a while," he told them. "I feel comfortable leaving now. I'll grow sales in the West, and you run the company."

Al said goodbye, got into his diesel-powered Oldsmobile Toronado, and headed West to Albuquerque. He drove for eighteen hours, finally getting a motel room in St. Louis, Missouri, at 3:30 a.m. the next day.

Although he was exhausted, Al was so excited about the prospects for Amigo West that he couldn't sleep. After three hours of tossing and turning in bed, he checked out of the motel

Amigo West facility, Albuquerque, New Mexico

and got back into his car. Twenty hours later, he arrived in Albuquerque.

•••

Three other people from Bridgeport soon moved to Albuquerque with Al to work at Amigo West: Dick Brookins, Marilyn Thomas, and Nancy Thieme, Alden's daughter.

"I was on Bridgeport Township's board," Nancy recalled. "I ran for re-election, and lost. Then my uncle asked me if I would be interested in helping him set up a plant in Albuquerque, because I had accounting and office experience. At Amigo's expense, a moving company packed my car and everything else I owned in a big semi and relocated me to Albuquerque. I rode with Marilyn Thomas, whom I didn't know until then. When we got there, Uncle Al had apartments ready for us. They were at the Paradise Hills Country Club. It was wonderful!"

A few months later, Al hired Maria DeSantis as his executive assistant and Anthony Garcia to work in service and assembly.

•••

After spending all of his life in green, humid Michigan, the forty-three-year-old Al Thieme acclimated quickly to brown, arid New Mexico. He bought a pair of Tony Lama cowboy boots, wore Levi's, and listened to KRST, Albuquerque's most popular country western station. With its broadcasting tower located atop 10,000-foot-high Sandia Peak, its signal could be heard all the way to El Paso, Texas.

Up until this moment, Al always had somebody else cooking his meals for him. First, it was his mother. Then it was Marie. Al didn't know how to cook and wasn't about to learn. For lunch, he would have someone pick something up for him. For dinner, his favorite restaurant was the Fireside, located high on the foothills of the Sandia Mountains. While having a martini with dinner, Al could look out over the vast Rio Grande Valley, with city lights twinkling as far as the eye could see.

But he would go out to other restaurants as well. He frequented one of the Garduño's Mexican Restaurants in the city, where he learned that every meal could be ordered with red chili or green chili or a combination of the two, called "Christmas."

"There was also Gino's, on the west side," recalled Nancy Thieme. "It was between our offices and our apartments. And, of course, as a member of the Paradise Hills Country Club, he often ate there."

The only meal he would have at his apartment was breakfast: Wheaties with water! He didn't keep milk in the refrigerator, he said, because it would "get old."

Al and Nancy spent a lot of time together. Along with working eight to ten hours a day, they went to church on Sundays and often out to dinner.

"I would say," Nancy recalled, "that Uncle Al would go up to the Fireside Restaurant a couple of times a week, and I would go with him. We'd share dinners. It had this wonderful piano bar. David Barela was the piano player and singer. He was just a fabulous person. Sometimes Marilyn would go. She liked to dance. I'm a terrible dancer. I remember Al telling me that I was a terrible dancer! There was a long stretch of road that came downhill from the restaurant, and Uncle Al would get going fast and see how far he could coast."

•••

Busy building Amigo West, Al had no desire to visit the Michigan plant. In fact, he hardly gave any thought at all to Bridgeport, except for an occasional conference call, during which his executive team gave him an update on the condition of the company.

In early April 1981, Al got a call from Murl Hoppe, telling him that the 10,000th Amigo would be built sometime toward the end of the month, and he should be there to celebrate.

That milestone Amigo came off the assembly line on April 30, 1981, to very little fanfare.

"No, we didn't have a celebration," Al recalled. "The Bridgeport plant did doll up that Amigo. They applied a special floor mat, handlebar grips, and things like that."

Celebration or not, it was a significant achievement in Amigo's history. Who could have guessed, thirteen years earlier, that that many Amigos would *ever* be sold?

•••

Amigo's success prompted Marty Atkins to submit Al's name for Michigan's Small Business Person of the Year Award. In order to be considered, the company had to be privately held, be past the start-up stage, be facing issues of growth (not survival), and have annual sales of more than $750,000. Amigo Company met all those requirements, so Marty compiled the paperwork and, unbeknownst to Al, applied for the honor. In December 1980, Marty was notified that Al had won the prestigious award.

The ceremony was to be held on May 7, 1981, at the Mayflower Hotel in Plymouth, Michigan. The executive team was there, as well as family members, friends, and Bridgeport officials. In all, 125 people attended.

Al receiving the Small Business Person of the Year award
from Vice President George Bush, 1981

•••

Winning the Michigan award automatically put Al in contention with the other 49 state winners for the national award—and he won that one, too!

When Marty told Al that he had won the national award, he also informed him that he would be receiving it personally from the President of the United States, Ronald Reagan.

Al was a great admirer of Reagan's, and looked forward to meeting him.

Al and Marie flew to Washington, D.C., where the presentation was to begin at 11:00 a.m. in the White House Rose Garden. Al and Marie left their hotel in plenty of time for the ceremony. (As Al likes to say, "Early is on time, and on time is late!")

Just before they arrived at the White House, news of an assassination attempt was made on the life of Pope John Paul II.

A little after 5:00 p.m. in Rome, the pope had just entered St. Peter's Square in his popemobile, when four shots rang out. Four bullets hit the pontiff: one in his left hand, one in his right arm, and two in his abdomen. Although he was severely wounded, the pope survived, but the assassination attempt prompted the Secret Service to immediately cancel President Reagan's appearance at the SBA ceremony.

Michael Cardenas, the administrator of the Small Business Administration, greeted Al and Marie when they arrived at the White House, and told them that because of the attempt on the pope's life, Al would instead be receiving his award from Vice President George Bush. Al was a little disappointed, but he quickly brushed off the change in plans and looked on the bright side.

"Me, a high-school dropout, shaking hands with the vice president!" he explained. "I wasn't afraid to dream big, and I wasn't a stranger to setting high goals for myself. I just never could have expected or predicted that I'd be at the White House, winning an award for something that I had built. I was full of pride, not just for myself, but for every salesperson, manufacturer, distributor, and anyone else who had been an integral part of Amigo's success."

"The accomplishment of Allan Thieme," Vice President Bush said, "exemplifies the whole spirit of what we're here to honor today."

•••

As Al and Marie got off the plane at Saginaw's Tri-City Airport, they were met by a throng of employees and reporters and a banner exclaiming, "Welcome Home!" Al addressed questions about the awards event and the success of the company, and from there he and Marie drove to Bridgeport to attend a champagne reception at the company. As they entered town, a large banner was hanging across the Dixie Highway:

CONGRATULATIONS, AL THIEME!

Lt. Governor James Brickley was there, along with Roy Olsen, the assistant regional director of the Small Business Administration in Chicago. Both of them gave a few congratulatory words, as did Bob Zelle.

"The Amigo," Bob told the crowd, "is Al's whole purpose in life."

Then Al recalled some of the early days at Amigo, and extended his gratitude to many of the people in attendance.

"We wouldn't be where we are today," he said, "if it weren't for the support of some of our wonderful friends who had faith in me and in Amigo."

Some of the people key to his success were there, along with employees Bill Schroeder, Don Marquis, Marty Atkins, and Bud Thayer, whom he aptly named "The Four Wisemen."

The highlight of the day for Al, however, was not getting the award, or the banner across the street, or even Bob Zelle's gracious comments: It was seeing eighty-seven-year-old Mrs. Robertson, Al's elementary-school teacher, listening to all the accolades and speeches.

"Max and I picked her up from an assisted living home," recalled Emy, "and brought her to the party."

Al walked over and gave her a big hug.

CHAPTER 10

A Company in Transition

"You're stopping us from doing what's right for the company."
—Alden Thieme

While Al's business was growing and he was receiving accolades for his accomplishments, his personal life was not going well.

When Marie became ill, the couple bravely took on the challenge. But as time went by, the years took a toll on both Marie and Al, so he filed for divorce shortly before leaving for Albuquerque to open a western office and build sales in the West.

"Some people can handle a loved one's disability, and some people can't," commented John Layman, whose wife, like Marie, had multiple sclerosis. "Everybody's got to follow their own path, whatever it may be. I'm not going to be judgmental about Al Thieme or anybody else on how they handle their situation."

However, many people *were* judgmental, feeling that Al should not have left Marie.

"But Al took care of Marie," explained his close friend Bob

Zelle. "She didn't want for anything."

"Marie kept the house," Al said, "and retained 40 percent ownership in the Amigo Company and 50 percent ownership in the Amigo Leasing Company."

•••

After a tumultuous 1981, the following year started out much better. Amigo Company made the INC. 500 list, which is similar to the Fortune 500 list, only for privately held companies, and it is based on continual annual income growth.

Al had subscribed to *INC. Magazine* for years and always enjoyed reading about the top small businesses that made the list every year. With Amigo Company's meteoric rise over the previous few years, the accounting department filled out the necessary forms and submitted them to the business magazine for consideration.

"We knew," Al said, "that we had annual growth for a number of years, so wc would qualify."

However, whether or not his company would make the list was another question. But it did, and at a respectable #212.

•••

The INC. 500 listing solidified what Al had been seeing in the company's financial statements for years: Amigo had been growing at 50 percent per year almost since its inception. Because most companies are happy to grow by 3 or 4 percent every year, such staggering growth required cash to buy inventory, build additional workspace, and hire more people. And Al was doing his best to make sure that Amigo West was contributing.

"We beat the east and central regions in sales for the fourth month in a row," he noted in his journal.

Those sales were largely due to Beth Loichinger, who had rejoined the company after a nine-month absence. She had left Amigo in October 1980, and gone to live in Chicago.

No one else in the company—whether they had a degree in marketing or years of sales experience at a large corporation—

had the same passion and talent for sales as Beth, who loved the Amigo almost as much as Al did.

•••

While Beth was working to build sales, Al was working on ideas to generate more sales leads. Advertising is the primary way that companies normally do that, but with Amigo's limited advertising budget, the number of leads the company was receiving was miniscule at best. Of those, Al said, "only about 4 percent would turn into sales."

Over time, Al came up with several ideas, and settled on one that really got him excited. He drew circles on sheets of clear velum and overlaid them on top of each other to try to explain his idea to Beth, but she became glassy-eyed. It took twelve clear plastic pages stacked on top of each other just to show her how his idea might work in its simplest form.

"It just keeps growing and growing!" Al said.

While it was difficult to explain, the Amigo Plan (as Al called it) was even more difficult to implement. Essentially, it was a legal pyramid scheme—in mathematical terms, a geometric progression. An Amigo owner (A) would send in the contact information of someone (B) who might be interested in buying an Amigo. Amigo Company would then take that information, record it, and contact B. If B bought an Amigo, the company would send a $25 gift coupon to A, with which A could buy Amigo merchandise. If B joined the Amigo Plan program, and one of B's referrals resulted in a sale, then B would receive a $25 gift coupon, and A would receive a $10 gift coupon.

This example demonstrates how two levels of the Amigo Plan worked, but the Plan went on for two more levels, making it practically impossible to keep track of without a computer.

Usually, a company pays for its own advertising. But with the Amigo Plan, Al had the Amigo owners pay for it! There was a $10 membership fee, for which the owners received a supply of customer referral cards—essentially postage-paid postcards with Amigo Company's address on the front.

"An owner would hand a lead card to another potential owner," Beth explained, "and they could fill it out to get information. And the Amigo owner's name would be on the bottom of it, so that we could give them credit if the lead resulted in a sale."

"Back in those times," Al said, "when people were out and about on their Amigos, *people would come up to them.* 'Where did you get that?' they'd ask. It wasn't our customers approaching people trying to pedal the Amigo."

Although the scheme confused Beth, she was still supportive.

"I think companies that survive have a visionary," she said. "I truly believe that Al has always been the visionary in our company. That's why we have different things going on, because he can come up with ideas. Some are crazy, and a lot don't work, but the ones that do are game changing!"

The Amigo Plan appeared to be one of Al's better ideas.

For the first year, the Amigo Plan worked just as Al had anticipated: 1,490 Amigo owners became members, generating 3,005 leads, which resulted in 470 sales. According to Al's calculations, the cost per lead was only $22.

Obviously, the lead-generating plan was working well, although Al admitted that it probably wouldn't work well with any other product.

"When people saw someone driving an Amigo," Al explained, "they often stopped to ask, 'What's this? It looks like a lot of fun. Why are you using it? Where can I get one?'"

It was this face-to-face interaction between Amigo users and potential buyers that made the Amigo Plan so successful.

•••

In his journal, Al wrote that the years between 1976 and 1982 were "very good," and he was right. During those years, sales grew an average of 50 percent per year. While that was easy to do when the sales volume was low, it was quite an accomplishment as sales grew and grew. As we have seen, Al financed this growth internally; that is, he took out short-term loans with the banks around town and sold Amigo stock to friends and family members to raise cash. But when the company began pushing $12,000,000 in total annual revenues, not even Bob Zelle could help much. It was then that Murl Hoppe suggested to Al that the company apply for a line of credit at a bank.

"For how much?" Al asked.

"A million dollars," replied Murl, explaining that the loan would mostly be used during the winter months, when sales were low. When sales picked up again in the spring, the added cash infusion from sales would be used to pay off any amount that had been drawn against the line of credit.

Al didn't like it.

"I never learned to communicate with banks," he said. "I had Murl Hoppe work with the bank. Any papers I had to sign, I'd sign them, and away I'd go. And that was part of the problem of my building a business. I should have been more astute in accounting and financials."

Al realized that much later. But in 1982, when a discussion of expanding the company's line of credit was brought up, he was reluctant to give his approval.

"At first, I said no," Al recalled. "But Murl and Alden convinced me that we needed to do it."

•••

At the time, The National Bank of Detroit was Amigo Company's banker. Its headquarters were located in Detroit, but it had regional offices throughout Michigan, and its Saginaw branch was downtown on the west bank of the Saginaw River on North Niagara Street. The president of that office was Richard Parks, and the commercial loan officer was Bruce Cady.

"Parks was a real gentleman," Beth recalled. "He didn't come with opinions. He was a good listener. Calm."

Cady was admirable, too, and he was their primary contact at the bank.

When Murl Hoppe and Robert Boes asked Cady to increase Amigo's line of credit to $1,000,000, he readily did so, since Amigo's financials appeared strong. In fact, Amigo Company was on track to generate $14,000,000 in sales in the year ahead, 1983.

In subsequent meetings, Amigo's entire management team met with Cady.

"When Al was in Albuquerque," recalled Mel Shepard, "and the times we had meetings with Bruce Cady, Murl Hoppe was there, Robert Boes was there, Warren Light was there, I was there, and Glen [not his real name] was there. I was production, Murl was finance, Robert was general manager, and Warren was administration. Glen was with the leasing company."

It is understandable why all of the Amigo managers were there, but Mel had no idea why Glen, who was manager of Amigo Leasing company, was at those meetings as well, because Amigo Leasing Company was a completely separate company from the Amigo Company.

•••

With Amigo making a good profit, Murl wanted to mitigate the company's tax bill as much as he legally could. And the federal government had just provided the perfect avenue for him to do that.

Six months after taking office, President Reagan signed the Economic Recovery Tax Act, one of the largest tax cuts in US history, which slashed the top income tax rate and allowed for faster expensing of depreciable assets. It was this latter provision that interested Murl. Instead of depreciating an asset on a straight-line basis over the asset's lifetime, the new law allowed the asset to be depreciated over a much shorter time frame. In other words, the new depreciation schedule allowed a company to claim greater tax deductions in a shorter period of time, thereby reducing its tax liability.

By this time, Amigo's Bridgeport office had an IBM

mainframe computer. One day, the IBM representative mentioned to Murl that since computers cost so much money, there were a lot of companies looking for third-party lessees, and there was a company in Detroit called CMI that facilitated such arrangements. The CMI representative said that Citibank in Delaware was looking for such an arrangement. While the computer that Citibank was interested in cost $1,600,000, Amigo Company could purchase it by making a down payment of $106,000 and finance the balance. The company would get paid back over time by Citibank, plus get the accelerated depreciation write-off. As far as Murl was concerned, that offer was too good to pass up, and Amigo had the money to make the investment.

Murl called Al to tell him what he wanted to do.

"No," Al said. "Why would we do that? We should be investing in marketing, advertising, and improving the product!"

Murl explained the whole scheme as best he could, but Al would have nothing to do with it.

"I remember Robert Boes calling me," Al recalled, "to say that we should invest in that computer, and I said no. Then they put Alden up to calling me. 'See, Al,' Alden complained, 'this is what we figured. You say that you're letting us run this company, that you're going to handle the West. You're not! You're stopping us from doing what is right for the company!'"

Obviously, Al didn't want his managers to make that investment (or to get the million-dollar line of credit, for that matter), but Alden was making a good argument—testing his brother, really—so Al capitulated.

"Alright," he said. "Invest in that computer."

•••

Then, out of the blue, Ray Weigel, the president of the Kysor Corporation, called Al to tell him that Al's competitor, Ralph Braun, the maker of the Tri-Wheeler in Indiana, had called him to say that he wanted to buy the JET product line.

"What did you tell him?" Al asked.

"I told him that I wouldn't sell it to him unless you said OK."

"Amigo should buy the JET product line," replied Al. "What do you want for it?"

"Just pay me for the finished product and the parts. It's not a product we want to spend any more time on."

That was an offer Al was not expecting or could pass up. He had been buying JET parts from Kysor for fifteen years, and Weigel knew that Al couldn't build Amigos without the JET parts, at least not in the short-term. Weigel could have asked for a lot more, but he had known Al for a long time, and, as he said, he didn't want to be bothered with the JET anymore. The arrangement worked out well for both of them.

Interestingly, Bob Zelle had advised Al to buy the JET line way back in 1968, shortly after Al had started the Amigo Company, but Al didn't have the money at the time.

Once the deal was consummated, Kysor continued to make parts for Amigo until Al was able to find new suppliers. Fortunately, there were many machine shops and metal fabricators in and around Saginaw that catered to the automotive industry. One of them was Grover Machine Products, which produced prototype parts for General Motors plants in the area. Roger Grover, the owner of the company, was looking for a way to diversify his business, and making production parts for Amigos was a perfect fit. In fact, he was a much better supplier than Kysor because he reacted to product issues faster than Kysor ever had, and he freely made suggestions about how to make the parts more easily and less expensively. Amigo Company also saved a significant amount in shipping costs, since Grover Machine was only six miles away, compared to 115 miles for Kysor.

•••

One day, Al got a call from Marty Atkins, who told him about an exceptional young lady whom he had just interviewed.

Ruth List was originally from Frankenmuth, but she had

gone to Oklahoma State University, where she had earned a BS degree in marketing. When Ruth walked into Amigo Company's office in Bridgeport, looking for a job, Marty told her about Amigo's facility in Albuquerque, and she said she would be willing to move there. That's what prompted Marty's call to Al.

Al didn't make any promises, but he told Marty that if Ruth wanted to make the trip to Albuquerque, he'd be happy to talk to her.

As it turned out, Al was highly impressed with Ruth, and hired her on the spot.

During their conversation, Ruth mentioned that her boyfriend's mother was an Amigo owner.

"What does your boyfriend do?" Al asked.

"He's a pilot," she replied. "He's working in Maryland right now, but not as a pilot, so he doesn't like it there."

"Well, if he wants to come out here," Al said, "tell him I'll give him a job in production. Someday we might get a plane."

When Mike Martin, Ruth's boyfriend, moved to Albuquerque for the job, Al put him to work in the production department. But Mike didn't like working in production. He was a pilot, and that's what he wanted to do. Four months after arriving in Albuquerque, he had a proposal.

"Al," he said, "could I look at how much you're spending on commercial flights? You and Beth have been traveling a lot, and I think your company would be better off financially if you had your own plane."

Obviously, Mike had an ulterior motive, but if he could find a way to save the company money, Al would be all for it.

Mike went through a year's worth of airline receipts to see what he could find.

Based on the amount of flying that Al, Beth, and the salespeople had been doing to build sales in the West, it appeared that the company could buy a plane. If nothing else, it might be a break-even proposition.

Al and Beth with their new company plane, 1982.

When Mike showed Al his analysis, Al was hesitant, because the type of plane that Mike was recommending cost close to half a million dollars!

"Send your idea to Murl Hoppe," Al said. "He'll have to be involved with this decision."

Even though Murl agreed with Mike's analysis, Al was still not convinced.

Mike was disheartened, but every time Al came back from a trip, Mike would tell him how much money he had just wasted.

"OK, Mike, you win," Al finally said. "Go find a plane."

Mike was elated, and it didn't take him long to find a plane exactly to his specifications: a twin-engine, seven-passenger Cessna 421 Golden Eagle. The asking price was $495,000, but Mike was able to negotiate the purchase of the plane for $371,000. It was white with maroon accent stripes painted on the sides. Al had the Amigo Company logo put on both sides of the plane.

$$\bullet\bullet\bullet$$

Although Al had approved the purchase, buying the plane still bothered him. For some reason, he recalled, "it didn't seem quite right."

In fact, he didn't even go look at the plane for two weeks!

But Mike finally convinced Al and Beth to go for a ride in the new plane. When the two of them arrived at the airport and saw the airplane for the first time, all Beth could think of was her own mortality.

"I looked at the mountains," she said, "and I looked at the plane. I said to myself, *This is how I'm going to die! In an airplane crashing into the mountains!*"

But after that first flight, she changed her mind.

"Mike was a phenomenal pilot," she said. "I felt extremely comfortable flying with him. It gave us tremendous flexibility. We could leave for a meeting in the morning and be back in Albuquerque in the afternoon, or we could go to our next destination. We weren't always in an airport, waiting for a plane. The plane connected our two plants better. Six passengers could ride in it, and we'd fill the plane with people from Bridgeport, and they would come here, and people from Albuquerque would go there. I think that helped our people communicate better together."

CHAPTER 11

A Company in the Dark

"I wasn't paying attention."
—Al Thieme

Toward the end of September 1982, Glen (the man whom Mel Shepard couldn't understand was at Amigo Company meetings), called Al and said that he wanted to fly out to Albuquerque to meet with him and Beth.

Al was surprised by this call "as he was never close to the family at all."

"I was really nervous about having him coming out to see us," Beth recalled, "because we had no relationship with him. None."

However, after some pleasant small talk, Glen told Al and Beth that he had heard a sermon at church that touched him, and he wanted to change his ways.

"He was pretty nice actually," Beth said.

Then he asked Al for a job.

Not that he needed one, since he was a CPA, had an MBA,

and was working for the Internal Revenue Service. Why he was looking to change careers is not known.

"I never talked to him too much about that," Al explained.

Be that as it may, it seemed odd that Glen would want to quit the IRS to work for Al. That would mean that he would be leaving the security of a government job, and if anyone knew the insecurity of the private sector, it was Glen—given all the audits he had conducted of small businesses.

Al didn't commit to Glen one way or the other, but told him that he would be back in Bridgeport in a week or so, and they would talk about it again.

"Interestingly," Al explained, "one of the books that I had read said that if you really want somebody to watch your dollars and work on your taxes, hire a person who worked at the IRS. *Oh, that's a good idea!* I said to myself. So I hired Glen, and put him in charge of Amigo Leasing Company."

It wasn't too long afterward that Al began to have second thoughts. Glen was indeed "a numbers man," as Al liked to say, but many of the employees didn't get along well with him.

"He was a real character," recalled Murl Hoppe. "He worked for the IRS before he came to Amigo, so he had an IRS aura about him."

•••

Although Glen worked for Amigo Leasing Company, he had nothing to do with the Amigo Company.

"But he always wanted to know more about Amigo Company and its financials," Al said. "He was doing a very good job with the leasing company. I appreciated his interest in our family businesses, and I trusted him."

It wasn't long after Glen arrived, however, that he began to tell Al that he should get rid of Robert Boes. Apparently, Glen had been analyzing Amigo Company's financial statements and didn't like what he was seeing: poor cash flow, high receivables, and low profit margins, and he blamed Robert Boes for those problems.

Nevertheless, Al pretty much ignored Glen's advice.

"Robert Boes was very close to me," Al explained. "I had a good team working with Robert, and they were qualified to run Amigo Company."

●●●

Shortly after Glen had returned to Michigan following that visit to Albuquerque, Al looked at September's sales report, which indicated that year-to-date sales had only increased 16 percent over the previous year. To most businessmen, such an increase would have been reason for celebration. But to Al—who was used to seeing 30 to 50 percent annual sales increases—that was a sign of trouble.

Although the sales numbers told the story, *INC. Magazine* confirmed the news in January 1983: Amigo Company had barely made the INC. 500 in 1982, coming in at #428.

●●●

Al contacted Bob Jensen, his new found friend in Albuquerque, and asked him if he would like to work at Amigo Company.

"I'll make you national sales manager," Al told him.

Under normal circumstances, that would have been a daring move, for Jensen had a good job with Pitney Bowes. But Al's offer intrigued him, because he might have been disenchanted with his job.

"I think Bob was looking for a change," Al recalled. "I think he was kind of tired of Pitney Bowes, wanting to do something else. They had their house up for sale when I first went out to Albuquerque. They were looking for something in their life."

The timing could not have been better.

"We were growing 50 percent per year then," Al explained, "and it was really exciting what we were doing for people—giving them mobility. Everything was so positive. Beth and I were excited about it, and we shared that with Bob, who thought he wanted to be a part of a small company. It was exciting!"

But before Jensen had a chance to accept the offer, Al threw in a dose of reality.

"You're really going to have to make a difference," Al told Jensen, "or I can't continue to keep you employed."

Fully aware of what he was getting himself into, Jensen quit the security of Pitney Bowes anyway, and joined Amigo Company in February 1983.

Not only that, but Jensen's wife joined the company, too. She had been a stay-at-home wife, and was looking for something to do.

"I had her work on special projects," Al explained.

•••

Three months later, on May 21, 1983, Al Thieme married Beth Loichinger. Not surprisingly, Al worked until noon that day and arrived at the Faith Lutheran Church in Albuquerque at 4:00 in the afternoon. (It certainly was a coincidence that the Lutheran church in Albuquerque had the same name as the Lutheran church in Bridgeport.)

Many employees of Amigo West attended the wedding as well as friends and employees from Bridgeport and several of Amigo's top salespeople.

Robert and Wendy Boes, Murl and Irene Hoppe, and Bill and Bea Schroeder flew in from Michigan for the occasion, as did Al's longtime friends Bob Zelle and Dick Vance. Two of Amigo Company's top sales teams—John and Donna Layman, and Pete and Jean Lodes—also attended. Bob and Joyce Jensen, and Henry Dominguez and his wife, Pat DeHerrera, were also there.

Al was delighted that his brother Alden was there, and Beth was overjoyed that her sister, Anne, and her cousin, Wendy Skonie, flew in from Chicago. In fact, Anne was Beth's maid of honor, and Alden was Al's best man. Ed Myslik, the owner of the Paradise Country Club, walked Beth down the aisle.

Pastor Russell Lee performed the wedding, and Dave Barela from the Fireside Restaurant played the music.

The reception was held at the Paradise Country Club.

"We had a live five-piece band for dancing," Beth said.

Al and Beth were the last ones on the dance floor to leave.

For their honeymoon, the newlyweds spent five days in Boston, a day in Newport, Rhode Island, and three days in New York City. While in New York, they spent time with Al's son Jess, who was selling Amigos there.

•••

While Al enjoyed his honeymoon, the drop in sales that he had noticed back in September continued to weigh on his mind. Now it was time to find out why sales were slowing down.

Al got out a roadmap and plotted a trip around the West. He wanted to meet not only with many of his salespeople in the region, but also with medical supply dealers, to find out why Amigos were not selling as they had been.

His first stop was to see the Laymans in Mesa, Arizona. Then he attended a medical equipment show in Los Angeles, where he talked to many manufacturers and dealers. From there, he visited several salespeople, including Dick Heup in Oregon, Alice Kaiser in Washington, and Kathy McAuliffe in Vancouver, British Columbia.

Everybody was glad to see Al, and when he asked them why the sales of Amigos were slowing down, they all gave the same three reasons: a change in Medicare's reimbursement policy; increased competition; and the lack of a rear-drive Amigo.

Al was not only surprised by their answers, but frustrated as well.

"We weren't looking into the future," he explained. "I was so focused on increasing sales in the West that I wasn't paying attention to other things!"

"The perfect depiction of our situation at that time," Beth explained, "was described in a cartoon in which a guy is walking across a bridge, and the surface looks great, but underneath it's falling apart! We thought we were on a pretty good path, but we were naïve about what was going on underneath."

•••

Up until the time that the Amigo Company was formed, medical equipment had been sold by medical supply dealers that operated out of storefronts. Then Al started selling Amigos through members of a sales force who—for the most part— worked out of their homes—selling Amigos "out of the trunk of their car," as he liked to say. When Medicare finally realized that Amigo was using that approach, the agency abruptly changed its payment policy.

"I remember," recalled John Layman, "that selling out of the trunk of a car, or out of somebody's house, didn't amount to credibility in the eyes of Medicare."

In other words, Medicare would no longer pay for Amigos that were sold by individual salespeople; the sales had to come from real "brick-and-mortar" facilities. The way John Layman put it: "I guess in the eyes of Medicare, you had to be more businesslike."

Medicare enforced this new policy by requiring every entity that sold durable medical equipment to be "accredited," which meant having a store, providing parts and service, and agreeing to regular inspections.

"There would be a little gal," Layman recalled sarcastically, "who would come out and tell us how to run our business."

Amigo's ignorance of Medicare's new policy was understandable, for Medicare sales had never been that significant for the company—no more than 15 percent at best. When customers could not be reimbursed by Medicare, they usually bought an Amigo with their own funds. But Medicare's requirement that Amigos had to be sold by bona fide businesses threw Amigo's multilevel distribution system into a tailspin.

Al immediately began thinking about using medical supply

dealers to sell Amigos. He didn't want to, since they were notoriously late in paying their bills, but it would be the quickest way to comply with Medicare's requirements.

"It seemed like the logical thing to do," Al said. "But that thought was overridden by the fact that we had so many Amigo owner-families selling Amigos—it was their passion—and it just seemed like the right thing for us to do would be to set them up in business so they would have a store."

The increased competition, however, could not be so easily explained away.

One particularly strong competitor was a rear-drive product coming out of New Jersey, called the Rascal. Al mentioned that machine in his journal in December 1982, so he was aware of it. But by that time, the Rascal had been on the market for almost a year and was making significant inroads into Amigo's market.

There were two reasons the Rascal was making such inroads: (1) it was a rear-drive machine, which allowed it to go places that the Amigo could not, such as over grass and up steep inclines; and (2) the Rascal had a substantial advertising budget, which was bombarding print media and even television.

As far as Al was concerned, however, the Rascal's maker, the Electric Mobility Company, was exploiting a false need.

"Rear-wheel-drive carts," Al told his salespeople, "aren't the right thing for our customers. They need a cart that will keep them active in their career, in their home, and to be transportable. The original front-drive Amigo is still the most practical, functional, and useful mobility cart for people with walking limitations."

One of Al's most supportive and long-term salespeople, who prefers not to be identified, found that point-of-view "unfortunate."

"I do think it was a mistake not to pursue a rear-drive unit," he said. "Al had kind of a dogmatic attitude about it. I think that was an error on his part, and it left the door open for competition to come in. That was a major mistake that Amigo made."

However, in Al's defense, Mel Shepard said that "Al had a good reason for being against a rear-drive Amigo. He had lived with Marie, so he *knew* that a rear-drive was too big, too clumsy, and too heavy to be a good cart to use indoors at home or on the job."

Most of Amigo Company's management team agreed with that salesman's argument, but three years later nothing had been done. In a memo written on July 29, 1986, one of Amigo Company's executives, who also wished not to be identified, wrote a page-and-a-half document to then president Bob Dixon, urging him to press forward on a rear-drive Amigo.

"The Amigo Company," that executive wrote, "could execute a major and significant marketing coup, one which would affect all of our competition, by developing a high-quality, reasonably-priced REAR-WHEEL-DRIVE Amigo. All necessary resources should be allocated to develop this unit, which would simply be an Amigo with rear-wheel-drive, and which would retail for no more than $1,640.00 (Michigan Medicare prevailing rate). Over the past several years, our competition has made substantial inroads into the market that Amigo initiated. Not by building a superior product or even providing better service, they gained market share by building a product that customers want: a rear-wheel-drive unit."

The memo ended with the most insightful piece of information: "All indications are that the Amigo Company could begin offering this cart no later than January 1, 1987."

•••

When Al returned to Albuquerque from his tour of the West, he was frustrated but determined. He just couldn't believe that the company had ignored the competition and had no idea that Medicare had changed its policy.

The challenges were daunting, to be sure, but Al was confident that he and his management team would come up with solutions. He believed that the company had the resources to do whatever would be required to get sales back to their lofty levels of years past.

CHAPTER 12

Amigo Mobility Centers

"They didn't like it, period!"
—Al Thieme

When Al said that he wanted to "set our sales force up in business so they would have a store," he meant franchising. Over the years, he had read many books on franchising, including Ray Kroc's *Grinding It Out: The Making of McDonald's; Finger Lickin' Good: The Story of Colonel Sanders; and The Mary Kay Way: Timeless Principles from America's Greatest Woman Entrepreneur.* Those books got him to thinking that franchising might be the way to go.

"Those concepts," Al said, "were based on people helping other people grow, to earn money, and to be in business. I thought that was the right thing to do."

But Al was taking a big chance. To change a well-entrenched distribution system that had worked so well for so long would be a daunting task, and building a franchise system would be even more overwhelming. Maybe the transition would work, and maybe it wouldn't. But there was only one way to find out, and that was to move ahead.

"In my opinion," Al explained, "we had three choices: (1) stay with multilevel marketing and not work with Medicare; (2) have medical supply dealers be our distribution network; or (3) help our multilevel sales force move into store locations to be mobility dealers, which would meet Medicare's requirements. I chose number three because franchising seemed to be the best way to make the change."

As we have seen, Al had never shied away from challenges or hard work, but with this decision, he was about to undertake one of the most challenging endeavors he would ever face in his long business career.

•••

The first step was to create a name for the new franchises. When Beth submitted the name "Mobility Center" to the Federal Trade Commission, which oversees franchise companies, the FTC turned it down, saying it was too generic. Beth talked to an attorney, Gregory Huffaker, and the two of them decided to add "Amigo" to the name, and the FTC approved that. Therefore, the name of each franchise would be "Amigo Mobility Center."

The next task was to develop a Uniform Franchise Offering Circular (UFOC). Also controlled by the FTC, the UFOC had to be highly detailed and meet specific guidelines. Actually, it consisted of two parts: the legalese section and the colloquial section. The first section was written in typical contract language, incorporating all of the legal requirements and stipulations that the franchisor wanted. The second section, which was required by the FTC, had to take all the items mentioned in the first section and rewrite them in "plain English."

Normally, an attorney would draw up a UFOC, which would have been expensive. Since Amigo Company wanted to save money, one of their employees put it together. Spending time at the law school library at the University of New Mexico, he found a manual that explained what was required by the FTC.

Using that information and analyzing several sample UFOCs, he was able to draft a UFOC for Amigo Mobility Centers.

Once the UFOC was written and Beth had made sure that all of the restrictions and requirements that she wanted were incorporated in the document, she gave it to Huffaker. He went over the UFOC thoroughly, made the necessary changes to make the document "bulletproof," and approved it.

The UFOC had one unique clause in it: "You are not restricted in the customers to whom you may sell your products and services, except that you may not solicit customers outside of your territory." That clause was not incorporated in the contract to penalize franchisees, but simply to have them concentrate on their local areas.

"We didn't object to a franchisee selling an Amigo at a *local* VA hospital, for example," Beth explained. "They just couldn't contact the Veterans Administration headquarters in Washington, D.C."

The next step was to hire a franchise manager. For that, Al and Beth placed ads in *The Arizona Republic* and *The Denver Post*, calculating that they would have better results in those larger markets than in Albuquerque. They got a number of phone calls and résumés, and one candidate, Greg (last name deliberately left off), actually drove 400 miles from Phoenix to interview in person. Interestingly, he was originally from Saginaw.

"During the interview," Al recalled, "Greg asked a lot of questions. But we had no interest in that man."

In fact, the entire interview disturbed Al, but he didn't know why.

Later on, he found out through Marie that Greg had moved back to Saginaw. How did she know that? Because he went to Amigo Company's Bridgeport office and talked to her, wanting to know more about the company and its future plans.

After seeing several other candidates, Al hired Jimmie Murphy, a bright and congenial manager, who had previously been with the National Cash Register Company.

The next position that had to be filled was that of the all-important franchise sales manager.

The first candidate was a man who was a native of Albuquerque, living at the time in Washington, D.C. He was in town, making plans to return home, when he saw the ad for the position. Al and Beth interviewed him, took him and his wife out to dinner, and hired him. He paid his own way back to New Mexico, since he was returning anyway, and it was a good thing that he did, for he rarely showed up at the office. After he had been "on the job" for only a week, he was asked to leave.

The next person hired for the franchise sales position was Terry Boulanger. Tall, handsome, personable, and persuasive, Terry was a native of Waterbury, Connecticut, and had moved to New Mexico eight years earlier. A graduate of Sacred Heart University in Fairfield, Connecticut, he became a sales manager for AT&T right out of college in 1969, and the company transferred him to Albuquerque in 1978. When AT&T was going through the downsizing fiasco of the early 1980s, the company wanted to transfer Boulanger to New Jersey, but he decided to stay in Albuquerque. When he saw the ad for a franchise salesperson for Amigo Mobility Center, he was interviewed and hired. Unlike the previous sales manager, however, Terry showed up to work early and went home late.

While Al and Beth were building the franchise team, Jimmie Murphy and Terry Boulanger were developing training courses and standard operating procedures manuals (which covered sales, service, parts, and administration) as well as selecting other products to be sold by the franchisees. The main idea behind franchising, of course, was to sell Amigos, but as the name Mobility Center implies, the company also offered a whole array of mobility products: regular wheelchairs, sport wheelchairs, a large-wheeled outdoor mobility vehicle imported from Israel called the Sportster, and the Tri-Wheeler, the Braun

Company's power cart, which was essentially a larger version of the Amigo, but with rear-wheel-drive. Along with those products, the Mobility Centers also sold all of Amigo Company's accessories, which included the Trunk Lift, the Hitch-hiker (an Amigo drivehead and battery that could be attached to a manual wheelchair), and the Bac-Pac (a rear-drive module that could be attached to an Amigo). The centers could even convert ordinary vans into vehicles for the handicapped.

To ensure that the franchisees would be successful, Al gave them a 46 percent discount and free shipping on all the products they bought from Amigo Company. While they would have to pay a 5 percent royalty and a 1 percent advertising fee to the parent company, Mobility Center, Inc., or MCI for short, the net discount would still give the franchisees a 40 percent margin, which was 10 percent *more* than what Amigo distributors were receiving at the time.

While the discount was substantial, potential franchisees had to pay a franchise fee to buy the territory or territories they wanted to own. MCI divided the country up into "franchise territories" delineated by county or counties, charging a fee based on the population of the territory. The base franchise fee was $20,000 plus $500 for every 50,000 people over 500,000 in the area. For example, someone interested in 1984 in the Albuquerque market, which had a population of 680,000 people, would have paid $21,800.

•••

On January 1, 1984, Al notified his sales force that Amigo Company was changing its distribution system to franchising. Before the days of email and teleconferencing, this notification was sent out by US mail, and listed all the reasons for making the change. For the distributors, the document said, franchising would lend credibility to their business and make it easier for them to attract salespeople because they would now be associated with a nationwide chain. For the area managers and independent salespeople, franchising would give them the opportunity to own their own business. But the primary reason for franchising, of course, was that Medicare's policy had changed, and unless the distributors, area managers, and salespeople had a bona fide place of business, they or their customers would no longer be reimbursed by Medicare.

"I thought," Al recalled, "that at least ten or twenty of our distributors and area managers would want to be franchisees right away. But that didn't happen. I don't recall that even one of the sales groups agreed with going into franchising. They didn't like it, period."

•••

The distributors' pushback was quick.

"The first thing they didn't like," Beth explained, "was the franchise fee. They said, 'I've been selling Amigos for a long time, and now you want to *charge* me for this? You want to tell me *how* to sell and *what* to do?'"

As for needing a storefront, a few of the "big hitters" *already* had storefronts, such as Earl Gottfried in California, Jean Lodes in Florida, and, most importantly, Joe Thieme in Chicago. They saw no advantage to putting a Mobility Center sign on their building, as opposed to their company name.

And when they found out that they would have to pay royalties, that sealed Al's fate as far as converting his distributors into franchisees was concerned.

"I was completely sold on this change," Al explained. "And I realized that we should have made a change sooner. I should have involved the top ten or twenty salespeople, worked with them, talked with them, and worked it out over a few months. Go back and forth, negotiate, and talk. But I didn't do that."

Looking back on that period, Al admits that he was too impatient.

"I felt that we had to move fast," he said. "I had read that you had to get up to twenty-five or thirty franchises before you started making money as a franchisor. I wanted a hundred, two hundred, three hundred franchises! That was my goal. Big mistake!"

But Al's real "big mistake" was not having a lofty goal—after all, that's what entrepreneurs do. The mistake was not implementing it properly.

"Why did I do it that way?" Al asked. "Partly because that's my nature. For most of my life, I worked for myself, I called the shots. I'd say this is what we're going to do, and we did it. When I started my plumbing business, and then the Amigo Company, I did the same thing."

Shooting from the hip was probably Al's greatest weakness. Sometimes it worked, as in those early years when he was starting the Amigo Company; and sometimes it didn't, as when he tried to change the company's distribution system.

Al had made a tactical mistake, and he knew it. But as he always says, "I'll find a way to fix it."

In this case, he came up with what he considered an ingenious plan, which he should have used from the outset. He wasn't about to entice his distributors by forfeiting the royalty fee, since that would be the source of MCI's income. However, he was willing to exchange the *value* of their businesses for the franchise fee.

•••

Three years earlier, Al had devised the Equity Plan as a means of establishing a "saleable" value for his distributors' businesses. The idea behind it was twofold: (1) he wanted his distributors to understand that he was interested in their success; and (2) if they wanted to sell their business, he would buy it from them, based on a standard formula used to sell a business.

At the time the Equity Plan was released, Amigo sales were strong, so none of the distributors were interested in selling their business.

Since no distributors had taken advantage of the Equity Plan to sell their business to Amigo Company, Al capped the value of their equity on January 1, 1984. But they "could use it to get into the next phase of the Amigo business," Al said. In other words, the distributors could apply 100 percent of their Equity Plan value toward the franchise fee for the area or areas they would like to purchase. With an average equity of $125,000, each distributor could have "bought" up to six franchise territories—more than enough to cover the area that they already controlled.

This seemed like the perfect solution to convert the Amigo distributors into Amigo Mobility Center franchisees, and they wouldn't have to pay a dime to do it.

•••

Al was making it as easy as he could for his distributors to change. As he explained, they could use their Equity Plan money to pay for all or most of the franchise fee, and while they would have to pay royalties, the generous discount structure would more than offset those payments. In fact, the distributors would be making *more* money as franchisees than they were making as distributors! But all of them except the Laymans in Arizona still refused to become franchisees.

Why?

Because Joe Thieme was not interested in the franchise plan, and "because he was the best salesperson out of all the salespeople," Al explained, the rest of the distributors followed his lead.

Obviously, Al would have wanted the support of his son and the other distributors, but he just chalked their resistance up to business and pressed forward with the franchise plan. Allowing distributors, area managers, and individual salespeople to continue selling Amigos just as they had always done, MCI started the task of selling Amigo Mobility Center franchises in the "open" territories of the country.

Now Al and Beth had to run two sales distribution arms—the original Amigo sales force and the new franchisees—but they also had to run two separate corporations: Amigo Company (the manufacturer) and Mobility Center, Inc. (the distributor).

"Show me," Beth said, "another franchisor who R&Ds their own products, manufactures their own products, sells and services their own products, and franchises their business! It's way too hard to do."

•••

One such franchisor was Mike Flowers, the owner of the Electric Mobility Company, the maker of the Rascal, which was Amigo Company's major competitor. When Flowers tried franchising a year or two before Amigo tried it, he ultimately gave up.

Flowers' first two stores—one located in Long Beach, California, and the other one in Largo, Florida—were owned by his company. His subsequent stores, however, were bona fide franchises, such as the one in Phoenix.

"It took me a whole year," Flowers recalled, "to put together the Uniform Franchise Offering Circular, so they were all legit."

But the endeavor quickly became unwieldy. The managers of the company-owned stores were cooking their books for Flowers in order to cheat him, and the franchisees were constantly "chirping" in his ear about needing more leads or that the quality of the leads was poor.

"It just got to the point," Flowers explained, "where I said to myself, *This is too much work! I don't need the aggravation!* Part of my problem as a businessman is that I always did those things that gave me the most excitement—the most jazz. And I lost interest in franchising."

•••

But Al's interest in franchising was just beginning, so he wanted nothing more than for Terry Boulanger to start selling franchises anywhere and everywhere.

However, Beth reined him in a bit.

"Let's do this strategically," she said.

Beth's plan was to first start a franchise in Albuquerque, then expand regionally.

Al, Beth, and daughter, Jennifer, outside
the Amigo Mobility Center franchise in
San Diego, California, 1985

"You have to visit the franchises and work with them," she explained. "Building the network region-by-region would keep expenses low. We're in Albuquerque, and the first guy who waves a check to buy the first franchise was in Tennessee!"

•••

Casper Hensley was a wealthy fifty-nine-year-old Amigo owner, who lived in Knoxville. He had a walking disability of some kind, and so had been using an Amigo for years. Hensley owned a chain of auto parts stores, and when he saw that Amigo Company was offering franchises for their products, he thought that would also be a good business to get into.

In fact, Hensley did buy a franchise, set it up in Knoxville, and was anxious to start selling Amigos. As an Amigo user himself, he was confident that he could sell a lot of them to a lot of people.

However, he wasn't as good at selling Amigos as he was at selling auto parts, because "every year he was the lowest in sales" of all the franchisees, Al recalled.

One day, after three years in the Amigo business, Hensley left his house on his Amigo with his young grandson on his lap, and as they went down a steep road, the drive pulley on his Amigo came off, causing him to lose control and tip over. Luckily, neither of them was seriously injured, but Hensley filed a product liability lawsuit against Amigo Company.

Disillusioned by the accident and frustrated by the fact that it was more difficult to sell Amigos than he had anticipated, Hensley closed the doors of his Amigo Mobility Center franchise.

"Casper Hensley," Al said, "was the first Amigo franchisee. The first franchise we lost pretty quickly."

•••

Terry Boulanger sold his second franchise to John and Donna Layman, the husband-and-wife team who had started with Amigo back in 1975. They, too, were Amigo distributors, but unlike the others, they decided to convert their business into a franchise.

"It sounded like a good idea," John explained. "We wanted to support Al and Beth. They gave us a business to do and a life to lead, and I'm very grateful for that. There are probably other things I could do to make more money, but I get a lot of satisfaction out of this, and you can't put a price on that. It's an important service, and it always has been. It makes a difference in people's lives."

The Laymans opened two franchises in Arizona: one in Mesa and the other in Glendale.

"We were the first to renew our ten-year franchise contract," John explained. "I remember we had one of our franchise meetings in Bridgeport, and I got up and made the announcement that we were going to renew the franchise."

CHAPTER 13

What a Rascal!

"We weren't shy about advertising."
—Mike Flowers

For fourteen years, Amigo had a lock on the power-operated vehicle (POV) market. From the ten Amigos sold in 1968, the company was selling almost 7,000 a year by 1983. The company grew from that little restaurant-turned-office into an office with an assembly shop in the back, with eventually two more large buildings behind those. And the company had 145 employees— seventy-five in Bridgeport and seventy in Albuquerque.

That kind of success, however, spurs competition, and by the end of the 1980s, there were at least twenty other competitors in the market that the Amigo had created. These included the Bravo, Chairmobile, Commuter, Fortress, Master, Shuttle, and Tri-Kart, just to name a few. Some were front-wheel-drive, and some were rear-wheel-drive; some had small wheels, and some had large wheels. But there was no question about which POV they were all imitating.

For example, the Tri-Kart, which was made by Alpha

Unlimited in Tampa, Florida, was a blatant copy of the Amigo: the same size, same wheels, same platform, same handle, and same seat. The company even copied the wording from Amigo's owner's manual, simply changing the name on the booklet from Amigo to Tri-Kart. In fact, if one put an Amigo and a Tri-Kart next to each other, one would be hard-pressed to identify which was which.

"The Tri-Kart," Al recalled, "was the first one that copied us. This lady bought an Amigo for her husband, who had multiple sclerosis. She even sold Amigos for us for a little bit. Then her husband got together with a boat manufacturer in Florida, and they started building what they called the Alpha Tri-Kart."

Surprisingly, Al was flattered by the imitators, not threatened. First of all, individual entrepreneurs like him were building those machines. Second, the imitations confirmed that the Amigo concept was valid.

"I found it interesting," Al said, "that so many people wanted to build something like an Amigo. For a while, I thought we were just building a hula hoop that was here and then would be gone. But it showed that the Amigo was right, which I always felt in my heart."

Although the Tri-Kart looked like an Amigo, "it was poorly built," Al said. "They used low-cost parts, and after three years, they had many service problems. Their advertising did help our sales, though."

•••

By the time Mike Flowers came out with the Rascal in 1983, he already had a lot of experience making battery-powered mobility equipment. In fact, his father had been making electric power conversions for bicycles and adult tricycles since 1974.

Francis "Frank" Flowers was a "serial entrepreneur," as his son called him. Over the years, he started ten companies, three of which are still in business today. His first successful business, which he started in 1950, was making and selling a hand-operated cinderblock press through mail order.

As a World War II veteran in 1950, Frank thought that other young, strong veterans would want to build their own homes, and his cinderblock press would help them to do it economically.

So, Frank started running the ad: "Build your own home! $99.95."

To promote the cinderblock press, Frank placed ads in *Popular Science*, *Popular Mechanics*, and *Mechanics Illustrated* magazines, the three most popular men's magazines after World War II—and sales took off!

"He sold them all over the world!" Mike exclaimed proudly.

That's how Frank Flowers made his first fortune.

Between 1950 and the late 1990s, mail order was the Internet of budding entrepreneurs, who would invent some product, advertise it in magazines, and sell it by mail order. They would start out with a small, inexpensive ad. If that generated sales, they would move on to larger ads or expand into other magazines.

"Mail-order advertising is a science," Mike explained. "The way you run these ads is an experiment, and your job is to generate the most amount of leads out of a publication at the least amount of cost. You're always testing, testing, testing."

With the money that Frank Flowers earned from the cinderblock press, he went into the "transportation business," as Mike liked to say. He bought a Case Tractor dealership and also started a business that manufactured massive construction trailers, which were big enough to carry backhoes, bulldozers, and cranes.

But Frank wanted to develop another product that he could sell through mail order. Since he was involved in other wheeled devices, he developed a simple electric drive system that could easily be attached to a bicycle or adult tricycle.

To build the power conversion kits, calling the new product Pedalpower, Frank started a firm called General Engines Company. As with his earlier cinderblock press, he advertised

Pedalpower units in popular men's magazines. To give people confidence in what they were buying, Frank offered the conversion kit with a full money-back guarantee.

•••

As time went on, Frank realized that people who had some type of walking disability were buying the majority of his Pedalpower units. In order to get around, they would purchase an adult tricycle and add his motorized kit.

Eventually, Frank began making complete battery-powered tricycles and selling them through mail order. One of the magazines he advertised in was *Accent on Living*, a small publication run by a man who was handicapped himself and geared his articles toward readers who also had walking disabilities.

"We were running full-page ads in that magazine," Mike recalled, "and really doing pretty well with it."

•••

In the meantime, Mike and his father attended an electric vehicle show in Chicago, where they saw a few small electric cars, quite a few electric bicycles and tricycles, and a little motorized wheelchair called the Amigo. After they looked it over carefully and drove it around, Mike told his father that the Amigo might be a good complement to his powered tricycles, and his mother, Josephine, could use one as well.

When they returned home, Mike called Amigo, talked to Beth, and told her that he wanted to sell Amigos, so she set him up as an Amigo sales representative.

By this time, Mike had a mailing list of over 100,000 people—all potential Amigo customers.

"Every quarter," he explained, "I would put out a seasonal mailing that would generate tons of business. So I put together a black-and-white catalog with a third of the front page showing an ad for the Amigo, with Marie Thieme sitting on it!"

But Mike only sold twelve Amigos from his mailing list, and

three of those were returned!

"People didn't like them," he recalled, "because they were underpowered. I couldn't make any money on the Amigo. I lost money on the twelve that I sold, and I put it aside. I didn't do much with it after that first mailing."

•••

Aside from the Amigo not doing well for Mike, many Pedalpower customers were returning their powered tricycles, complaining that they couldn't raise their leg over the crossbar.

"Listen, Mike," his father told him, "if we don't do something about this, we're going to be out of business. Tell me all the reasons people can't use them."

Mike took his father and engineer Albie Kalachich to lunch to discuss his dilemma.

"Remember that Amigo you tried selling?" Frank asked.

"Yeah."

"Why don't we develop something that has a flat platform like that?" He flipped his placemat over and began sketching out his idea. "We'll use a flat platform, and make it out of aluminum so it's lightweight. Let's put sixteen-inch wheels on it, and it should be pretty good for outdoors and getting around indoors, too."

"What kind of drive system do you want?" asked Kalachich.

"Put in a rear differential drive," Frank directed.

"I can take that little differential that we use now on the tricycle," Kalachich explained, "and put a motor on it with a chain and belt."

"OK," said Frank, "build a couple of them."

A few weeks later, Kalachich had samples of the new powered tricycle. With its flat platform and padded seat and armrests, it looked like an Amigo, except with large diameter tires and wheels, as well as a D-shaped steering handle that extended back toward the rider.

"I've got the perfect name for this!" exclaimed Frank. "We'll call it the Electric Chair!"

"Dad!" Mike exclaimed. "*Nobody's* going to buy a product with that name!"

Instead, they ended up calling their new vehicle the Cyclechair.

"When we came out with that," Mike recalled, "it was hot! We sold 6,000 of them that first year, and we were off to the races! As I said, we had this mailing list of 100,000. We weren't shy about advertising. I was religious about keeping that mailing list fresh and always growing. By 1982, I had the mailing list up to 300,000."

With his new Cyclechair, Mike Flowers had just entered the handicapped mobility market in earnest, for he advertised it as a mobility device for people who had a difficult time walking, not for the general public.

•••

Because the Cyclechair was geared toward handicapped people, Mike contacted Medicare to see if it would reimburse customers for the vehicle as a type of durable medical equipment. That would add another sales tool to his marketing toolbox, since he could advertise the Cyclechair as "Medicare approved."

"Back then," Mike explained, "every state had a different insurance company that ran the Medicare program for the federal government. In New Jersey, we had Prudential. So we submitted claims to Prudential on behalf of customers, and they started paying them. This is great! People are getting paid! That was in March of 1982."

A few months later, however, Prudential stopped paying customers' claims because Medicare said that the Cyclechair was too big for indoor use.

Just as Beth Loichinger had done, Mike asked one of his senators for help.

In August 1982, Mike met with Prudential representatives at their headquarters in Newark, New Jersey, with Medicare

Mike Flowers, president of Electric Mobility (courtesy Mike Flowers)

representatives there, too. He rode in on a Cyclechair, circled the conference table a few times, and stopped.

"What do you mean," he said, "you can't use this indoors?!"

"We're sorry, Mr. Flowers," replied one of the Medicare representatives, "but those wheels are too big. They're designed for outdoor use, and we have a regulation that says medical equipment has to be for use indoors. Prudential has been reimbursing people for something that's not approved."

"OK, if that's the way you're going to play," Mike replied, pretty certain that he was going to lose this battle. "But what are you going to do with all those people you've already paid?"

He thought that question would lock them into a corner.

"We're going to get all our money back from them!" asserted one of the Prudential representatives.

"You're heartless!" Mike replied in amazement. "*You* made

the mistake, and you're going to these people to ask for your money back?"

No one replied, but Mike found out later that they did just that.

•••

After the meeting, Mike called his dad to tell him what had happened. By the time he got back to the company, Frank already had a plan of attack.

"Why don't we do a small version of the Cyclechair?" he said. "Make it the same size as that Amigo you tried selling a few years ago."

Mike thought that was a great idea and couldn't believe that he hadn't thought of it himself, especially after seeing his mother struggle with her Amigo. She liked its compact size, but "we noticed that it lacked power, could not go up steep ramps well, and got bogged down going over grass. It was ideal indoors, but my mom liked to go outside, too, and the Amigo was not good for that."

By downsizing the rear-drive Cyclechair to the size of an Amigo, Mike said that "it was not only great outdoors, but could maneuver well indoors, too!"

Mike had just discovered the Amigo's Achilles' heel: it was *not* an outdoor machine, and the market, as correctly noted by Mike's mother, wanted machines that could go indoors *and* outdoors—in other words, an Amigo-sized machine with rear-wheel-drive.

•••

Excited about his new concept, Mike immediately called Beth Thieme.

"Beth," he said, without giving her any specific details, "I'm going to build my own cart, and I can do it better."

"I don't think you can ever do it better," she replied confidently. "Let's just say you can do it differently."

Beth didn't know how prescient she was, for Mike did

230

everything differently, from the design of his POV to its marketing.

•••

To come up with a name for the new product, Mike devised a contest for his employees, telling them that he would give a $50 savings bond to the person who submitted a suitable name for the smaller Cyclechair.

"Put in as many names as you want!" he told them. "There's no limit!"

When 200 names had been submitted, Mike and two of his marketing people sat down at a table to go through all of them.

"Rascal jumped out at me right away," Mike recalled. "I was a big fan of *The Little Rascals* TV show when I was growing up. Alfalfa and Spanky, they were just great!"

The name was fun and recognizable, especially with the age group that Mike was going after.

"They all knew it!" he exclaimed.

•••

With his extensive knowledge and experience in mail-order marketing, Mike Flowers was not afraid to spend money on advertising, because he knew that was the best way to find customers. He ran full-page ads with detachable postcards in *Modern Maturity* magazine at a cost of $27,000 per issue and half-page ads in *AARP Magazine* at a cost of $12,000 per issue.

"Those two ads," Mike explained, "generated over 20,000 inquiries!"

Mike also began advertising on television.

"We were the first people in the country to advertise anything medical on TV," Mike said. "All those pharmaceutical commercials you see on TV now. There weren't *any* in 1983."

Electric Mobility's first Rascal TV commercial appeared in 1983, and unlike most television commercials at the time, which were meant to simply make people aware of a product or service, Mike's commercials asked for action.

The commercial started out with an elderly man in his workshop, standing next to a workbench, but then sitting down on his Rascal wheelchair.

"Hi, I'm Ray," he said, "and this is my Rascal scooter. This Rascal changed my life! But let me tell you why I almost didn't buy. See, I wasn't getting around as well as I used to, but I thought riding a scooter would be like giving up. Then, one day, I realized all the things I was missing out on: parties, graduations, even hobbies. Now *that's* giving up! I called for a catalog that day, and *now* look at me! My wife calls me 'Rascal Ray'! If you're sitting around like I was, don't wait! Check out a Rascal for yourself."

Then the scene changed, showing a portly woman riding a Rascal along a sidewalk, and then across some grass. All the while, the narrator explained the crux of the ad.

"Now," he said, "you can win a Rascal free! Call and enter Rascal's Monthly Mobility Sweepstakes. Every month, we give away another free Rascal. When you call, you'll get this free full-color Rascal catalog and up to twelve chances to win your free Rascal! Call now! You could be next month's lucky winner! Call 'em, because there's too much you can't afford to miss! Call 1-800-MOBILITY."

•••

The catalog that the potential customer received did have product information in it, but it was primarily a booklet made up of twelve large raffle tickets, and as the TV commercial touted, the customer could enter the contest once a month for twelve months. The ticket asked for the customer's name, address, and telephone number.

What was only a raffle ticket to the customer was a lead for Electric Mobility, which got thousands of leads a month. Not even Al Thieme's Leads Plan could compete with the sheer volume of leads that Electric Mobility got from its extensive advertising.

"It was never about the product, or the quality, or the features," Beth said. "It was always *win*! *Win* a free Rascal! That was the common theme throughout all of their advertising."

But didn't the prospect of winning a free Rascal discourage the customers from buying one?

"Not at all!" exclaimed Flowers.

The "free" aspect was simply a way to get people's attention. In marketing parlance, it was name recognition or product awareness.

"There were very, very few people," Mike explained, "who would respond to an ad for a free mobility scooter who didn't need one. Most of those people *needed* a walking aid, and they weren't about to wait around to see if they would win one."

Mike described the situation this way: "What would you do with a Rascal if you won it?" he asked rhetorically. "What would you do with it today that you couldn't do yesterday? Where would you go today that you couldn't go yesterday? The answer: 'I'm going to see my grandkids play ball! I'm going to take it out to my mailbox! I'm going to go with my daughter to the mall!' In other words, they start selling themselves. And you would just remind them: 'You know, it's only a small investment to buy one now. Why wait until you win one?'"

Beth Thieme calls that "high-pressure selling."

Mike, of course, would disagree. As far as he was concerned, the customers had already signified their desire and need for a Rascal by responding to his ads; all his salespeople were doing was closing the sale. A similar thing happens in the automotive industry.

"Nobody," explained a long-time dealer, "goes to a car dealership just to look at cars. They're in the market to *buy* a car!"

•••

With his massive advertising budget and his "Win a Free Rascal" campaign, combined with the power of his rear-drive

*Frank Flowers on a Rascal scooter in
front of the company's headquarters*
(courtesy Mike Flowers)

machine, Mike was soon selling thousands of Rascals a month. And it didn't take long for other manufacturers to figure out his formula for success. Very few companies could afford Electric Mobility's advertising budget or give away free machines, but they certainly picked up on the advantages of a rear-wheel-drive POV. In fact, of the thirty-five or so competitive machines that eventually came on the market, 90 percent of them were rear-wheel-drive models.

"The evolution from a front-drive to a rear-drive happened this way," Beth explained. "When Al started the Amigo, people who were disabled weren't getting out the way they do today. I

Fortress
2001 LX
RS #329

Golden Technologies
Golden Regent
RS #331

Golden Technologies
Golden Scoota Bug
RS #332

Golden Technologies
Golden Scoota Plus
RS #333

Golden Technologies
Golden Sterling
RS #334

Golden Technologies
Golden Sterling XL
RS #335

Invacare Corp.
Tri-Rolls
RS #336

Invacare Corp.
Tri-Scoot
RS #337

Leisure Lift
Pace Saver Plus II
RS #339

Ortho-Kinetics Inc.
Bravo! 434
RS #355

Ortho-Kinetics Inc.
Pony 4312
RS #356

Ortho-Kinetics Inc.
Sierra RWD 446
RS #359

Ortho-Kinetics Inc.
Triumph
RS #360

Pride Healthcare
Shuttle
RS #341

Pride Healthcare
Sidekick
RS #342

Ranger All Season Corp.
Solo
RS #343

Just a few of the myriad of Amigo's competitors, 1991

235

think the first thing was putting them in mobility equipment that they could use to move around in their house. In the 1980s, you got the Americans with Disabilities Act, you got the President's Committee on Employment of the Handicapped, and the world of the disabled started to expand. So now they would say: 'Yes, I use it in my home, and I'm happy with that. But now I want to go out on the grass. I want to cut my flowers. I want to go down a walking path.' Now the world is theirs! In hindsight, we were extremely slow in adding a rear-drive model. People were saying: 'My world is bigger, and I want to go farther.' A lot of this you see in hindsight. I think the companies that take off are the ones who are gifted and see that."

"I took my eye off the ball," Al admitted candidly. "I should have offered a rear-drive Amigo sooner. We didn't see it because we were so sold on the function, transportability, and serviceability of our little front-wheel-drive Amigo."

Unfortunately, not having a rear-drive Amigo sooner had dire consequences for Amigo Company. In fact, sales of Amigos *peaked* the same year that the Rascal was first introduced.

CHAPTER 14

The Call

"They were good, honest people."
—Al Thieme

Just when Al thought that he was righting the Amigo Company ship, he got a disheartening call from his brother.

"Al," Alden said, "something's wrong."

At that point, the company had been planning to buy new Toronados for key employees, since the cars that they were driving were four years old. Buying the cars wasn't the problem; *how* the company was going to buy them was.

"I know we've always paid cash for our cars," Alden said, "but we're going to have to finance them this time."

"No, we can't do that!" Al said. "Why would we do that?"

"Because we don't have the cash!"

"Why?" Al asked

"I don't know. And nobody else seems to know, either. I think we need to have an audit done to figure out what's going on. We'll get an independent firm to come in and go through all of our numbers.

"OK," Al agreed.

Alden hired Yeo & Yeo, a well-respected accounting firm in Saginaw, to perform the audit.

●●●

While Yeo & Yeo's auditors were busy scouring for information, Mel Shepherd, who was general manager of the Bridgeport facility at the time, called Al to tell him that he couldn't get along with Emy.

Al's older sister could be a little abrasive.

Mel Shepard is strong-minded also, so the two of them clashed.

Although Emy was just trying to help Al and help the company, Al supported Mel, nonetheless. He had put Mel in charge of the Bridgeport plant, and if he had to let Emy go, then he had the authority to do so.

It seems a little harsh, but the way Beth explains it: "We made a conscious decision, saying that in a family business, do you want to be family first or business first in your decision-making? We are a business first."

Mel did let Emy go, but that proved to be more difficult than he had expected. Emy had worked for Amigo Company since the beginning, had done her best to help her brother and the company, and now was being asked to leave.

"She was in tears," recalled one of her coworkers.

"I was asked to leave on September 22nd," Emy recalled. "I know that because that's when my second grandson, Joshua, was born. I thought God is working here, because now I can go out and stay a week or so in Virginia with my daughter and grandson."

When Emy came back to Bridgeport, she got a job with Al's former IT manager, Bill Loeffler, who had left Amigo Company a year earlier to start his own freelance computer programming firm with a partner. For the next fifteen years, Emy traveled the country to teach computer accounting systems.

When Emy was asked to leave, Robert Boes decided to leave as well. He wasn't under any pressure to quit. In fact, he and Al were very close.

"I trusted Robert Boes completely," Al said.

The reason Boes decided to move on was that he just couldn't see the company transforming from a one-man entrepreneurial business into a formal corporation run by professional managers. He had started with Amigo just when Al moved to Albuquerque and hoped that he would be able to watch the company grow into a multi-plant corporation. But now he had concluded that that wasn't going to happen.

"Unfortunately," Boes explained candidly, "I didn't think that Al had the capability to continue on as an organization versus an entrepreneurship."

•••

During this time, other problems developed as well. Despite Bob Jensen's best efforts, sales continued to drop. By the summer of 1984, the company had used up its $1 million line of credit with the National Bank of Detroit.

"Taking plane to Michigan to sell," Al noted in his journal. He also ordered that all the company cars be sold. The managers would have to purchase their own cars.

"Beth and I sold our cars, also," Al explained. "It wouldn't be fair if we kept our cars but didn't let our managers keep theirs."

As it happened, it was Beth's birthday at the time, and since she now needed a car, she and Al went shopping for one.

They went to a Datsun dealership and then to a Chevrolet dealership, but neither one had a car that Beth liked. They went to the Mercedes-Benz dealership, which also sold Porsches. They probably wouldn't have gone to that luxury car dealership, but they had attended a fundraising event there at one time and knew about it.

"The salesman took us to the used car lot to show us several cars," Beth recalled, "but we didn't like any of them. As we walked through the showroom to leave, I saw a car that caught my eye. When I sat in it, I told Al, "I like *this* car!"

She didn't know what it was, but it fit her well.

"That's the biggest thing for me," she said, "to be able to sit in the seat and reach the pedals."

She could in this one, a 1984 Porsche 928S, with a big sticker price.

"Oh, no!" Beth said. "We're not going to get this."

"Take it home with you," the salesman quickly interjected, hoping to save a possible sale.

"No, we can't do that," Al said. "We would feel committed."

"The owner of the company has one just like it," said the salesman. "You can use his for the weekend."

"OK," Al said. "Happy Birthday, Beth!"

They drove it on Saturday and Sunday, and took it back to the dealership on Monday.

"We told the salesman," Beth said, "that we would take the one on the showroom floor."

They took out a personal loan, and signed the paperwork for $46,783. When they were ready to leave, Beth was too scared to drive it!

"Al, it's too expensive! What if I get in an accident?"

So Al drove it home from the dealership. Beth eventually got more comfortable with the car, and drove it until they needed to add a second car seat to the vehicle.

•••

Not long after the Thiemes got their new cars, Greg Barber joined the company. Tall and handsome, with a wicked sense of humor, Greg had attended the Anderson School of Business at the University of New Mexico, where he had majored in accounting and financial management. He was also a CPA.

After college, Greg worked for the large nationwide accounting firm of Peat Marwick, and then went to work in the savings and loan industry. When that industry practically went bust in the early 1980s, Greg went to work for a small company owned by a friend's father.

"The business was really messed up," Greg recalled, "so I convinced him to prepare it for sale. When he sold it, I was out of a job again."

Then he saw in a newspaper ad that Amigo West was looking for an accountant.

After being interviewed by Al, by John Blumberg (Amigo West's accounting manager), and by several other managers, Greg was offered the job and joined the company in the fall of 1984.

"I would always stay later at work than John Blumberg," Greg said, "because his wife would be yelling at him to come home. So I'd be in the accounting department, everybody's gone, the lights would be out, just my light in the cubicle."

Al liked it when his employees put in extra effort, and after seeing Greg's light on for several days in a row, he dropped by his cubical to ask him what he was working on.

"There's a couple of things that don't make sense to me," Greg replied. "Murl said that we had this much in receivables and this much in cash. Well, there's this gap. The way financials work, you can't have a gap."

He didn't tell Al anything more than that, because he hadn't yet figured out the discrepancy.

•••

In the meantime, the results of the audit came in, and they showed that the company was in serious financial trouble.

"The audit revealed," Al explained, "that our in-house financial statements showed much better results than what was actually happening. That was such a shock to me because the financials I was getting—the ones that were put together in Bridgeport and sent out to me in Albuquerque—showed that we were doing well. The company was growing, and we were very profitable. So, to get this audit, I never expected anything like that!"

••••

There were two primary reasons why the financials were incorrect. One was obscure, but the other should have been apparent.

The obscure reason was that the "cost of goods sold" number—typically the second line item on a company's income statement and the number that is subtracted from "sales" to generate the all-important "gross profit" number—was wrong. It was artificially low, causing the gross profit to be artificially high, which resulted in an artificially high "net income" number.

And that was the fault of the company's computer software.

"The problem," Greg explained, "was the way that the inventory program operated. It was an 'average costing system,' instead of a 'last-in, first-out' system; it just averaged the cost of goods. Every time an entry was made into the inventory, the system just put it into a pool and averaged it."

Normally, that would not have been a problem, but in a period of high inflation—which the 1980s were—the computer software was not keeping up with the prices Amigo Company was paying for parts.

"So that was the problem," Greg said. "The system was misstating how much our gross profit really was. We never knew how well or how badly we were doing!"

When Bill Schroeder ran the accounting department, however, the company always knew how it was performing.

"Bill was hired very early in the company," Al explained, "and he was used to working with spreadsheets and paper."

And so was everyone else in accounting.

"Back at that time," Emy explained, "we had about sixty employees, and I had to do the payroll by hand. I did the hour multiplications and the deductions on a big spreadsheet."

Joyce Bennett, who also worked in the accounting

department, recalled similar processes before a computer was brought in.

"I used to do my accounting on ledger cards," Joyce said. "Every month, I had to balance, and if I was off, I had to go through all of my ledger cards to see if I had transposed a number or whatever. But I always balanced!"

The work was time-consuming, but the results were accurate.

When Emy was asked if it were challenging to convert the paper accounting system to the computer, she said, "It's like anything new, you know, a difficult thing."

But Murl wasn't so generous. "It was a fiasco!" he said.

When Amigo purchased its first computer, Al said, "Bill Schroeder told me, 'Al, I'm not a computer man. You have to hire a person who understands computers.' And that's when we hired Murl Hoppe."

The second problem that Yeo & Yeo's audit brought to Al's attention was his Equity Plan, which could cost Amigo Company $500,000 if the key distributors ever decided to sell their business to the Amigo Company.

"Our in-house financials," Al said, "did not list this as a liability, but the audit did list it as a possible liability."

During this time, receivables were also high. While that line item on the income statement was accurate, it also helped to explain why the company's cash flow was so poor.

"My good friend Bob Zelle," Al said, "had told me numerous times, 'Al, watch and control receivables! Poor collections have destroyed many companies.' Unfortunately, I was overly focused on building the West, and not watching receivables."

The worst offender of receivables was Amigo-Europe, which owed Amigo Company a staggering $550,000! That amount had built up relentlessly. Amigo-Europe would order one shipping container of Amigos, and while that container was crossing the Atlantic Ocean, it would order another. At that rate, it didn't take long for receivables to get out of hand.

"Along with this," Al explained, "many of Amigo's top salespeople were slow to pay us. Their businesses were growing, and growth eats cash flow. They expected the Amigo Company to be their bank."

Unfortunately, if receivables are high, most likely payables are, too.

"I surmised that," recalled Joyce Bennett. "I worked with June Racquepaw. She worked in payables, and I know they were trying to figure out how to get enough money to pay the bills on time. That was a struggle for us."

Additionally, Amigo Company was suffering from runaway expenses. Warren Light, for example, was spending thousands of dollars a year on patent applications, not only domestically, but internationally as well.

"Warren loved the legal stuff!" exclaimed Beth. "He loved working with lawyers, applying for patents and trademarks."

However, when Beth laid out all the patents on the table, she found that very few sales occured on the many ideas.

She also discovered other outrageous expenses, including $45,000 to a sales consultant, $15,000 for unneeded office furniture, $19,000 to buy a dubious mailing list, and $40,000 a year for a directors and officers insurance policy.

•••

Why was all this allowed to happen?

"Because there wasn't one person running the show," Beth explained bluntly. "You kind of want a tough person at the top sometimes. Someone who will ruffle feathers, say no and put some reins on them. I just think, looking back, knowing the people, we didn't have one person in charge who really understood the whole thing. A lot of people had management roles, but there wasn't one in control."

The one person who should have been in control, of course, was Al Thieme. But he had relegated that responsibility and authority to his management team in Bridgeport when he left for

Albuquerque.

Regardless of how and why it happened, Al blamed himself for the company being in the mess it was in—not Robert Boes, Murl Hoppe, or Warren Light.

"They were good, honest people," Al said.

•••

Glen, Amigo Leasing Company's manager, wasn't about to absolve all of Amigo Company's management team of responsibility. He didn't criticize Boes too much, because Boes was no longer there. But Hoppe was still in charge of accounting, so Glen placed the blame for the company's inaccurate financial statements squarely on his lap.

"We need to remove Murl," he told Al. "He's your financial guy, so he's the one responsible to see that you had proper accounting."

Al became disheartened when he heard that, but he couldn't argue against what Glen was telling him.

At a board meeting held on December 4, 1984, Murl was asked to resign.

"Murl was hurt," Emy said. "His family never talked to any of us again."

•••

Fortunately, the audit was done by the Saginaw accounting firm and only for the edification of Amigo Company's managers, who would use the information that they had learned from the audit to make the necessary changes and move on. However, if Bruce Cady at the National Bank of Detroit found out that the financial statements that he was getting from Amigo Company were overstated, that could have devastating results.

Nobody knew that better than Glen, so it's understandable why he became enraged when he came across some information that made even the audit results pale in comparison. He was so beside himself that Alden and Mel were compelled to call Al to ask him to come back to Michigan for a few days.

"They need help in handling Glen," Al noted in his journal.

What happened was that Glen had found out about the Equity Plan that Al had developed for Amigo's distributors. As far as Glen was concerned, based on all the audits he had done for the IRS, the Equity Plan created a half-a-million-dollar liability for the company.

"Glen was all over the place," Al explained, "driving people bonkers," complaining to Alden, Mel, and anybody else who would listen about that "concealed" liability.

When Al and Beth flew to Michigan, they had a late Sunday afternoon meeting with Alden, Mel, Warren, Glen, and Tom McNish, Glen's right-hand man.

"The meeting was grim," Al noted later.

All they talked about were problems, problems, and more problems: money was low, suppliers were getting restless, and there were rumors about the company going bankrupt.

Not surprisingly, the most heated topic was Amigo West. Glen wanted it shut down. To prove his point, he showed the group how positive the business plan that he and McNish had worked on was, which did *not* include Amigo West. But when Al tried to make his argument about leaving it open, Glen got upset and walked out.

On that Monday, Glen and McNish surreptitiously met with Bruce Cady and showed him their business plan minus Amigo West. Cady looked it over and gave a positive response.

"I was in meetings with our other managers and with Cady," said Mel Shepard. "And Cady said, 'Look, you guys better get this thing turned around, and if you don't ....' And he went through the process of describing what taking possession by the bank would be like, repossessing the company and selling off its assets. I don't know how dead serious he was. I think he wanted to paint a picture that would make us wake up and realize that things were serious. The times I remember interacting with Bruce Cady, Al and Beth were still in Albuquerque, and I think Cady realized that we were maybe just sitting there saying, 'Well, our leader's not here. This is really not our job to fix things. We need Al here to do that.' Cady spoke to us like we really didn't understand what was coming down the tube if we didn't change things."

●●●

With both Murl Hoppe and Robert Boes now gone, Alden asked Al to put Glen in control of the Bridgeport office. Alden didn't like Glen's tactics any more than Al did, but Glen was the only one at the Bridgeport facility who had the wherewithal to work with the bank.

Al trusted his brother, thought about what he said, and agreed to put Glen in charge. At an emergency board meeting on December 19, 1984, the board appointed Glen general manager and chief executive officer of Amigo Company, with the proviso "that all managerial decisions by the Chief Executive Officer are subject to advice and consultation of the management staff: Mel Shepard, Warren Light, Alden Thieme, and Tom McNish."

The one man whom no one ever thought would be leading Amigo Company was now its principal executive.

"The bank wanted us to take action," Al confirmed, "and what the company needed was somebody that understood numbers and could work with the bank. So, it was alright to put him in as general manager, or whatever we called him."

"I think Al was up against the wall!" Beth said.

The audit results were poor, negative publicity was hitting the newspapers, and Glen was now the general manager.

"I think, at that point," Beth explained, "Al put up his hands and said, 'OK!'"

Since the board now called Glen general manager and CEO, his position in the eyes of the law made him the highest-ranking executive in the company, who was ultimately responsible for making managerial decisions. Although Al remained chairman, he might as well have abdicated his own authority, because that "advice" clause in the board's resolution did not necessarily—and probably didn't—prevent Glen from doing whatever he wanted in terms of running the company.

•••

One of the pieces of negative publicity that Beth was talking about was an article that appeared in the *Albuquerque Journal*. Someone in the Bridgeport office called the newspaper to say that Amigo West would soon be shutting down. "Albuquerque Layoffs in Line with Recovery, Officials Say," ran the headline. The article wasn't exclusively about Amigo West, but mentioned it along with a number of other companies that were either downsizing or closing altogether. It said that Amigo West would be closing in January, and cited a slump in sales as the reason. Another company that was mentioned was the Plateau Corporation, an oil company that had a refinery in Farmington, New Mexico, with corporate offices in Albuquerque. About 100 employees were losing their jobs due to the company being sold.

When Al and Beth returned to Amigo West, they were met by a group of disheartened employees. Al tried to allay their fears, admitting that the company was in trouble, but emphasizing that he had not yet made up his mind about what to do with the Albuquerque facility.

But the employees weren't buying it.

"They were hurt, sad, and mad," Al wrote in his journal.

•••

While Al was doing his best to calm the waters in Albuquerque, Glen was ordering people around in Bridgeport. He and Tom McNish went to see Bruce Cady again to tell him that Glen was the new CEO of the Amigo Company. Cady was so pleasantly surprised that he asked Glen if he could send him a new organizational chart without Al Thieme's name on it!

Al had heard some pretty strange things lately, but when he heard from Glen about what Cady wanted, it was hard for him to believe. In fact, by this point, he didn't know what or whom to believe. To get some unbiased advice, he called Jack Wild for help.

The sixty-year-old Wild was the treasurer of the Wirtz Manufacturing Company in Port Huron, Michigan. After telling Wild what he knew about the situation, Al asked him to meet with Cady.

"I trusted Jack," Al said. "He was neutral. He had no alliance to anyone."

That was on December 21, 1984. On the morning of the 24th, Wild reported back to Al.

"The information," Wild said, "that you're getting from Glen and Warren Light is different from what Bruce Cady told me."

Not wanting to muddle things up worse than they already were, Wild simply replied, "Call Bruce Cady."

Since it was Christmas Eve Day, Al didn't have much confidence that Cady would be in his office, but he called him anyway. As he figured, no one answered, so he left a message.

Around 4:00 that afternoon, Al and Beth had just returned home from the office when the telephone rang.

"I wonder who that is?" Al asked, thinking that it couldn't possibly be Cady. But it was.

After making some small talk, Cady came to the point.

"If you don't close down the Albuquerque facility," he told Al, "I'm going to have to pull your loan. You need to come back to Bridgeport and run your company."

CHAPTER 15

Consolidation to

Albuquerque

"Being realistic is not one of my attributes."
—Al Thieme

Al waited until after Christmas to dig into what had prompted Cady's ominous call. Apparently, people had been feeding Amigo Company's audited financial information to Cady, and that's why he had returned Al's call.

Al understood that Cady had no choice and had to do whatever he could to protect the bank's position.

And in the short term, there was little that Al could do, either. Murl was gone, Boes was gone, and the person that he had put in charge had let him down.

•••

Why did this happen? Why would Glen give Bruce Cady sensitive financial information, knowing full well that could have a devastating effect on Amigo Company?

"Possibly," Al explained, "because many people wanted me and Beth out of the picture to give the company to Marie. And they would help her hire the right people to run the business."

Essentially, what Glen and some of the people at the Bridgeport facility were saying was: "Al and Beth, stay in Albuquerque, do whatever, but we're going to get the business."

"For a while," Al explained, "the people in Bridgeport thought that I was going to shut Bridgeport down completely and move everything to Albuquerque. Alden had told me that. I can understand why people would feel that way. I transferred sales management to the West when sales continued to slide in the East and Midwest. Next I was going to transfer financial control to the West when cash flow problems surfaced, and we had Murl leave. Bridgeport was left with manufacturing and shipping Amigos to the East and Midwest. That gave people in Bridgeport more of the feeling that they had to keep this in Michigan and keep it in Marie's hands."

Keith Christiansen, a longtime and trusted employee, whom Al said was like a son to him, confirmed that these were the sentiments at the Bridgeport plant.

"I heard Glen say in conversations to others," Keith recalled, "'Al doesn't need to be running the company anymore, and he shouldn't be in charge. This company's Marie's.' I'm not sure if Glen wanted to take over, but he basically felt he and the others in Bridgeport could run the company better without Al."

There was one more person who would have loved to see Al Thieme go, and that was Greg, the "strange" fellow whom Beth had interviewed for the franchise manager position. Al and Beth knew, of course, that Greg had ended up back in Michigan, but in the meantime, he had struck up an association with Marie Thieme, and for some curious reason he was now going by a different first name. When he originally applied for the franchise manager position, he used the name Greg. In Michigan, he used the name David.

Regardless of what name he was using, apparently, he was consulting Marie on business matters, and one of their ideas may have been to get Al out of the company.

Charlene Zorn did not know any details, but recalls that "there was a divide there between Al and Marie. I could see where Marie and whoever she was working with…, and I don't remember what his name was…, I do remember there was a lot of not-so-good things happening."

•••

At the time, Al was unaware of those factions. All he knew was that he was not about to let acts of disloyalty go unanswered. As in a scene from *The Godfather*, he first called Warren Light and had him leave. Then he called Glen.

"Glen, he said, "you no longer will be a part of the Amigo company."

"Are you firing me?" Glen asked.

"No," Al replied. "You can continue to run the leasing company, but stay totally out of Amigo Company's business. I'm transferring all corporate financial control to Albuquerque."

With no financial expertise left in the company, Al began looking for "a good financial person." After putting the word out in Albuquerque's business community, he got a lead from the Arthur Anderson accounting office.

•••

Tall, tanned, and mustachioed, with a deep, melodic voice, Bobby Gene Dixon could have easily played the brother of movie heartthrob Sam Elliott.[1] He was born on December 17, 1927, in Parsons, Kansas, a railroad town in the southeast corner of the state, where he was raised. After serving in the Navy during World War II, he attended the University of Colorado, earning a bachelor's degree in business administration.

---

1 Bobby, not Robert, was the name on his birth certificate, although he went by Bob.

"Dad worked for the Plateau Corporation," explained Bob's daughter, Jennifer. "Plateau was a refinery with gas stations in the Southwest."

Bob joined Plateau's office in Albuquerque in 1965 and worked his way up to be its vice president of finance and administration. When he started with the company, it was worth $3 million; when he left, nineteen years later, it was worth $325 million.

In 1984, when Plateau was put up for sale, Bob and several partners tried to buy it, but another investment group outbid them. So Bob's dream of owning an oil company came to a screeching halt, and he became one of those 100 laid-off people mentioned in that *Albuquerque Journal* article.

The staff at Arthur Anderson knew Bob well, were aware that he was out of a job, and notified him about Amigo West.

•••

Al and Beth were immediately impressed with Bob Dixon.

"He was a pure financial guy," Beth recalled.

They told him why they were looking for somebody with his experience and brought him up-to-date on the condition of the company.

"Bob asked tough questions," Al recalled. "I didn't sugarcoat anything."

He told Bob that the company was in financial trouble, and that they needed a strong financial person to help them turn it around.

The three of them spent most of January 1985 talking back and forth, weighing the pros and cons, but eventually Al and Beth made Bob an offer, and he accepted it.

"He so strongly wanted to make a difference," Al recalled. "He really, truly wanted to help me, Beth, our employees, and Amigo Company."

On Bob's first day of work, Al gave him a pile of folders to go through, and Bob, who was a hard worker, learned quickly.

"I would be in on Saturdays," Al recalled, "and Bob was there, also. He was doing everything possible to help our company."

And so was Greg Barber.

"I was hurt and disappointed that Al didn't make *me* his top financial guy," Greg recalled, "but I was only twenty-seven at the time. However, when I met Bob Dixon and saw the tons of experience that he had, his nature, and what a smart guy he was, I came to accept that he was the right choice. We worked well together."

•••

Not long after Bob joined the company, however, Al began to have second thoughts about hiring him.

"I had some instinct about him," Al explained. "I had a feeling that something wasn't right. A lot of things I do are by intuition. I don't know where it comes from. I just have these feelings."

While Al had his doubts about Bob, he let them pass. There was nothing that Bob was doing that was questionable. In fact, his performance was exemplary.

Furthermore, Al and Beth soon developed a friendship with Bob and his wife, Jeanne.

•••

A month after Dixon joined Amigo, Robert "Bob" Shrode was hired as the company's personnel director, and then Wolfgang Price was recruited as a business consultant.

Shrode was a graduate of the University of New Mexico with a degree in business administration and had recently been laid off from the Public Service Company of New Mexico, due, he said, to "a big political upheaval."

While Shrode was looking for a new job, some close friends of his bought an Amigo for their little girl who had muscular dystrophy, and now she could play with the other kids on her cul-de-sac. Shrode was so impressed with how that machine changed the girl's life that he thought to himself, *That would be a good company to work for.*

As luck would have it, a friend of a friend of his worked at Amigo, and she arranged a meeting between him and Al.

"I went to see Al on a Friday afternoon," Shrode recalled. "He had a stand-up desk. 'You can start on Monday,' he told me."

As for Wolfgang Price, he was a few years older than Al, had a bachelor's degree in industrial engineering from Marquette University, a master's degree in labor economics from Cornell University, and had worked for both the US Atomic Energy Commission in Los Alamos, New Mexico, and the Sandia National Laboratories in Albuquerque. In the early 1980s, he had worked for the national accounting firm of Peat, Marwick, Mitchell & Company as a business consultant, before establishing his own consulting firm, Price & Associates.

"As I understand it," Wolfgang explained, "Dixon was the one who had an influence in my then coming in as a consultant to Amigo."

Like Bob, Wolfgang was highly personable and a hard worker.

"I liked Wolfgang," Al said. "I like people who are aggressive, and he was very aggressive. It was my idea to bring Wolfgang onboard because things were in disarray, and I needed someone from outside to give me a fresh opinion about what was going on."

Al now had two high-powered professionals working with him—one to help him get the company's finances back under control, and the other to help with additional problems in the company.

•••

Wolfgang conducted interviews as part of developing an all-encompassing business plan for the company.

"That's what I was mainly paying him for," Al explained. "To put a plan together to understand where we were going wrong."

In March, Wolfgang traveled throughout the country to meet with Amigo salespeople, distributors, and Mobility Center franchisees in order to develop a marketing plan as part of the overall business plan. Appreciating Wolfgang's interest and autonomy, the salespeople provided him with a lot of feedback—both negative and positive—which he then passed on to Al. In fact, the salespeople got along so well with Wolfgang that Al hired him as part of the company's sales staff.

"Yes, we hired him," Beth said, "in true Al Thieme fashion. He was to work with our sales staff, distributors, and Mobility Centers. Al makes everybody an employee. He believes every soul of every human being is good. If they say they can do it, or they say they can help, he believes they can help! It's his optimism. But putting the right people in the right seat is an area he struggles with."

And that's what happened with Wolfgang Price.

Initially, the Amigo sales force liked working with Wolfgang, but then they began to complain to Al about him. Apparently, according to one employee, Wolfgang "made promises, but did not follow up on them."

Al was becoming disenchanted with him as well. He kept asking Wolfgang for the business plan he was supposed to be working on, "but he just wouldn't do it," Al explained. "I couldn't get him to finish that, and I told him that I was very disappointed in him. Finally, he did finish it, and when he did, it was of little value."

•••

Bob Dixon, after learning as much as he could about the condition of the company from Al and Beth, made a trip to Bridgeport to talk to people at the company and at the National Bank of Detroit.

256

"Dixon was a very collaborative guy," Greg Barber explained. "He was friendly and nice, so everybody talked to him."

Murl Hoppe and Robert Boes, the two people Bob should have talked to, were no longer with the company, but he met with the other key players at the Bridgeport facility—Marie, Alden, and Glen, and they all told him the same thing: "The company is messed up."

Bob soon learned that the bank felt the same way.

"I should have called this loan a long time ago," Cady confessed to Greg Barber.

Understanding their concern, Bob used his western charm to assuage the situation. Just as what had happened with Al and Beth, both Parks and Cady took an immediate liking to him.

"You know," Greg explained, "Murl handled that whole situation with the National Bank of Detroit, but he was gone. So Parks and Cady were feeling bad that the person they did trust was gone, and there was this piece of the puzzle, and that was Bob Dixon. He was a very experienced executive. Knew finance. Knew banking."

Obviously, Parks and Cady liked that.

Cady came right to the point with Bob by telling him that the bank was furious that Amigo had maxed out its line of credit and that they were not getting the reports they wanted.

"The bankers were really kind of tired of all the pie-in-the-sky Al Thieme-talk," Greg explained.

And so were a lot of other people, including some of Al's own managers.

"It's good to be positive," explained Mel Shepard, "but Al was *so* positive that he missed a lot of reality. In the business world, there's a lot to be said for going forward and expanding and building, but in Al's world, that's all there is. There's no, 'Maybe this isn't the right time. Maybe we ought to wait for a while.'"

•••

One example of Al's ambitious dreams was to develop a vehicle into which Amigo users could enter on their Amigos and drive away!

In June 1983, Al had met a young businessman in California by the name of Todd Takasu who had built a crude prototype of a small front-wheel-drive car that could possibly be converted for handicapped use. The back of the car folded down into a ramp, on which the Amigo user could then drive into the car, positioning the Amigo behind the steering wheel, locking it down, and driving away on it. Al couldn't wait to tell his management team all about the concept.

"We had an executive retreat," recalled Bill Loeffler, one of Al's executives at the time, "where we were supposed to plan out the future of the company. We're all at this retreat, and we all had our own agendas to present. We're sitting around the table, and Al says, 'Nope! Let's not talk about this. I want to talk about building cars!'"

Everyone looked at each other in amazement as Al proceeded to tell them about his new idea.

"Al," Loeffler said candidly, "do you have any idea what the requirements are—just the legal requirements or the safety requirements alone—to build a car?"

Al knew that it would be challenging, of course, but that had never stopped him before.

"It would be fun!" he said. "It would be exciting! Another mountain to climb!"

Al was used to hearing negative reactions from others, but that is what separates entrepreneurs from ordinary people. Where average people see obstacles, entrepreneurs see opportunities.

"That's what entrepreneurs do!" exclaimed Al's sister, Emy. "They don't think about all the things that can go wrong."

•••

Cady didn't make any promises, but he told Bob that if he could come up with a reasonable business plan with realistic sales projections, the bank would probably maintain the line of credit and possibly even expand it. In fact, Cady was probably *hoping* that Bob could come up with a plan, because, as Greg explained, "from the financial information that we were giving the bank, they wouldn't be able to recoup their investment anyway!"

And nobody knew that better than Cady.

"Bruce was always telling me," Greg recalled, "'You gotta make it happen, because I got my neck out. If we don't collect on this loan, I'll get fired!' He was pretty nervous about it."

Bob Dixon did not want *anybody* to get fired. He just wanted the bank to continue to work with Amigo Company. He told Parks and Cady that he would do everything he could to win back their trust.

•••

When Bob returned to Albuquerque, he and Greg went into "panic mode" to develop a reasonable pro forma income statement and business plan that Parks and Cady could believe in. First, Bob and Al developed the overall strategy, and then Bob and Greg worked on the numbers and, in Greg's words, "parleyed that into a forecast."

Bob and Greg then went to Michigan to meet with Parks and Cady to show them Amigo Company's new improved business plan, and both bankers were impressed. They didn't like the up-and-down profit numbers, but those didn't surprise them. What they appreciated most was Bob's and Greg's candor.

But Bob, as the seasoned executive that he was, noticed that Cady was still not yet convinced that things were going to change that much between Amigo Company and the bank.

"Bruce," Bob asked Cady, "what do we need to do to make this a better relationship, to make this thing work for you?"

Cady told Bob that the bank would continue its line of credit for a while, but it wouldn't do it for the long term unless there were an increase in sales and Amigo obtained a loan from the

Small Business Administration.

• • •

In early March 1984, Bob and Greg applied for a $500,000 loan from the Small Business Administration, and the SBA approved it in mid-April. In order for the agency to release the funds, however, both Al and Marie would have to sign the loan. Although Marie knew that the company needed these funds, she refused to sign the loan papers. Month after month, Bob pleaded with Marie to sign the loan documents, but she continued to refuse.

Bob told Parks and Cady he was confident that Marie would sign the papers sooner or later, hoping that would be enough for them to extend Amigo's line of credit. But their hands were tied. Unless Marie signed off on the loan, they told Bob, the bank would not extend any additional funds.

"We had nowhere to turn," Al recalled. "We figured something would happen. Some order would come in."

• • •

Throughout all of this drama, Al and Beth did have some good days. On July 8, 1985, Beth gave birth to Jennifer Thieme after a long and arduous labor.

"Jennifer was always my favorite girl's name," Beth said. "So I told Al, 'When we have a daughter, I really like the name Jennifer.' It wasn't after anybody in particular. Her middle name is after me—Elizabeth—even though my name is Beth."

"Jennifer is a darling," Al wrote in his journal.

• • •

The joyous occasion of Jennifer's birth may have been a bellwether for better things to come. In August, for example, after months of traveling back and forth to Michigan and meeting with Richard Parks and Bruce Cady, Bob Dixon finally got the National Bank of Detroit to renew its $1 million line of credit, albeit at a very high interest rate.

A little later that same month, The Sunrise Medical

Corporation, a large wheelchair manufacturer in Fresno, California, contacted Al about a possible purchase or merger with Amigo Company. Although Al was not interested in either deal at the moment, Sunrise's interest gave him confidence that if worse came to worst, the company would not be altogether lost.

Then, in October, Al received some more good news. When September's financial statement was compiled, it showed that the company had a year-to-date profit of $440,000! Part of this newfound wealth came from reduced expenses, and part of it came from reducing accounts receivable, but most of the income came from increased sales.

That was a relief for everybody, especially Bruce Cady. A month later, when Al was in Bridgeport, he and Cady went out to dinner, which in and of itself was a testament to Cady's new outlook. He told Al that he "was very pleased with the progress" the company was making.

When Al returned to Albuquerque, he told Bob Dixon what Cady had said. To show his appreciation for all of Bob's hard work, on December 31, 1985, Al promoted him to executive vice president.

The Thiemes and Dixons went out to dinner to celebrate.

CHAPTER 16

A Company in Turmoil

"Fine! I don't care who's president!"
—Al Thieme

Almost a year after the Small Business Administration had approved the loan for Amigo Company, Marie still had not signed the loan papers, and Bruce Cady's patience was all but exhausted. He was still waiting for Bob Dixon's "sooner or later" to happen.

At Amigo Company's board meeting in early February 1986, Bob Dixon presented a sobering report about the bank's displeasure with Amigo. He said the bank's loan committee had voted unanimously to approve the SBA loan and the bank's own line of credit, but when the loan went before the bank's full board, it was flatly voted down. In fact, Bob explained, "they discussed calling the line that day, but what they have done is given us ninety days to find a new bank. They no longer want to do business with us."

Bob asked Cady why the loan committee had approved Amigo's request, but the board had then rejected it. According to the minutes of the Amigo's board, this is how Bob described what had happened: "Cady asked two bankers on the board who voted to renew the loan if it was a good loan, and they said yes. But, after some questioning, it finally got down to a personality-type decision, rather than a business decision."

In other words, the executives of the National Bank of Detroit did not want to give Amigo Company a loan, not because of the condition of the company, but because of their feelings about Al Thieme.

•••

There was nothing Amigo Company could do but start searching for a new bank. Bob and Greg called on all the banks in Albuquerque, but none were interested. Some hinted that if the company were relocated entirely to Albuquerque, they might consider it. But unless and until that happened, there was nothing they would do.

Bob and Greg faced a similar negative reaction from the banks in Saginaw. One of those banks was the Second National Bank, the largest bank in the area. As noted earlier, Amigo Company had received small loans from that bank in the past, so Bob and Greg were hopeful that it would take past history into consideration.

However, when the executives at Second National reviewed the company's history, they didn't like what they saw and declined the loan.

"When a bank looks at whether or not a loan can be repaid," explained Jim Van Tiflin, the then senior vice president of Second National Bank's commercial loan division at the time, "there are a lot of things they take into consideration. Obviously, having a history of making money and having cash flow to be able to pay the loan is key, and at that point in time, Amigo didn't have any history of that. The other thing was that Al was what I'd call a seat-of-the-pants kind of guy. He didn't have a real strong organization. It was more of 'We'll show up every day, and we'll do what we have to do to get the job done' kind of a thing,' as opposed to having a chief financial officer or a chief operating officer. Those are the things banks look for that give banks confidence that they are going to be repaid. Al is a typical entrepreneur."

Bob also contacted William Blair & Company, a large investment bank in Chicago, and Citibank in New York. Bob thought that the executives at Citibank in particular might be receptive, since Amigo was leasing a computer to them.

But neither bank was interested.

•••

As the prospects for finding a new bank dwindled by the day, Al began thinking seriously about selling the company. Over the years, quite a few businesses had expressed an interest in buying the Amigo Company.

"That's why I wasn't too worried about Amigo," Al explained, "because we would get two or three offers a year."

In March 1984, for example, the Amedco Corporation, a major medical equipment supplier headquartered in Hialeah, Florida, contacted Al for a possible purchase. A year later, Invacare and Sunrise Medical were interested in buying Amigo.

In each of those instances, Al and Beth had said no.

"The only offer we really looked at," Beth recalled, "and it wasn't for long, was a $4 million offer we got in the autumn of 2006 from Creative Technology Services Corporation in Detroit. They built an electric wheelchair that could go up and down stairs, and they wanted to buy us. I remember talking to Al about the offer. I said, 'OK, let's play this through. Let's say we do that. What would we have after taxes? Probably half that much, roughly. We have a young family. We both have to work, and that amount wouldn't carry us through the rest of our lives. So what are we going to do? We're going to take that money and we're going to start a business. We already know *this* business. Why don't we just stay with what we have and what we know?"

But those days in the past had been better times. Now Al was concerned.

"We may have to sell to E&J," he wrote in his journal.

Everest & Jennings was the world's largest manufacturer of wheelchairs, both manual and electric, but it had yet to enter the three-wheeled market. Al was confident that he could get E&J interested in some kind of business arrangement—either a merger or an outright purchase. On April 21, 1986, he called the president of E&J and left a message.

But no one ever called back.

The one glimmering light was that Mobility Center, Inc., made a profit for the first time, although it was only $46,030.

•••

Then, as luck would have it (or, according to Al, the Almighty intervened once again), Grace Berger made an unannounced visit to Amigo Company.

Grace was an account representative from the Saginaw Area Growth Alliance (SAGA), a government agency charged with diversifying the local economy and making sure that the companies that were in the Saginaw area *stayed* there.

"The year 1986 was a tough time in Michigan," she explained. "Businesses were moving to Texas!"

Through an initiative started by Governor Jim Blanchard, the State of Michigan provided funds to SAGA, and Grace's job was to call on companies and let them know about those funds.

Grace told Al that SAGA could provide some funds to Amigo, and the State of Michigan could provide additional funds.

Al asked Grace to explain the application process to him, which turned out to be similar to applying for a regular commercial loan. He would need to provide two years of historical financial statements and two years of projected financial statements with the new debt included in them. She would then put a loan proposal together, which would include the financial information plus a history of the company, who the owners were, who the managers were, what amount they were requesting, and who their banker was. Whatever the loan amount was, it had to be collateralized, but SAGA took a subordinate position.

The proposal would then be submitted to the SAGA board of directors for evaluation and, with any luck, approved.

Al was indeed interested in Grace's proposal and told her that he would have Bob Dixon contact her to provide all the information she required.

•••

As a government agency, SAGA could not lend money on its own; it needed the support of a banking institution.

"Our role," explained JoAnn Crary, a former SAGA employee, "was never to take the place of bank financing. Otherwise, the bank could say, 'What's the government doing loaning money to a company that we would loan to?' That would be competing with the private sector, using taxpayer dollars. We were subordinate financing, which meant that a business would have to pay the bank back before they ever paid the county back. SAGA's role was to fill in the gap."

The SAGA board was made up of a number of highly qualified members, with Jerry Breen as its executive director.

"Jerry wasn't a touchy-feely kind of guy," recalled JoAnn. "He was a rough Irishman, and he looked after SAGA's money as if it were his own. If a hundred dollars were owed to the bank, and twenty dollars were owed to SAGA, Jerry wanted the County to get its twenty bucks."

The other members of the board were Dave Wierman, publisher of *The Saginaw News*; Angelo Guerriero, president of the Saginaw Business Institute; and Marvin Hare, Saginaw County's longtime and well-respected treasurer. Like Breen, Hare "protected the County's money like nobody ever did," said JoAnn. The last member of the board was none other than Richard Parks, the president of the Saginaw branch of the National Bank of Detroit!

Grace Berger compiled all of the information that Bob Dixon had given her and presented the package to Jerry Breen. After Jerry reviewed the material thoroughly, three things bothered him about Amigo Company's application. The first problem he had was why Al Thieme was operating two companies: Amigo Company for manufacturing and Mobility Center for distribution. As far as Jerry could tell, a part of Amigo Company's financial woes was caused by Mobility Center siphoning off profit from the Amigo Company.

The second problem Jerry saw was Al's insistence on having a western facility.

And the third problem was Al himself.

Breen didn't know Al personally, but what he had heard about him over the years was not good. Bruce Cady told him why his bank was disassociating itself from Amigo Company, and it wasn't because of the company's financial condition. In a memo that Jerry sent to his board, he explained the real reason why the National Bank of Detroit did not want to lend Amigo Company any more money.

"What appears to be the case," he wrote, "is that the NBD-Saginaw Board of Directors has a dislike for Allan Thieme, based on his personal conduct."

That was Breen's attitude as well. He didn't like the fact that Al had left Marie.

•••

Whether Breen liked Al or not, he was obligated to present Amigo's loan request to the SAGA board, which he did on the 13th of June, 1986, a Friday. Normally, not all of the board members would be present at a run-of-the-mill loan presentation, but this loan request was far from ordinary, so Breen insisted that *all* of the board members be present for this one.

"Holy Moses!" exclaimed a SAGA employee. "That was a meeting with some pretty powerful people. SAGA must have been trying to use their influence to involve the National Bank of Detroit."

And that must have been the case, for the SAGA board—which included NBD's Richard Parks—agreed to lend Amigo Company $215,000 on twelve conditions, the following five being the most salient:

- Restoration of all operations to Michigan within 60 days
- A merger of Amigo Company and Amigo Mobility Center
- Jerry Breen would become a part of Amigo Company's board of directors
- Bob Dixon would be named president and chief executive officer of Amigo Company
- Al and Beth Thieme would personally guarantee the loans

Now that SAGA had approved Amigo Company's loan request, the State of Michigan kicked in an additional $215,000, and the National Bank of Detroit, no doubt at Parks's recommendation, renewed Amigo's line of credit, giving the company $1,430,000 of available cash!

Plus, Marie Thieme finally signed the Small Business Administration loan papers.

But Amigo Company was not yet in the clear. Not by any means. All of the $1,430,000 that the company received was immediately used to pay suppliers.

•••

While Al wanted dearly to stay in Albuquerque, and tried to think of ways to keep the western facility open, he finally capitulated.

"I see no better solution," he wrote in his journal on April 18, 1986, "to get back on top of the business. It's quite clear that we are unable to get sales up enough to cover expenses. We need to consolidate."

"I thought about it a lot," Al recalled, "prayed about it, and all of a sudden it hit me—like a light went on. I didn't talk to anybody. I didn't ask anybody. I had an epiphany: *Al, you gotta go back to Bridgeport*."

•••

Marie was not happy when Al informed her that he and Beth were moving back to Michigan.

"If you're coming back," she told Al, "I don't want to be involved with Amigo Company. You and Beth run Amigo. Let me run Amigo Leasing Company."

Al exchanged all of his Amigo Leasing stock for 617 shares of Marie's Amigo stock. While she still had 650 shares of Amigo Company stock, she was now sole owner of the Amigo Leasing Company.

Glen the manager of the leasing company, was now working for Marie. At that point, Amigo Leasing bought a Mobility Center franchise in Grand Rapids, Michigan. Glen also hired Al's son-in-law, Chuck Priest, to work out of the Grand Rapids store as a salesman. (Chuck and Jill Priest had been living in Albuquerque, but had separated. Jill stayed in Albuquerque, while Chuck moved to Grand Rapids.)

"Glen had done very well building and running Amigo Leasing Company," Al recalled. "It was a financially strong company."

•••

Bob Dixon was in Bridgeport when he heard the good news from SAGA, whose stipulations didn't surprise him. How Al was going to take them was another matter.

On his flight back to Albuquerque, Bob thought about how he was going to explain to Al what had happened with SAGA.

"SAGA will give us a loan," Bob said with a little hesitancy in his voice, "and NBD will continue our line of credit if you make me president of the company."

"Fine!" Al said. "I don't care who's president!"

Beth agreed. If making Bob Dixon president of Amigo would facilitate the loan, they saw no reason not to make him the company's president.

"Al and I have never cared about titles," Beth explained. "We had no problem making Bob Dixon president. Al would be chairman."

•••

At an Amigo board meeting held on June 6, 1986, at the offices of Amigo West, the topic of appointing Bob Dixon as president of the company was discussed. Bob brought the members up-to-date about why SAGA and NBD wanted him appointed president, and Al said that he supported their recommendation.

"I am confident," Al said to the board, "that Bob Dixon can do a better job as the key person in our company. It will relieve me to do the things I am better at."

Then Bob mentioned that he was working on contracts to entice certain Amigo West employees to move to Michigan, and that he was also "putting together an investment group to give us some working capital." He said he hoped that he could get a number of Amigo employees to invest in the company.

"How much of that is put together now?" asked Joyce Godwin, one of the board members.

"About $90,000," Bob replied. "If I don't find enough people at Amigo Company, I am working with some outside people."

(According to the minutes of the meeting, no one on the board asked who those "outside people" might be.)

Then Ted Royal, another member of the board, asked: "No employment contracts will be done without the approval of the board, right?

"That's correct," Bob replied.

With no further questions, Bob made the motion, and the board duly appointed him president and chief executive officer of Amigo Company, effective as of July 1, 1986.

But that wasn't the end of the meeting. Ted Royal then brought up the subject of Bob's employment contract. Although Bob said that he would present his contract to the board for approval, Royal made a motion to that effect: "RESOLVED, that the management agreement between Bob Dixon and Amigo Company, be presented to the Board, to be approved, effective July 1, 1986."

Joyce Godwin seconded the motion, which then carried.

•••

Normally, Al didn't like using contracts, but as we have just seen, one was written up for Bob Dixon. It's not clear who wrote it up. In any case, with all its *therefores* and *whereases*, the contract looked as if it had been professionally done, but it contained clauses that an attorney would find troublesome. The very first clause was the most problematic: "Dixon shall have full and complete responsibility and authority for the day-to-day operations of Amigo."

The agreement then went on to specify certain other terms: the contract would be for three years; Bob's salary would be $70,000 per year, with annual increases; Bob was eligible for a cash bonus at the end of each year, and he would receive a bonus of 1 percent of the authorized capital stock of Amigo Company at the end of each year (totaling 3 percent). Additionally, the contract allowed Bob to purchase up to 3 percent more of Amigo Company's stock at any time.

The agreement also addressed what would happen if Bob left the company before the contract ended, either by termination or of his own volition. If he were terminated, Amigo Company would still be obligated to fulfill its financial obligations to him. However, if he quit, the contract would "immediately terminate."

The contract was signed by Al, Beth, and Bob, and witnessed by Al's secretary, Beverly Allen. Therefore, it appeared to be a bona fide contract, and would probably stand up in a court of law, even if an attorney hadn't drawn it up.

"Had a little party to congratulate Dixon as president," Al wrote in his journal. "Today is his first day."

Al had just handed complete control of his company over to Bob Dixon. Although Al had said that making Bob president didn't bother him, the thoughts that he had had about Bob shortly after he started with the company resurfaced.

"It seems like Dixon is setting things up to get me out," Al wrote in his journal.

•••

On the morning of June 3, 1986, all of Amigo West's employees awoke to headlines in the *Albuquerque Journal*: "Wheelchair Company Moves Headquarters."

When the reporter who wrote that article asked Bob Dixon why the company was leaving, Bob replied, "Amigo needed a finance package, and was unable to get it from New Mexico financial institutions. In Michigan, the company got the financial support it needed from city, state, and financial institutions. This state needs to take a closer look at things. It's easier to keep jobs than to bring jobs to the state."

When Al asked all the employees to gather in the conference room, they knew what he was going to say.

•••

The only people from Amigo West who moved to Michigan were the Thiemes, the Dixons, the Barbers, and the Shrodes.

Al and Beth knew it was necessary to move back to Bridgeport, and the Barbers were taking it as an exciting change.

"Jane and I were recently married," Greg Barber explained. "We didn't have any kids, so we looked forward to moving to Michigan as our next adventure!"

The Dixons and Shrodes, however, were not so eager about the change.

"My mother had lived in the Southwest all her life," the Dixons's daughter, Jennifer, explained, "and she didn't want to go to Michigan."

And neither did Marilyn Shrode.

"Marilyn wasn't happy about it," Bob Shrode recalled. "But she was willing to put up with it for a few years."

•••

Both Bob and Joyce Jensen had left the company by this time, and so had Wolfgang Price. Al was sad to see them go, but things just didn't work out.

"Bob Jensen was a good sales manager," Al recalled. "Unfortunately, none of us realized that we had to change our distribution plan. Had we realized that a change was needed, Bob would have implemented the new system. Bob and Joyce were great people. Well, all of us back then thought that this was the way to sell Amigos—the way we had been successful using Amigo owners. So that's what Bob Jensen did, and he did that well. But it was the wrong thing. We should have done an analysis to find out how things were changing. Things were totally changing, and we didn't realize it. We kept working hard on what *had* been successful, instead of looking at the changes we should have made in our distribution system."

Al thought highly of Wolfgang Price, too, but he just wasn't doing the job that Al had hired him to do, so shortly before Al returned to Michigan, he asked Wolfgang to leave.

•••

The moving van arrived at Al and Beth's home on the West Mesa early in the morning of July 28, 1986. After putting some of their belongings on one side of the back seat of their Porsche and strapping one-year-old Jennifer in a car seat on the other side, the Thiemes were on the road by 2:00 p.m. As they headed east on Interstate 40 over the Sandia Mountains, Albuquerque receded in their rearview mirror.

"I had a lot of time to think during that ride," Al recalled. "We were going to turn things around. I knew darn well that I wasn't going to give up!"

The Thiemes bought a home on Hamlet Drive in the Westbecker Woods subdivision in Saginaw Township, fifteen miles northwest of Bridgeport.

At the same time, the Dixons bought a home just around the corner and down the street from Al and Beth. In fact, in order to get home, Bob Dixon had to drive right past the Thiemes' house. And the neighbors couldn't miss him when he entered the subdivision, because he was the only one in that GM town who owned a Saab!

Greg and Jane Barber moved into a handsome contemporary two-story house on the same side of town, ten minutes south of the Thiemes and the Dixons. Bob and Marilyn Shrode bought a place in Frankenmuth.

•••

News of the Thiemes' return to Michigan quickly spread throughout the Bridgeport facility and the whole area. Some people were looking forward to their return; others were not. Al and Beth got their first inkling of that while they were still in Albuquerque, when Amigo West received an anonymous phone call from a man who said that he was from the Bridgeport office.

"Tell Al we don't want him back," the man said.

"There were people who didn't think very well of Al and Beth," explained Jim Van Tiflin, "because of the fact that Al had divorced Marie."

•••

Al moved back into his old office on the main floor of the facility, which had been vacant ever since Robert Boes had left, two years earlier. Beth worked at a desk upstairs among her sales staff. They had been gone almost seven years, but they acclimated quickly. It soon seemed like old times.

Greg Barber, Bob Shrode, and Mark Campbell also worked upstairs, taking over Bud Paffrath's, Robert Boes', and Murl Hoppe's old offices, respectively. Bob Dixon had a large office built upstairs in the southeast corner. If they wanted to bounce an idea off each other or just chat, all they had to do was walk to the office next door.

"In Albuquerque," Beth recalled sadly, "we worked as a team. When we got here, it started out OK for a month or two, but then Dixon changed—and relatively quickly."

When Dixon was at Amigo West, "he was a financial person," Beth said. "He looked at costs, and he helped us make financial decisions."

But shortly after he moved to Michigan, Bob stopped working long hours and began to spend money that the company didn't have.

"He didn't act like a financially conservative person in a turnaround situation," Beth explained. "It was a totally different Dixon."

One day, for example, Beth saw a large office furniture truck pull into the parking lot, and men began unloading some beautiful office furniture. She went downstairs and told them that they must have the wrong address.

"Who's this for?" she asked.

"A Mr. Bob Dixon," came the reply.

Beth immediately went to Bob's office and asked him to send it back.

"You can have *my* furniture," she told him. "It's not important to me."

"No," Bob said, "I've got it all taken care of."

But that was just the tip of the iceberg. Bob began traveling a lot, meeting with suppliers, Amigo distributors, and Mobility Center franchisees. He would take them out to lunch or dinner, order expensive cigars, and have nice wines brought to the table.

"He was spending *our* money!" Beth exclaimed. "Our lives were in the company! It was a terrible feeling."

But perhaps Bob was spending money lavishly to give people confidence that the company was strong and viable. A case in point was his hiring Mark Campbell, the former vice president of sales for Everest & Jennings. Although Beth was the head of Amigo's sales at the time, Bob wanted someone with more "horsepower" to head up that crucial part of the company.

"Bob Dixon wanted more critical mass in Amigo sales volume" is the way Mark Campbell explained it. "A headhunter contacted me from Amigo, at that time, and a gentleman by the name of Bob Dixon appeared to be running it. I joined Amigo through Bob Dixon."

Bob was excited to have "stolen" Campbell from E&J, but Campbell was expensive: $70,000 in salary and $46,000 to move him to Michigan.

"We were not part of that decision at all," Beth recalled. "We didn't even know that Dixon was doing that."

But as far as Bob was concerned, they didn't need to know. He was president of the company, after all. Nevertheless, the Thiemes were having a difficult time adjusting to the new reality.

"Things like that started to put cracks in our relationship," Beth explained. "If you're put in charge of a company that's financially strapped, you look for ways to stretch the dollars, and when I saw all those expenses, there was no intention on Dixon's part to save money…, none whatsoever. That's when it changed for me. It kind of confirmed suspicions for me that something had changed in Bob's mind. And it was a sinking feeling knowing that we had personally guaranteed the loans. There was so much at stake."

That "something" just might have been a takeover of the Amigo Company.

•••

When Bob traveled back and forth from Albuquerque to Bridgeport, he would talk to Richard Parks, Bruce Cady, Jerry Breen, and Glen.

"He'd talk with Marie a lot, also," Al recalled.

Over time, Bob realized that many employees and people in

the community were very much against Al and Beth.

"I think he saw the opportunity to take over the company," Al said, "to get me and Beth out of it. And that temptation was too strong."

Beth agrees with Al's assessment.

"I believe in my heart," she said, "that Bob Dixon started out with all the right intentions, but I think people felt sorry for Marie, and I think Glen didn't like Al. I think Bob Dixon started to listen to some of those people, and his motivation changed."

Al and Beth were not the only ones who had that perception. Greg Barber had it, too.

"Bob Dixon changed when he moved to Saginaw," Greg said. "When we were in Albuquerque, we went out to lunch often and talked about business. Then, when we moved to Saginaw, that rarely happened."

•••

"Al was the owner of the company," Beth explained, "but Dixon didn't spend much time with him."

"Was it *his* fault?" Al asked rhetorically. "No, it was *my* fault."

"Al came home one Saturday," Beth recalled, "and he said to me, 'Honey, just tie me up! I don't think I want to ever run a business anymore, because I can't trust people.' And I said, 'Al, you can trust people, but you can't *entrust* them. You give them the whole thing…, lock, stock, and barrel. You go too far with trust. You should trust but verify.'"

CHAPTER 17

A Company on the Brink

"There's something called lender liability."
—Herb McLachlan, CPA

Beth was probably right when she told Al that he tended to give people too much leeway. Bob Dixon had the legal authority to do whatever he wanted, and he didn't hesitate to use his newfound power. For example, as Mark Campbell was on his way to Michigan to start his job with Amigo, Bob had Beth's desk moved from Sales downstairs next to Al's.

"He didn't talk to me about it!" Beth exclaimed. "It just happened. I was sitting at my desk, and all of a sudden two guys from production came up and were looking at me, and I said, 'What do you need?'"

"We're moving your desk."

"Where to?"

"Downstairs, where Al is."

"But my team is up here!"

"Well, we were told to move your desk."

"Who told you?"

"Mr. Dixon."

Since Mark Campbell would be working upstairs, Bob didn't want Beth up there to interfere with their discussions or planning. That's why he had her moved downstairs.

"Just work on franchising," he told Al and Beth.

From then on, Bob and his team worked upstairs, and Al and Beth worked downstairs.

•••

Since Bob had told the Thiemes to work on franchising, the first thing Al did when Mark Campbell arrived was talk to him about franchising. But Campbell would have nothing to do with it.

"My perception," he explained, "was that the idea of franchising wasn't a bad idea per se, but franchising in and around the Amigos and the other products that we could contrive for them was a bit of a stretch. What Al wanted was someone who was passionate about developing this franchise concept, and I thought we should focus on the Amigo and making it better and selling it wherever it could be sold because of the goodness of the product."

Coming from E&J, Campbell knew full well how most of the Amigo's competitors—especially Electric Mobility—were selling their products, which was through Medicare. And that was the marketing scheme he wanted to deploy at Amigo.

"I'm not saying they were 'gaming' Medicare," Campbell said, "but I was more for product development and selling more product."

•••

Not surprisingly, the first meeting between Al Thieme and Mark Campbell did not go well.

"In my judgment," Campbell recalled amusingly, "Al and I were already at odds by the time my furniture had reached the Rocky Mountains!"

And since he and Al were on opposite ends about how to market Amigos, their relationship never improved.

"If I'd say white, he'd say black," Campbell recalled. "If I said black, he'd say white. This would go on and on."

Campbell later admitted that he realized early on that his days at Amigo were numbered, even though Bob Dixon was the president and had hired him personally. It really didn't matter to Campbell, because he had confidence and experience, and knew he could get a job elsewhere. The important thing to him was that Amigo Company had paid to move him and his family back to the Midwest, where they were originally from.

Until the inevitable happened, Campbell recalled, "I started doing stuff that I knew would get under Al's skin, such as smoking in the office."

"Throughout Amigo Company's history," Al explained, "I didn't allow any of our people to smoke around customers or inside the buildings. But when Mark Campbell got here, he'd be in a big chair in his office, feet up on his desk, smoking a cigar!"

That irked Al to no end, but he couldn't do anything about it. Campbell worked for Bob Dixon, and Dixon smoked cigars, too!

●●●

All the talk about people not wanting the Thiemes back in Michigan didn't bother Al and Beth too much, until they started getting phone calls in the middle of the night.

"We'd pick up the phone, and nobody would be there," Beth recalled. "And it kept continuing—night after night after night."

Eventually, they contacted a police officer whom they knew, and he agreed to put a tracer on their phone to try to find out who was making those crank calls. But it wasn't going to be easy to do. The officer said that there would have to be three calls in a row from the same phone in order to charge the perpetrator. Apparently, the culprit knew that, because he or she would call from different phone booths.

Al and Beth didn't know for sure who was making those menacing calls, but they suspected that it was David.

•••

When the Thiemes left Albuquerque, Beth was already seven months pregnant. On October 9, 1986, she gave birth to a son, whom she and Al named Adam Edward Thieme. For the first time, the name of one of Al's children did not start with the letter *J*!

"We had Jennifer," Beth explained, "and then Adam was the second one, and I said to Al, 'Your grandfather had an *A* name, and you have an *A* name. I think we should pick an *A* name. It's kind of the lineage of the men in your family.' So we named our son Adam, and his middle name was after my grandfather, Edward."

To celebrate the occasion, the Dixons gave the Thiemes a beautiful christening outfit for Adam to be baptized in. It was such a gracious gesture, and indicated just how close the two couples had become.

Tragically, little Adam caught a virus while he was still in the hospital and died fifteen days later.

Al was devastated over losing Adam. After all, this was the second son he had lost. And Beth was equally devastated. She was depressed for days after that, wondering over and over in her mind what she could have done differently that might have prevented such a tragedy. But there was nothing she could have done about a virus.

Little Adam Edward Thieme was interred at the Roselawn Cemetery in Saginaw, buried in the christening outfit that the Dixons had bought for him.

•••

Interestingly, the late-night calls that the Thiemes had been getting before Adam was born stopped for a while after he died, but started up again shortly after his funeral. That gave Al and Beth some indication that whoever was making those crackpot calls knew them personally.

If those calls weren't disconcerting enough, the Thiemes

also began to get hate mail. Those were not messages compiled from cutout letters in newspapers and magazines, as in the movies, but magazines would arrive addressed to "Adolf Hitler" or "Al Hitler Thieme." Al and Beth still suspected that David was behind all this troublemaking, but they could never prove it. They would have had to catch the perpetrator red-handed in order to press charges. But that was highly unlikely.

Then, early one Sunday morning, June 26, 1988, Alden Thieme was driving by Amigo Company around 6:30 a.m., after having picked up a copy of *The Saginaw News* at a local convenience store, when he saw a car drive into the company's parking lot. In and of itself, that was not unusual, since many cars pulled in there just to turn around. Nevertheless, Alden pulled over and waited for the car to come out, but it didn't. So, Alden slowly pulled in and found David looking through the dumpster!

Alden did not detain him, but he did call the police and had them file a report on the bizarre incident.

"We didn't file charges against him," Al said. "We knew the guy was goofy, doing silly things, and this was just another one to add to all the other goofy stuff David was doing."

●●●

The Thiemes never could prove that David was the culprit (although the dumpster incident came pretty close), but a chance meeting that Al had a short time later all but confirmed his and Beth's suspicions.

When Al was at a medical equipment trade show in New Jersey, he met Jacques Dallery, the US distributor for a wheelchair called the Lifestand. As the name implies, the unique wheelchair mechanically extends, allowing the user to stand up. When Al told Jacques who he was and where he was from, Dallery said that he had recently been in Saginaw to meet with a David, and asked Al if he knew him.

"Yes, I know him," Al replied. "He's bad news!"

Then Al told Jacques about the phone calls and magazines, indicating that he was sure they were David's doings.

That didn't surprise Dallery, because he was also having problems with David.

"He started to build his own standup wheelchair," explained Dallery, "as a copy of the original Lifestand, and I brought a legal suit against him. After the suit started, I began to receive phone calls at my house in the middle of the night without anyone talking, and getting many subscriptions to magazines that I had not ordered."

"That proved where this foolishness was coming from," Al said.

•••

"I look back on that time frame," explained Beth, " we were getting hit from every direction possible. Moving back to Michigan was traumatic. Floods hit the month after we moved back, the following month was Adam's arrival and passing, then these calls were coming in the middle of the night, and the ugly subscriptions started. It was unsettling!"

"We were concentrating on saving the business and making a profit," Al explained, "because we were so focused on that, all these other things were like swatting a mosquito: 'Oh, here's another mosquito! Let's just work on getting our business profitable.'"

"The interesting thing about me and Al," Beth said, "is that neither of us is a worrier. You would think that going through all this for so long from all directions, we'd have ulcers. But we don't. We just live day-to-day; we don't dwell on the negative. We might lose sleep once in a while, but we're similar characters. We just ask ourselves, 'What do we have to do? Let's figure it out. Let's do it!' And what's unique is that we're both like that."

•••

While all this was going on, Bob Dixon was having challenges that he hadn't expected. Whether or not he and whoever else may have had plans to overthrow Al Thieme and take over the company, there was one person whom no one ever suspected, who brought the plans of a coup d'état to the fore.

Bob Shrode, Amigo Company's personnel director, was fed up. Like Bob Dixon and Greg Barber, he had received a contract that stated that if he stayed with the company for five years, he would get 100 shares of Amigo stock. And those shares could become quite lucrative if the company turned around or were sold.

But as time went on, Shrode saw that possibility fading away before his eyes. He was not a marketing or a finance man, but since he was part of Dixon's management team, he participated in all of Dixon's strategic-planning meetings. The team came up with a number of good ideas that could help Amigo, but with the company so short of cash, most of those ideas were too expensive to implement. That is, all of them except one.

While Al had the engineering team working on a rear-wheel-drive Amigo—which everyone thought was needed—that project was going to take time that the company probably didn't have. During the vehicle's development, the purchasing department sent bids out to companies all over the world, especially South Korea, seeking the best prices for parts. It was during this prolific search that a representative of one of those Korean manufacturers told Amigo's purchasing department that his company could produce the *entire* rear-wheel-drive Amigo for pennies on the dollar!

"There's a billion people over there that will buy this thing!" Shrode said. "We were going to try to pedal it overseas. So we started pursuing that, and, of course, Al wasn't involved in those discussions because Dixon kept him out of the day-to-day things. But when he found out about it, he just became incensed!"

In fact, Al was so upset that all of this was happening behind his back that he quashed the project before it had a chance to get off the ground.

The reason Al became so infuriated wasn't just because his executives were meeting behind his back; it was because just a few months earlier, Amigo Company's board of directors had passed a resolution specifically stating that a "complete Amigo unit should NOT be built off-shore."

•••

Nevertheless, that was the breaking point for Bob Shrode, who walked into Dixon's office shortly thereafter and dropped a bombshell.

"Bob," he said, "we got to put together a leveraged buyout, or Al's going to destroy this company!"

"Well, I don't know," Dixon said hesitantly, surprised that a guy in personnel would come up with such a scheme.

"Let's talk to Barber," Shrode said. "Let's talk to Boulanger. And see what *they* think."

Apparently, Barber and Boulanger were also irked with Al because they both agreed to take the next step.

"We couldn't deal with any of Al's relatives," Shrode explained, "because the word would get back to Al."

And they certainly didn't want to meet at the company to do their scheming, so, according to Shrode, they "met in the back of bars," where he could lay out his plan in relative secrecy.

"Because we've got all this borrowed money to keep the company afloat," he explained to Dixon, Barber, and Boulanger, "my suggestion is that we force the company into bankruptcy. We go to the bank and tell them that we want them to call the note, and then we'll go to the judge, and we'll ask that you, Bob, be assigned as the administrator. We'll tell the judge about our plan to go overseas and that the company is going to be extremely viable."

•••

Bob Dixon may have had that same idea in the back of his mind, because not only would it be easy to do, it was also the only way that the company could be wrestled out of Al's control.

"I think that was a strong possibility," explained banker Jim Van Tiflin. "The bank could have forced Amigo Company into what is known as involuntary bankruptcy, forcing the company out of Al's hands."

Apparently, Bob Dixon had several investors lined up for a scheme like that.

"He knew guys with a lot of money," Greg Barber said.

•••

Dixon may have had money waiting in the wings, but he wanted to make sure that Shrode's scheme of forcing the company into bankruptcy would work, so he went to see a bankruptcy attorney.

The attorney told him that he had two options: Chapter 7 bankruptcy or Chapter 13 bankruptcy. Under Chapter 7, the company would be liquidated, and Al and Beth would be left with whatever was left over, if anything. Under Chapter 13, the court would allow the company to reorganize, restructure its debt, and pay off its creditors over time. Of the two options, Dixon preferred the former. If he already had investors lined up, and the judge ordered Chapter 7, the investors could quickly buy up the assets, and Amigo Company would be theirs.

•••

Although Al had absolutely no proof that anybody was out to take over the company from him, his intuition began to kick in around this time.

"I had a feeling that something like that was going on," he recalled. "Did I try and find out? No, because we had a business to run, and I was working non-stop to turn it around."

But then Al was warned by a neighbor, which made him change his mind.

Gordon and Angie Marinoff lived across the street from the Thiemes and on the same street that the Dixons lived. Al enjoyed talking to Gordon because he was a retired plant manager of one of the GM factories in town. When Al would tell him his business woes, Gordon would tell him "war stories" of his own.

Up to then, the Thiemes and Marinoffs had not been that close. But after Angie heard about Adam's death, she began visiting Beth more often, "helping me through that," Beth explained. "She was like a mom to me." Angie would go see Beth, or Beth would go see Angie, and she would bring Jennifer with her.

One time, when the Thiemes were at the Marinoffs for dinner, Al and Gordon began talking business.

"And then," Beth recalled, "Al confided to him about our struggles and how Bob Dixon came to help us turn things around."

Marinoff could hardly believe what he was hearing!

"Al," he said, "this guy is going to try to take over the company!"

"Gordon," Al replied, "look what he has done, how he has helped us!"

"If Bob Dixon is president, and he was hired to turn around your company," retorted Marinoff, "why is he consistently coming home around 3:00 in the afternoon? I'm in the front yard working, and he's waving at me and smiling! It doesn't add up."

"He's out to take over your company!" Marinoff said emphatically. "That's all I can say."

•••

There's no doubt that Gordon Marinoff got Al to realize what was happening, but there was no one in the company Al could turn to for help. So he brought in an outside "numbers man" whom he had used in the past.

Forty-seven-year-old Herb McLachlan was a graduate CPA of Michigan State University and a managing partner of Ernst & Ernst, one of the country's "Big Eight" accounting firms.

Al and Beth invited McLachlan and Marinoff over to their house to talk about what they should do or, more importantly, what they *could* do. After all, based on the agreement that Al had with the National Bank of Detroit and the Saginaw Area Growth Alliance, his options were extremely limited.

McLachlan listened carefully to what the Thiemes had to say, asked a lot of questions, and, in Beth's words, "really believed in us."

"Al," he said, "there's something called 'lender liability,' which says that banks and loaning institutions cannot dictate who manages your business, because then they become liable for the management of the business. In fact, there has been recent litigation about that. I want you to do something. Ask for a meeting with the bank and with SAGA, and we'll talk this out. Let's have Dixon there, the bankers, and I'll go with you and Beth."

● ● ●

That meeting was held at the bank. When Al, Beth, and Herb McLachlan arrived, Richard Parks and Bruce Cady were already there, as was Jerry Breen. Then, a few minutes later, Bob Dixon walked in with his attorney, and right behind them were Mark Campbell with his attorney.

"We just talked," recalled Beth. "We had a conversation around the table."

They talked about Amigo's line of credit, whether or not the bank would continue to extend the company credit, and what Amigo Company would have to do for the bank to continue to support the company.

Then Cady brought up the subject of Bob Dixon. The bank was pleased that Dixon was president of the company, Cady said, and liked hearing his plans and strategy for the company. But Cady also mentioned that he had heard rumors that Al was unhappy with Dixon's performance and was thinking of firing him.

"If you fire Mr. Dixon," Cady said bluntly to Al, "we will pull your loan."

Up to this point, Herb McLachlan just sat back and listened,

Herb McLachlan, business consultant to
Al Thieme (courtesy Herb McLachlan)

but when Cady mentioned why he might pull the loan, he spoke up.

"I've been reading some articles about lender liability," he said.

"The room went silent," Beth recalled.

The reason that Cady and Parks were taken aback by McLachlan's comment is that they were fully aware why he was bringing up this subject. McLachlan was clearly suggesting that the bank had no right to interfere with Amigo Company's management—and if it did, it could be held liable for future trouble.

"Herb didn't accuse them of that," Beth explained. "He just hinted at it."

It may have been only a hint, but McLachlan's tactic worked. Cady quickly changed the subject, and the meeting was adjourned.

"SAGA and the bank," Beth said, "knew they had made a mistake by insisting that Dixon be president."

Looking back at that episode, Herb McLachlan commented: "We all went out of our way to make things work. Back during those times, when you got certain players around, there could be backstabbing going on, I'm sure. You're just doing what you think you had to do in advising them. I was just using whatever professional skills I had at that point. You reach in the bag for different things sometimes."

•••

Al saw the National Bank of Detroit's retreat as an opportunity to reassert himself. On Monday morning he went up to Dixon's office and had a three-hour talk with him.

"We got into some heavy items," Al wrote in his journal.

First on Al's list: get rid of Mark Campbell and Bob Shrode.

Dixon listened politely, but did nothing. In fact, when he told Campbell and Shrode what Al had said, they just laughed. But Dixon knew that it was a serious matter: Al Thieme was going to reestablish his authority.

In an effort to thwart that possibility, Dixon had his attorney write Al a letter, reminding him that Bob Dixon, not Al Thieme, was the CEO of Amigo Company and had "total control of the company."

Al knew that, of course, but he was getting tired of hearing about it. Amigo Company was his, not Dixon's or Shrode's or Campbell's. Al had tried working with them and the bankers, but all he was getting was resistance. No one cared about what he wanted to do or even listened to his arguments. He decided to take action.

"We made the decision that we had to take away Bob Dixon's authority," Beth explained.

Al came up with the method of doing precisely that.

"We won't fire Bob," he told Beth. "We'll just rewrite the bylaws to give the powers to the chairman and not to the president. I'm majority shareholder, and we can get that done today."

They wanted to make sure that whatever they did was legally sound, so they told their attorney, Tom, what they wanted to do, and he wrote up a legally tight resolution that they could present to the board of directors.

The resolution that Tom drew up was five paragraphs long, but it can be summed up like this: Amigo's board had previously given Bob Dixon authority over the company. Now the shareholders were going to vote to transfer all authority of the company back to Al Thieme.

Instead of bringing all the shareholders in for a meeting, Beth simply called them on the telephone to get their vote. Beth was able to reach everyone except Dixon, who didn't answer the phone. Since everyone else voted yes, they didn't need Dixon's vote anyway.

The next day, Al put a copy of the resolution on Dixon's desk and sent off a three-page letter to Bruce Cady at the National Bank of Detroit, explaining what had happened and why. Since agreeing to make Bob Dixon the president of Amigo, Al wrote, "we have had eight consecutive months of losses, and numerous expensive sales/marketing decisions have been made with poor results. We cannot continue on this path, and a change in management was requested by the Amigo shareholders."

Al expected sparks to fly, and they did. Bruce Cady immediately called for a meeting with Al, Beth, Dixon, and Breen.

Dixon's first stop was his attorney's office.

CHAPTER 18

Taking Back Control

"I want this resolved so Al can run his company,
and I can run mine."
—Marie Thieme

The first thing that Al did with his newfound authority was to fire Mark Campbell and Bob Shrode.

"Then," Beth explained, "Al started reviewing where we were at and running the company. Our focus every day was to grow sales. Then he began loading Dixon up with menial tasks, hoping that he would leave."

But Dixon was stubborn and was not about to go without a fight. In an effort to reclaim his authority, Dixon had his attorney, Richard Smith, send Al a scathing letter, demanding that he reinstate Dixon in his position as CEO of Amigo Company:

We request that Amigo's breech of its contract with Mr. Dixon be cured immediately, and that Mr. Dixon be restored to the office of Chief Executive Officer with full responsibility for running the day-to-day operations of

Amigo Company.

The recent history of corporate acts suggests that Amigo's bylaws are used as a shield when it suits Mr. Thieme's and the Board's purposes and are ignored when it does not suit their purposes.

This, of course, started a war of letter writing that lawyers love, and Al's attorney, Tom, responded in kind:

Mr. Dixon was not fired. Mr. Dixon refused to work with the Board and Mr. Thieme, despite significant efforts on their behalf. A change had to be made, as Amigo Company and Mr. Dixon were not performing as contemplated.

Then Tom mentioned Dixon's employment contract, which Dixon no doubt had given to his attorney:

You have also not explained who negotiated and drafted this instrument for Amigo Company, as opposed to Mr. Dixon, nor have you satisfactorily explained why it was not reviewed by Amigo's corporate counsel.

In that one sentence, Tom had just earned every penny that he was being paid. He had read through all of the board meeting minutes during Dixon's tenure at Amigo Company, and nowhere did they say that Dixon had submitted his employment contract to the board for approval, as he had said he would. As far as Tom was concerned, Dixon's lack of follow-up made his contract null and void.

•••

Al was pleased when Tom told him that Dixon's contract was unenforceable. But Al wanted to avoid more legal maneuverings, hoping that Dixon would eventually leave on his own. However,

Dixon continued to linger. Although he was stripped of his powers on June 12, 1987, he was still around two months later!

Now totally fed up, Al walked into Dixon's office on August 17th and told him, "You need to leave!"

Al knew full well that that action could cost him at least $140,000, because Dixon still had two years left on his contract. But Al didn't care. He wanted Dixon gone and would accept the consequences.

Dixon left the very next day. But before the month was over, Al received a letter from Dixon's attorney, stating that since Dixon had been fired, he "is entitled to the continued payment of salary and fringe benefits through June 30, 1989."

Tom's response to Smith was the same as it had been before.

"Dixon was not fired," he wrote, and the company could not and would not pay anything more to Dixon, because essentially the company was broke. "Amigo and its employees," he wrote, "are struggling for the corporation's basic survival. It will not voluntarily pay Mr. Dixon such luxurious benefits. Indeed, it cannot."

That, of course, opened the door for a lawsuit.

•••

After two arduous years in Saginaw, Bob and Jean Dixon returned to Albuquerque in the latter part of 1987, and they were glad to be back in the Southwest. At sixty-two, Bob was still too young to retire. So, he did "consultation work for a number of companies," explained his daughter, Jennifer. He did that for several years, and then he and Jean retired to Las Vegas.

"Mom had a sister there," Jennifer said, "and dad liked to golf, so it was a good spot."

•••

A few weeks after Dixon's departure, Glen left Amigo's Bridgeport facility and worked on the Mobility Center in Grand Rapids. A few months later, David, who was now firmly aligned with Marie, showed up at the store, and was more than happy to inform Glen that he was now his boss.

Playing off Amigo Company's slogan, "The Friendly Wheelchair," Marie and David purchased the franchise store in Grand Rapids and named it "The *Frendly* Company," deliberately leaving out the *i* to avoid legal complications with Amigo Company. They also opened another durable medical equipment store in downtown Saginaw, right across the street from the Saginaw General Hospital, calling it Marie & Company.

David and Glen tried to work together, but since both of them had such strong personalities, it wasn't long before they butted heads. Not long after David resurfaced, he fired both Glen and Chuck Priest.

•••

Through all that turmoil and drama, Al and Beth's third child came into the world. Jordan Allan Thieme was born on October 2, 1987, fifty-one weeks to the day after his late brother, Adam.

The fact that the new boy's name started with a *J* was just a coincidence.

"We were on a business trip in Texas," Beth explained. "As we were going down the expressway, I was talking about the baby and that we didn't have a name yet. Then we saw a billboard off the side of the road, advertising the Jordan Marsh store. 'What do you think about Jordan?' I asked Al. 'Oh, I like it!' he replied. So that's how that happened."

And just to prove that he had no hard feelings toward Al, Bruce Cady called to congratulate him and Beth on the birth of their new child.

•••

Perhaps Cady was just trying to reingratiate himself with the Thiemes with that phone call, because he called Al again a few months later to say that he had a buyer for the Amigo Company, and that he wanted to be the broker. Despite the obvious conflict of interest, Cady probably figured that Al had put him through enough grief over the years that he might as well be compensated for his aggravation.

Al would have been interested in that proposal if Cady had presented it two or three years earlier, when the company was in the midst of crisis, but Al was no longer interested in selling the company. He believed that the worst was now behind him, and to sell the company would be heresy.

Deep down inside, Al never wanted to sell the company in the first place.

"Quitting wasn't an option for him," Mark Campbell explained. "I think Al would have said to himself, 'If I'm not doing this, what am I going to do? If I throw in the towel, I wake up and do *what* tomorrow?'"

Who Cady's potential buyer or buyers were was never revealed, but it could very well have been a consortium put together by David. Or perhaps by Bob Dixon. Or even the two of them together.

"David," Al recalled, "told us that he had people here in Saginaw who wanted to buy the company. He had people lined up, and he kept on us about that."

●●●

While Al and Beth were waiting to learn the repercussions from a disgruntled Bob Dixon, Amigo's accounting department told them about problems with both The Frendly Company and Marie & Company. As independent medical supply dealers, the two companies bought Amigos at wholesale prices, but they weren't paying for them, and now they owed Amigo Company $96,000. With such a substantial amount outstanding, Al got involved.

He and Beth drove to meet with David at his office in Saginaw.

"Is there something wrong with the Amigos that we sold you?" Al asked rhetorically.

"No, of course not," David replied.

"Well, then, you need to pay us for them!"

"We're not paying you anything!" David said defiantly.

"Then, we're going to have to sue you," Al replied.

"Go ahead!" David exclaimed.

From Al and Beth's perspective, this was strictly a business matter.

"It was a pure collection suit," Beth explained. "You owe Amigo Company this much money for these goods. End of story!"

But it wasn't the end of the story. In fact, it was just the beginning.

•••

After repeated attempts to collect on the account, Amigo Company filed a collection suit for approximately $96,000 on May 26, 1988. Al and Beth didn't want to sue, but they had no other option. And they expected the suit to be a long, drawn-out process.

What they didn't expect, however, was a seven-count countersuit from The Frendly Company, alleging, among other things, unlawful conversion of assets and violation of Michigan franchise statues. Marie and David were seeking damages of nearly $400,000.

The Frendly Company was asking the court to dismiss Al and Beth as corporate officers of Amigo Company and for the court to take jurisdiction over the corporation. Specifically, they were claiming that the Thiemes "improperly transferred assets from Amigo Sales, Inc., to Mobility Center, Inc.," and that they "have manipulated the financial obligations of Amigo and Mobility to the financial detriment of Amigo and its shareholders."

To explain the legal basis for the suit, Arthur Lippert, Marie's attorney, stated in a newspaper interview that there was "a special statute to protect the rights of minority shareholders from inappropriate acts. The court can issue an order to sell off the company's assets or reorganize the business." The minority shareholder in this case, of course, was Marie.

"It was just unbelievable!" Al recalled. "There was never anything that we did to manipulate funds. I don't know how to do that, to begin with!"

While Al dismissed the suit as a "smokescreen," Frendly's action could have dire consequences.

•••

Until now only the parties directly involved were aware of these disconcerting events. But then someone, perhaps, David notified the press.

"'Oust officers,' says AMIGO exec's ex," read the headline in *The Saginaw News* on the morning of September 2, 1988.

But once again, Divine Providence intervened on Al's behalf. Instead of vigorously pursuing the case in court, Arthur Lippert agreed to settle through mediation.

Also working in Amigo's favor was that Marie apparently wanted mediation, too.

"I want this resolved," she said to a reporter, "so Al can run his company, and I can run mine."

•••

Mediation is a step prior to trial in an attempt to settle disputes. It is much less expensive than going to court and much quicker. A neutral party, usually an attorney, listens to both sides of the argument and then recommends a solution. If both parties agree, their decision is just as binding as if it were handed down by a judge or jury.

"Our attorney read the recommendation," recalled Beth, "and said, 'We accept it in part. We accept that they owe us money, but we reject that we owe them money.' He signed it and filed his response."

At first blush, it seemed as though Amigo Company had just won the case. But Al and Beth's attorney had just made a serious blunder. According to the laws of the State of Michigan, if one side in a mediation case accepts a decision in part, they accept it in whole.

"The whole purpose of mediation," Beth said, "is to get the case resolved. So, if you accept in part and reject in part, you're not resolving anything!"

For whatever reason, the Thiemes' attorney missed that point. So, although he was agreeing to only part of the mediator's solution, he was in fact agreeing to the whole solution. And by doing so, Amigo Company lost the case!

In a convoluted settlement, the mediator awarded The Frendly Company $395,055 and the Amigo Company, $95,991.91, with the net result being that Amigo Company ended up owing The Frendly Company $299,063.09!

"We were just trying to get paid on equipment!" Beth explained. "It was a simple collections suit. And now our attorney is telling us that we owe all this money! Well, that would put us out of business! We didn't have it!"

But Al and Beth were still not ready to give up.

"Wait a minute!" Beth told her attorney. "This is not our fault! You're the lawyer! We don't know the law!"

At first, the attorney just shrugged off Beth's protestations, explaining to the Thiemes that sometimes you lose, but they weren't about to accept that.

"We got hit with a judgment," Beth said, "because our attorney made a mistake. We pushed him harder, and eventually he turned the case over to his malpractice insurance company, and they paid a settlement."

While Al and Beth were relieved about that, they still lost their collection suit.

"We didn't collect any money!" lamented Beth. "We never got the $96,000 that The Frendly Company owed us."

•••

Some years later, Beth ran into Arthur Lippert.

"Why did you go after us for manipulation of funds?" she asked.

"Because we had no other defense," he replied.

Later that year, Marie Thieme, in conjunction with Bob Dixon, filed a lawsuit against both the Amigo Company and Al and Beth personally. Marie was seeking payment of a $126,000 promissory note from Al, and Dixon was seeking lost salary and benefits payments from Amigo Company in the amount of $200,000.

Marie's promissory note arose out of the various negotiations that Amigo Company had had with the National Bank of Detroit over the last few years.

"The bank," Beth explained, "would not lend money to pay off vendors. They said they would do a debt-for-equity loan, so Al and Marie sold the buildings and put the money in promissory notes."

Marie and Dixon could have filed their own separate lawsuits against Al and the Amigo Company, but Dixon (or maybe David) convinced Marie that they would have a better chance of winning if they joined forces as minority stockholders.

After three years of litigation, a settlement was reached in November 1991. The court ruled Dixon's employment contract null and void because, Beth explained, "Dixon had said to the Board that they would get a chance to look at his contract, but he never did share it with them, so it was dismissed." As for Marie's action, she graciously agreed to accept Al's offer of allowing him to pay her for the note over time.

While Dixon lost a significant amount of money from his now voided employment contract, Al agreed to have Amigo Company buy back all of Dixon's Amigo stock for the price he had paid for it ($100,000), but the company could only do that over time, and Dixon agreed. The National Bank of Detroit facilitated the transaction, agreeing to hold Dixon's stock until it was paid for in full.

"There were no shenanigans with Marie's and Dixon's suit," explained Beth. "It was just simply ..., she wanted 'paid' on her promissory note and Dixon wanted 'paid' on his employment contract. The contract became null and void, and we agreed to buy back his shares of stock. And we did it over time, because we didn't have the money. Then we made monthly payments to both of them."

•••

Except for the Frendly lawsuit and its associated negative publicity, 1988 ended pretty well for Amigo Company. Sales dropped some that year, but the company still posted a strong profit of $350,000. It looked as if Amigo Company had finally turned the corner.

With Al and Beth back in control, they started doing things that Bob Dixon should have been doing to turn the company around.

"We made a list of things that we could live without," Beth explained. "We laid off some people, and we focused on sales. I don't know how we got through that! It was by the grace of God. And our relationship was never in jeopardy; we always stuck through it and figured it out."

•••

The last year of the 1980s also started well. The lease on that Citibank computer finally ended in March 1989. It didn't affect the company's bottom line one way or the other, but Al was glad to finally get it off the company's books. However, as if in some demented last act of defiance, Citibank "wanted to ship the computer to us," Al recalled, "because we owned it!"

No one at Amigo can recall what happened to that computer. Someone at Amigo Company probably told the Citibank executives to do whatever they wanted with it. Al would have loved it if they just threw the darn thing in the Delaware River! What is known for sure is that the computer never showed up on Amigo's receiving dock.

In the meantime, sales continued to drop, but at a slower rate, and then began to pick up again in the fall. The company hit $900,000 in sales for September alone.

●●●

But what about SAGA's requirement that Amigo Company and Mobility Center, Inc., be combined?

"That didn't happen," Beth said. "SAGA never followed-up on that."

CHAPTER 19

The SCOOTER Store

"Al Thieme could have had me as the
top franchisee in the world!"
—Douglas Harrison, founder of The SCOOTER Store

Probably the most ambitious person to inquire about an Amigo Mobility Center franchise was Douglas Harrison of New Braunfels, Texas. If Al is a Type A personality, Harrison is an A+. Highly intelligent and articulate, Harrison not only wanted to start a business, but to build a "business of scale," as he put it.

Harrison was a petroleum engineer for the Conoco Oil Company. He and his wife, Susanna, had been talking for years about starting their own business. In fact, they had saved a goodly sum of money and were looking around for the perfect business opportunity. However, the one who found it was Harrison's father, Otto.

Like his son, Otto was in the oil business, except with the Exxon Corporation. He traveled a lot and read a lot on the road. While reading *Entrepreneur Magazine* one day, he saw a listing of franchise offerings. The Amigo Mobility Center franchise caught his attention—so much so, in fact, that the next time he was in Dallas, he dropped by the Amigo Mobility Center there to further investigate the business opportunity. After looking around the store, he talked to the owners, asking a lot of questions, and became even more intrigued with the operation. As soon as he left the store, he called his son.

"Hey, Doug," he said, "take a look at this company."

•••

It was early 1991, and President George W. Bush had just signed the Americans with Disabilities Act (ADA) a few months before. An extension of the Civil Rights Act of 1964, which made discrimination based on race, sex, religion, and national origin illegal, the ADA additionally prohibited discrimination based on physical disability. Among other things, the act required all public and most private facilities to remove "barriers to access," which included adding ramps next to steps and adding curb cuts between sidewalks and streets. Up until that time, people in wheelchairs often were able only to go as far as the next step, the next curb, or the next driveway.

The new law was sure to open up a whole new world for people with disabilities, including Douglas Harrison's paternal grandmother, who resided in an assisted living facility. She was spry and alert, but she had endurance problems.

"I can't tell you specifically what her illness was," Harrison said, "but she just couldn't ambulate far enough to be independent."

So Harrison bought her an Amigo, which changed her life.

"Now," Harrison recalled, "she was able to do the stuff she needed to do. She could get to the bathroom, and she could go down the hall to get to the dining room. She still hated not being in her own house, but she was OK with staying in an assisted living environment now that she wasn't confined to her room. She had fun driving the Amigo around, and it made her happy to be able to get out and be mobile. 'I love my little scooter!' she would exclaim."

Her reaction, in fact, got the Harrisons thinking that the "mobility field" was the business for them. The passage of the ADA, they thought, was sure to drive up the demand for wheelchairs, and the huge baby boomer market, which was getting older by the minute, would simply add to that demand. Harrison saw an opportunity that was too good to ignore.

•••

Without hesitation, Douglas and Susanna flew to Michigan to visit with Al and Beth. Harrison told them right off the bat that he wanted to acquire the San Antonio and Austin markets and have options for eight more territories in Texas.

"I told Al," Harrison said, "that I eventually wanted to buy the *entire* state of Texas. Al would sell us a franchise for New Braunfels, but nothing bigger. We wanted to start really big, but he wanted us to start very small."

With Al's goals and Harrison's goals on different tracks, the only deal the two men made was that Al would sell Amigos to Harrison as an independent medical equipment dealer.

That night, the Thiemes took the Harrisons out to dinner at the Bavarian Inn in Frankenmuth. Afterward, they went to Bronner's Christmas Wonderland, "the world's largest Christmas store." With more than seven acres under its roof, Bronner's had Christmas trappings of every size, shape, and description: Christmas trees, Christmas cards, and more than 6,000 different kinds of ornaments. Even Douglas Harrison was impressed.

As a memento of the visit, Al bought the Harrisons a beautiful angel ornament to put on top of their Christmas tree, with "1991" molded onto its base.

However, the ornament was little consolation to the Harrisons, who had come to Michigan with high hopes and money in their pockets, but had to leave frustrated.

"We were disappointed," the ambitious Harrison said. "Al Thieme could have had me as the top Amigo franchisee in the world!"

•••

Al doesn't remember the events quite that way. In fact, if Al had met with the Harrisons, it was only briefly, because at that time, Mobility Center was utilizing the services of Franchise Development Resources, a company in Detroit that specialized in selling franchises. One of its brokers was Frank Flack.

"I do remember Frank Flack coming to me and Beth," recalled Al, "saying that the Harrisons were coming in to attend our franchise training. He assured us that they would sign the franchise agreement."

However, on the last day of the franchise training—the day that the Harrisons were supposed to sign the franchise contract—they had "an emergency" and returned to Texas without signing the contract.

Regardless of how the events transpired in Bridgeport, by the time the Harrisons landed back in San Antonio, they had decided to abandon any ideas of owning any type of franchise, let alone an Amigo Mobility Center. Instead, they decided to go into business for themselves, and that decision forever changed the industry.

•••

In the spring of 1991, the Harrisons opened up their first SCOOTER Store in New Braunfels.

"We chose the mobility field," Harrison said, "not the medical field. So, unlike a lot of other people who were selling a whole line of medical equipment, we just did mobility—scooters and power wheelchairs. We very specifically said that we were in the mobility business."

Doug's company did not manufacture any of the products that it sold.

•••

Back in 1991, Doug Harrison had quite accurately predicted the expansion of future health care expenses. In 1968, when Al Thieme started the Amigo Company, Medicare expenditures totaled $7.5 billion. In 1992, Medicare expenditures totaled $110 billion. Ten years later, total Medicare expenditures had doubled to $220 billion. Harrison had entered the booming health care market at just the perfect time.

When Harrison went into the durable medical supply business, he didn't know anything about Medicare. Although he soon learned that Medicare would help to pay for POVs, it was hardly worth the effort to submit the necessary paperwork. As Mike Flowers had learned earlier, Doug discovered that every state had its own Part B Medicare carrier. Therefore, there were fifty different sets of rules.

"They were all crazy," Doug said, "and it was nearly impossible to get something approved."

•••

Like Mike Flowers's Electric Mobility Company, The SCOOTER Store did not accept Medicare assignments for years. Harrison's salespeople would help customers to fill out the necessary Medicare forms, so that they could get reimbursed, but the company expected cash from the customers at the time of delivery. While his sales were adequate, they were not what Doug had hoped for or wanted. As he thought about ways to expand sales, he took another look at Medicare and came up with an idea.

Since the vast majority of people in his target market were on Medicare, and most would probably get reimbursed from Medicare if they needed a mobility device, Doug decided to do what both Al Thieme and Mike Flowers refused to do: accept Medicare assignments from his customers. From his point of view, the risk of not getting paid was low, and the potential gain in sales was enormous. In any case, it was definitely worth a try. After all, his salespeople knew how to fill out the necessary paperwork. All they had to do was instruct the government to send the money to The SCOOTER Store, instead of to the customers.

•••

To promote his new marketing scheme, Doug increased his advertising dramatically. Like Mike Flowers, he started out doing a lot of print advertising. As we have seen, a full-page ad in a magazine that specifically targeted the elderly could cost tens of thousands of dollars per month, and The SCOOTER Store did not have that kind of money to spend on print media—at least, not at the moment. Instead, Doug tried all different kinds of print media: newspapers, small-circulation magazines, and direct-mail pieces.

"Anywhere," he said, "that we thought we could get our message in front of our potential target audience, we tested it. We tested viciously and thoroughly. We would run an ad for a year to see what would happen."

Surprisingly, Doug never ran an ad with a "1-800-SCOOTER" phone number. While that figure had the appropriate number of digits, and the name would have fit his business perfectly, "it belonged to a bank!" he said laughingly. "Plus, if we had only one phone number, we wouldn't know where customers called us from. In our business, we had something like 2,800 toll-free numbers. So, when you called The SCOOTER Store, we didn't need to ask you how you found us, because, based on the number you called, we knew exactly what direct-mail piece, what print ad, what newspaper, what city, and what day it ran that you called us on!"

•••

There was a time in television broadcasting when there were only three national networks—ABC, CBS, and NBC—and they would broadcast only for eighteen hours a day. They would "sign on" at 5:00 a.m. and "sign off" at 1:00 a.m. At the end of each broadcast day, the image of an American flag flapping in the wind would show up on the TV screen, accompanied by playing "The Star-Spangled Banner," and then the screen would turn into hissy snow.

There was also a time when the TV networks had to run a certain number of public service announcements. The federal government required the networks to show these PSAs, as they were called, free of charge for organizations that had a "message of public interest" that they wanted to disseminate, which usually pertained to the public's health and safety.

With the rise of cable TV stations and the deregulation of the television airways throughout the 1980s, those PSAs were no longer required, and the three national networks began to broadcast twenty-four hours a day, providing a lot more time to play commercials. With the plethora of new cable stations entering the field, the price of commercials plummeted, especially during the off-peak hours. For example, while a thirty-second spot could easily have cost $80,000 in 1982, that same commercial could be run in the mid-1990s between the hours of 11:00 p.m. and 6:00 a.m. for less than $50.

To take advantage of that new advertising opportunity, Doug Harrison had a TV commercial produced and then instructed the major networks to play it whenever they had a spot that they hadn't sold. Using that technique, he rarely paid more than $50 for a thirty-second commercial.

"There were a lot of early-morning and late-night spots," Doug explained, "which worked well for our target market. Our average customers were in their eighties, and a lot of them are up early in the morning or stay up late at night."

Before long, Doug's company was spending $100,000,000 a year on print and TV advertising. That was ten times more than Electric Mobility was spending, and ten *thousand* times more than Amigo Company was spending!

•••

"Our marketing strategy," Doug explained unabashedly, "is fairly aggressive in getting the message out to who we think are potential customers."

And his television commercials proved that. The ads were

loud, direct, and to the point.

One of their typical commercials started out with a headline banner:

Attention!
All Medicare beneficiaries
who need assistance
getting around their
homes:
There is a Medicare
benefit that may
qualify you for a
power chair or
scooter at little to
no cost to you.

NARRATOR: Imagine one scooter or power chair that could improve your mobility and your life. One Medicare benefit that, with private insurance, may entitle you to pay little to nothing to own it. One company that can make it all happen.

COMPANY EMPLOYEE ON THE TELEPHONE: Your power chair will be paid in full!

DOUG HARRISON: Hi, I'm Doug Harrison. We're experts at getting the power chair or scooter you need. In fact, if we qualify you for Medicare reimbursement and Medicare denies your claim, we'll give you your new power chair or scooter free!

CUSTOMER: I didn't pay a penny out of pocket for my power chair. With help from The SCOOTER Store, Medicare and my insurance covered it all!

DOUG HARRISON: Call The SCOOTER Store for free information today!

NARRATOR: Call 1-800-501-5760 for free information.

The first scene in the commercial shows a power chair being removed from a van. The second scene shows an elderly lady sitting in a conventional wheelchair, being pushed into her living room to accept her new power chair. The third and last scene shows a man entering a living room on Christmas Day to join his grandchildren, again in a power chair.

Although the company's logo featured the silhouette of an Amigo-type cart, and although the company's name was "The SCOOTER Store" (with the letters for *scooter* deliberately capitalized), nowhere in the commercial was a disabled person ever shown using a scooter.

Why?

Because The SCOOTER Store made more money on power wheelchairs than on scooters. It's similar to new car dealerships. While they may offer low-cost compact cars, they want you to buy larger cars or even pickups, because there's more money to be made in those types of vehicles.

•••

The word *free* in The SCOOTER Store's advertising drove up customer inquiries exponentially, surpassing even Doug Harrison's expectations. The volume was so great, in fact, that Doug had to develop an electronic processing system to handle it all.

"Medicare's rules," Doug explained, "were long and detailed, but they weren't hard. So, we built a giant spreadsheet, and every Medicare rule was part of our intake form, and you checked off the box and made sure that if you were going to pursue a claim for this customer with Medicare, they had to meet *every* box. Every time we got a claim denied, we'd go back to the checklist and say, 'What did we screw up?' That meant that our checklist was wrong, so we'd go back and find out how to make the checklist better, so we wouldn't do that mistake again.

And we'd do that over and over and over."

Once Doug's state-of-the-art process was fine-tuned, the company was not only able to process orders quickly and efficiently, but, Doug said, "Medicare would pay us pretty fast. The SCOOTER Store got paid, on average, fourteen days from the time that we submitted our bill. The industry average was close to six months. We got paid on 99.8 percent of our claims, whereas the industry average was barely more than 50 percent."

Like Mike Flowers, Doug Harrison capitalized on the word *free*, but in Doug's case, his power wheelchairs *were* free! (But not free to taxpayers.) Nevertheless, Doug had hit upon the perfect formula for selling power mobility equipment. It took him ten years, but by 2010, The SCOOTER Store was generating $400,000,000 in revenue per year and, according to the company's website, had "changed the lives of over 600,000 seniors and people with disabilities."

●●●

As sales grew, so did The SCOOTER Store. By the summer of 2001, Doug Harrison had grown his enterprise into "a business of scale," just as he had envisioned a decade earlier. During that time, his business grew to 126 retail outlets and distribution centers in 42 states, and had 3,000 employees: 1,000 in the field and 2,000 at The SCOOTER Store's headquarters in New Braunfels. And all those employees worked directly for the company. Doug could have set up a chain of independent dealers or franchisees, but "because of Medicare's reimbursement rules," he said, "we knew they were tight, and we said we've got to control this internally. They were all our own people."

Although The SCOOTER Store opened in 1991, the company didn't start expanding beyond Texas until 1999.

"From 1999 to 2009," Doug explained, "we grew pretty fast. For the first ten years, we learned how to make the business work, hiring professional staff. In that first ten-year period, I got my executive master's degree to learn how to run businesses. I hired business coaches. I hired a guy that was a retired Harvard MBA, a professor at Southern Methodist University, to be my personal coach. I hired Verne Harnish to be the executive coach to my senior team. He wrote a number of business books, including *Scaling Up*; *Mastering the Rockefeller Habits*; and *The Greatest Business Decisions of All Time*. We hired Dr. Paul Metzger to be our medical director [he had been with Medicare], and we hired Leslie Norwalk, the lady who had been the assistant director of Medicare. We hired 400 nurses, who worked for us at the office on medical files, Medicare files, and billing, and we made sure that we were totally in compliance with Medicare's rules. We just did what it took to do it the right way. Once we got the formula, we grew faster. By 2003, we were coast-to-coast."

•••

Just like Amigo Company, The SCOOTER Store found a place on the INC. 500 list—not twice, but five times, placing it in the INC. 500 Hall of Fame. And it made *Fortune* magazine's 100 Best Places to Work list twice, once in 2004, and again in 2010.

As with all of his other endeavors, Doug made it his goal to be on that prestigious list, and he simply used *Fortune*'s guidelines to do it.

"They had this giant matrix," Doug explained, "that says what makes your company a great place to work, and we used it as our rubric. We did all those things that were on their matrix."

•••

The SCOOTER Store's presence became so powerful, so overwhelming, that it eventually forced Mike Flowers out of business.

"The market," Mike explained, "switched from being a cash market for scooters to being an entitlement market after President Obama was elected. Everybody thought, *I'm on Medicare, so I deserve to have one of these for free!* The SCOOTER Store started running advertisements on TV incessantly. Its ads said: 'If you want an electric scooter or a power wheelchair and we process your claim, and your claim is denied by Medicare, you can keep it on us!' That sure sounds like it's free to me! It was really hard to sell fully featured, top-quality electric scooters for *money* when you had somebody offering them for free."

And to make matters worse, customers got Electric Mobility's TV ads mixed up with The SCOOTER Store's TV ads.

"When we showed up at the door," lamented Mike Flowers, "they would say, 'Where's my free scooter?' It just wore us down."

CHAPTER 20

Near-Death Experience

"The medical market was like a race to the bottom!"
—Clarence Rivette

The death of Al's father on February 9, 1990, was a gloomy portend of things to come. Al never saw his father much over the years, and hadn't seen him in seven years. Had his father lived in Michigan, Al would have seen him quite often, but since he lived in Florida, he saw him very little.

The last time Al saw his father was in November 1983, when he and Beth went on a business trip through the South and stopped in to see Alfred. As during most of the previous visits, he and Al mostly talked about living in Florida.

"We just visited for a while, then we left," Beth recalled. "I'll never forget that, because we were in the car. He had hugged us goodbye, and we had said our goodbyes, and we start to back out. He kept walking alongside the car all the way out to the end of the driveway, waving to us. Then we turned to go out to the road, and he stood in the middle of the road, just waving. That was our last sight of him."

Three months later, Alfred Thieme died. He was seventy-nine years old.

Not long afterward, Al had an odd dream, in which he was having dinner with his family, and his dad appeared. "Hello, son," he said. Then Al asked him to sit down at the table.

Al didn't make too much of that dream, although he couldn't remember ever dreaming about his father before. The dream was probably an indication that Al missed his father more than he realized. Also, the birth of his and Beth's fourth child reminded him of how precious life is.

•••

Katelyn Joanne Thieme was born on August 20, 1990. Beth explained the choice of that name this way: "So, I'm half-Irish, and Al's grandmother's name was Kate. We went to her 100th birthday; she was a wonderful lady. We liked that name."

•••

In an effort to get international sales going again after the departure of Bud Paffrath, Clarence Rivette was hired to head up the company's international division. Born and raised in Saginaw, the twenty-nine-year-old former naval intelligence officer was looking for a job when he saw Amigo's ad in *The Saginaw News*, seeking a manager for "International Sales."

"I didn't know how to sell!" Rivette admitted candidly. "I had no business experience. But I had the confidence of having traveled to a number of countries overseas, and I had no fear. I speak Russian fluently."

Beth looked over Rivette's résumé, but discounted it, not because he didn't have any business experience, but because of his high-level experience. He had spent the previous three years in the military, working at the Pentagon.

"Wow!" she said. "I don't think we can afford you!"

"Yes, you can," Rivette quickly replied," because I'm not working!"

Beth and Al agreed that he was such a dynamic and gregarious person that they would hire him.

•••

Rivette began to bring the international department back to life. First, he flew to Europe to meet with Georges De Coster in Belgium, then with Ray Hodgkinson and Martin Corby in the UK. From there, he flew to Mexico City to meet with Federico Fleischmann.

"We ended up taking that base of salespeople," Rivette explained, "giving it the attention it needed, listening to them, bringing product ideas. The year 1997 was kind of exciting. We landed a joint venture with an Israeli company, and we obtained half a million dollars from the Bird Foundation, which supported joint product development between Israeli and American companies. We had a vision for the first-ever folding scooter, called the TravelMate. It really revolutionized scooters at that time. That led to much smaller, compact portable scooters, and it was a very, very successful product. It really put Amigo and the Tzora Company in Israel, which is actually an Israeli kibbutz, back on the map again. It reflected the international spirit that we had, working with others in different countries to create new things. TravelMate was a very exciting chapter."

•••

Rivette expanded Amigo sales into new foreign markets—almost every European country as well as Brazil, Chile, and Korea.

"Over the years," he recalled, "with the right attention, energy, and support, we grew and expanded foreign sales by 35 percent."

Foreign sales increased so much, in fact, that Al formally changed the name of the company to Amigo Mobility International, Inc. (Amigo Mobility for short.)

"Originally," Al explained, "I thought our company would likely have the majority of Amigos built by some other company, and Amigo Company would mainly be a sales company. Hence, the name Amigo Sales, Inc. As we grew and sold internationally, it seemed fitting to have our name better explain what we were."

•••

While Rivette was building up international sales, Al hired John Murphy in the spring of 1991 as the franchise manager of Mobility Center. After five years of mediocre growth, it was time to move this distribution network forward.

John Murphy had been the franchise director for the Tuffy Muffler Company of Toledo, Ohio, which had 175 locations throughout the country, so Al had high hopes that Murphy could expand Mobility Centers similarly. With the help of a salesman, an operations person, and two office personnel, Murphy got right to work. But even with all of his experience, it still took him over a year to sell his first Mobility Center franchise. It was located in Indianapolis—Chuck and Jill Priest's old territory.

Murphy wasn't particularly pleased with his slow progress, but he eventually got traction, adding two more franchises in 1993, and by the time the Mobility Center's tenth anniversary rolled around in June 1994, Murphy had seventeen franchises in operation.

"Franchising going great!" Al noted in his journal.

Murphy sold four more franchises in 1995, and another four in 1996.

•••

Another welcome addition to Amigo Mobility's executive staff was Mike Galer, who became the new controller. Galer, who was a CPA, had graduated from Michigan State University with a bachelor's degree in accounting. He was born and raised in the quintessential American town of Dearborn, Michigan, the hometown of Henry Ford and the Ford Motor Company. In fact, Galer's father worked at Ford Motors.

"I kind of spent my childhood at the Greenfield Village," Galer recalled. "We lived on a dead-end street, and there were about fifty kids on the block. It was just an awesome neighborhood—a Shangri-La!"

After college, Galer worked for Touche Ross & Company, one of the nation's largest accounting firms, before eventually joining Amigo Mobility.

•••

Alden Thieme was glad that things appeared to be turning around for Amigo. But life was about to take a drastic turn for him.

On the afternoon of March 18, 1993, after putting in a day's work at Amigo, he went home, a hundred yards away from the office, to fix a leak in the roof of his garage. It was the first nice day after a long winter, so he figured it was as good a time as any to climb a ladder and make the repair.

"I'll see you later," he told Carol Hackett, one of the company's service technicians, as he walked out the company door.

"It wasn't ten minutes later," she remembered, "when my sister called and said that Alden fell off the ladder, and they're flying him to the hospital. I walked outside just as the helicopter was landing."

His son, Jim, explained that Alden "was coming back down the ladder to get a tool, when the bottom of the ladder slipped out from under him, and down he came! He didn't fall that far, maybe twelve feet, but he landed just right and broke his back at the T10 vertebra and broke all of his ribs. They didn't think he was going to survive."

Alden did survive, but he was paralyzed from the waist down.

When Al went to see his big brother at the hospital, Alden was lying in bed, despondent. Alden had seen plenty of people in his condition riding around on Amigos—including Marie, of course—and he knew that he didn't want to be one of them.

Eventually Alden got over it—at least to the extent that anyone can.

"He took to the Amigo really well," Jim said. "He went through rehab faster than anybody else, and he went back to work. He took everything in stride. That's the way it started out, anyway."

•••

On October 17, 1994, Al and Beth's last child was born, and they gave him a strong, legendary name: Alexander John Thieme.

So over a forty-year period, Al engendered eleven children: Jill, Joe, June, John, Jess, Jack, Jennifer, Adam, Jordan, Katelyn, and Alex—the firstborn being old enough to be the mother of the youngest!

•••

A month later, just as Al was telling Clarence Rivette how well Alden's rehabilitation was coming along, Bob Dixon called. Al was surprised, for he hadn't expected to hear from his past president ever again.

"How are you?" Dixon asked. "How's business?"

Al was lost for words and didn't immediately respond.

"Bob," Al finally said, "I just can't talk to you. Goodbye."

Looking back on that day, Al regrets not talking with Dixon.

"Maybe he was going to tell me how bad he felt for what had happened," he said, "because he and Jeanie were good people."

The two men never talked to each other again, although they did exchange correspondence about the stock buy-back agreement that they had consummated at the end of 1991.

On May 25, 1995, Beth wrote a letter to Richard Smith, Dixon's attorney, noting that Amigo Mobility had made the last payment for Dixon's stock. A copy of that letter was sent to Dixon, ending forever any communication between the two men.

Jean Dixon died on July 1, 2004, and Bob lived for another fourteen years, dying of natural causes on March 29, 2018, at the age of ninety-one. Since Bob was a military veteran, both he and

Jean were interred at the National Military Cemetery in Santa Fe, New Mexico.

•••

If Beth thought that running six franchises had been challenging, managing twenty-seven located throughout the country became almost overwhelming. But Al and Beth were doing as much for their franchisees as any other franchisor.

"We were going out and seeing them," Al said. "We'd have sales meetings on a regular basis, and we gave the franchises a 50 percent discount off the suggested retail price. We wanted those franchises to be successful."

But Al learned what all other franchisors eventually learn.

"We could sell franchises, and they were doing pretty good," Al said. "But as the network ages, they think they know better and want to do it their way."

•••

Although international sales were up, and Amigo Mobility was gaining more sales as more Mobility Center franchises were added, that all took time, so for most of the 1990s, both Amigo Mobility and Mobility Center were on the brink of collapse.

"We were struggling to make money," recalled Mike Galer. "We went three or four years where we made almost no money, so cash flow was not good."

Amigo Mobility's persistent and relentless cash-flow problem was not only bothersome, but worse than ever. For example, in March 1992, the company lost $75,000, and over the next nine months, inventory increased by $300,000. That January, Galer asked the National Bank of Detroit for an additional $200,000, but the bank said no.

While the bank didn't end Amigo's line of credit, its refusal to extend any more credit forced Galer to look for another bank. Despite Amigo's poor financial condition, he was able to transfer all of the company's business from the National Bank of Detroit to the Comerica Bank, which had a branch in Midland,

Michigan, not far from Bridgeport. But that turned out to be a short-lived arrangement.

Six months later, Amigo overdrew its account by $200,000. "That was a major hiccup with them," recalled Galer. Unlike the National Bank of Detroit, the bankers at Comerica had no tolerance for a customer's noncompliance with their loan covenants, so they told Galer to either find another bank or "prepare for bankruptcy," because they would not hesitate to call the loan.

"It wasn't a slap on the hand," Galer said. "It was a fist to the face!"

He knew they were serious because, a few years earlier, Comerica had forced another local company out of business for nonpayment.

Fortunately, Galer was able to move the company's account to the Michigan National Bank, which was more lenient than Comerica had been.

"Oh, you overdrew again?" Galer said, paraphrasing the bankers at Michigan National. "Happens all the time!"

Galer appreciated their amiability, especially when Amigo was so cash-strapped, but all that changed quickly when Michigan National was bought by the Standard Federal Bank. Like Comerica, Standard Federal did not tolerate overdrafts, let alone insolvency. When the bankers saw that Amigo wasn't complying with the covenants of the loan, they told Galer that he needed "to find another bank, or we're going to close you down."

Fortunately, that never happened, but they put Amigo Mobility into what they called a "workout group," meaning they would work with them for a while, until Amigo found another bank.

But that was easier said than done. Amigo Mobility had gone through practically every bank in town, and none of the banks they had not yet used were interested in its business.

Right at that moment, Amigo Mobility was at a precipice. As we have seen, it had some serious financial challenges in the past, but none as serious as the one it was facing at the beginning of 1997. Al suspected that the company was in peril, but Mike Galer *knew* it.

At the time, Chase Bank handled Amigo's payroll account. Every two weeks, Galer would transfer funds to Chase Bank, which would then process the company's payroll checks.

Galer would normally call Kathy Ragan, the branch manager, to let her know that funds would be coming, so they knew each other well and had a good working relationship. In fact, they were on the board of the Bridgeport Chamber of Commerce together, where they met once a month.

"I trusted her, and she trusted me," Galer said. "I remember the company was struggling, and vendors were wanting money. I was trying to save money for payroll, but cash was not coming in. We got to the day before payroll, and I had to transfer $70,000, and I didn't have it! It reminded me of the movie *It's a Wonderful Life*."

So he called Kathy to plead his case.

"You know," he said, "you're going to get a transfer for payroll tomorrow, but we're not going to be able to meet it. You're going to have to reject it. I apologize. We're just not able to fund that payroll."

Galer was intending to tell Al that Amigo wasn't going to make payroll, when Kathy caught him off guard.

"Well," she asked, "what do you need?"

"What do you mean?" Galer replied.

"How long do you need?"

"I don't know. I might need a week."

"OK."

"What?"

"Yeah. I'll transfer the money, and you pay me when you can over the next week."

"I didn't even have a loan relationship with Chase Bank," Galer recalled. "I mean, Kathy went out on a limb! That lady saved us!"

Not only that, but she saved Al the embarrassment of having to tell his employees that they were not going to get paid!

"Al tells me," Galer said, "that he always had a little pit in his stomach when I'd come over to talk to him during those times, because he was never sure what news I was going to bring."

•••

What Mike Galer couldn't assuage was the tragedy that occurred a few months later.

Al was walking toward the showroom located on the north side of the building when he came upon his old friend, Dick Vance, lying on the service department's floor. Dick was only sixty-one years old, but he had just had a heart attack.

Al rushed over, as did several others. They did their best to revive him, but it was too late.

"My friend has died," Al wrote in his journal. "Dick and I did a lot together."

Vance's death came just six months after the death of Al's brother-in-law, Max Goodman, Emy's husband. Max had had a stroke some time earlier and was using an Amigo. But he never fully recovered, and died on October 2, 1996, from congestive heart failure at the age of sixty-seven.

•••

To help improve the condition of the company, Al promoted Clarence Rivette to president in May 1997. Rivette had done a laudable job in reviving and expanding international sales, so Al hoped he could work his magic on the rest of the company.

Rivette appreciated Al's confidence in him, and to show how committed he was to the company, he made a deal with Joyce Godwin, a former member of Amigo's board of directors, to buy her Amigo stock over a five-year period.

"I bought those shares for a very good price," he recalled.

"I think it was about 5 percent of the company back then. At that time, I wasn't picturing going anywhere else, and it was a wonderful relationship, so why not be a shareholder? That's how committed I was, and Al and Beth were comfortable with it."

In other words, the Thiemes never had second thoughts about Clarence Rivette, the way they did about Bob Dixon.

"It was a win-win," Rivette said.

•••

Al and Beth may not have had any reservations about making Rivette president, but Clarence began to have second thoughts as soon as he started to delve into the company's problems. Cash flow, of course, was practically nonexistent. Inventory was exorbitantly high. And profits were low.

But those were only the results. The basic underlying problem was the lack of sales.

"It was kind of a triple whammy," Rivette explained.

Electric Mobility and The SCOOTER Store were decimating Amigo's domestic sales, Asian imports were adding to the competition, both domestically and in Europe, and the franchises weren't buying product from Amigo Mobility as they had been.

"It really hurt us," Rivette said.

•••

Ever since Amigo Mobility had begun expanding its franchise network in the middle of 1991, annual sales from the Mobility Centers increased exponentially from $190,000 in 1991 to $2.7 million in 1997.

There was no question that the franchisees were doing everything they could to sell Amigos, but they were fighting a losing battle. Not only were Electric Mobility and The SCOOTER Store overwhelming them with their incessant advertising, but they were offering products that Amigo Mobility did not have—namely, power wheelchairs.

"Al built his business," Rivette explained, "based on the vision that people can be much more active, both in their physical aspect and their mental aspect, by being in on an Amigo versus being in a wheelchair or a power wheelchair."

But the market for Amigos had not only changed, it had collapsed. The way Rivette put it: "The medical market was like a race to the bottom!"

•••

The loss of sales had been worsening ever since Electric Mobility entered the market back in 1982, but the company was approaching its nadir in the spring of 1997. And things just continued to disintegrate.

John Murphy quit in March 1998, and by the end of April, the company had already lost over $130,000. In fact, cash was so tight that both Al Thieme and Clarence Rivette personally signed a note guaranteeing a $45,000 loan to keep the company going.

"My orientation with Al," Rivette explained, "was as long as I was there, I was by his side. We're in this together."

Throughout the early part of 1999, Al, Beth, and Rivette met almost every day to talk about cash flow (or the lack thereof), "negative profit" (Al's term), and low sales.

Then, right in the middle of those strategy sessions, Clarence Rivette quit. He wasn't planning on quitting. After all, he had just signed that note. But in early June, he was contacted by John Parker, the president of the Intercare Group, a durable medical equipment manufacturer with divisions in Canada and the UK.

"He had a publicly traded company," Rivette explained. "He made me an offer, I saw this global opportunity, and I took it."

On the one hand, Al was sad to see Rivette leave. He had been with the company for almost a decade, and, as Al recalled, "Clarence was very charismatic, wanted to learn everything he could, and we trusted him completely." On the other hand, Rivette's leaving would help the company's cash flow.

"I had limited business experience," Rivette said years later. "I learned from Al and Beth. I learned the industry from them.

What we did there for nine years was pretty amazing!"

Rivette left on Friday, June 18, 1999, and the following Monday, Al took back the reins.

"My first day of running our beloved company," he wrote in his journal. "Able to make decisions and take action."

It didn't take him long to make two monumental decisions, which would forever alter the course of Amigo Mobility—or destroy it in the process.

•••

During all those strategy sessions that Al had with Beth and Rivette, it became clear that franchising was not working, and the medical scooter market was all but destroyed. Henceforth, Amigo Mobility would put all of its emphasis on its motorized shopping cart, the Amigo Shopper, and Amigo would let the twenty-seven Mobility Center agreements gradually expire.

Although Amigo Mobility had been selling the Amigo motorized shopping cart for almost thirty years, it really hadn't promoted it much. Mart Cart was the only other similar device on the market at the time.

"We really felt that the Amigo Shopper market was the market to go into," Beth recalled.

But that would not be easy. First, there was no guarantee that the Shopper market was any bigger than the few hundred carts that they already sold every year. Second, whatever the market was for the Shopper, it would take time to develop it—time that Amigo Mobility did not have. Third, Al and Beth would have to overcome the objections of their franchisees.

Al wanted to "hit that market big," he explained, but the franchisees put a halt to that quickly.

"The franchisees felt that they were the only ones who could sell the Shopper," Al explained, and that raised a serious contention between Amigo Mobility and the Mobility Center franchisees.

CHAPTER 21

Avoiding Catastrophe

"Amigo Mobility has the right to sell the Shopper."
—John Layman, franchisee

When the indefatigable Shirley Beebe was Amigo Mobility's national sales manager, the company had the Amigo Shopper as a product, but, she explained, "we weren't doing much with it."

From that first Shopper that Jill Thieme sold to the Meijer Thrifty Acres store in Flint, Michigan, back in 1970, the Shopper had always been a low priority for the company, which sold only about one per week. Part of the reason that sales for the Shopper were so low was that the Amigo salespeople were more used to selling to individuals than to businesses. To combat that, Shirley Beebe solicited the services of the United Steel & Wire Company in Battle Creek, Michigan, which made conventional shopping carts and sold them through manufacturers' representatives. If United Steel could sell non-motorized shopping carts, Beebe figured, they could just as easily sell motorized ones!

•••

United Steel's top sales representative asked Beebe to bring a Shopper to a store that was already using Mart Carts, so he could compare the two.

As Beebe was setting up the Shopper, a lady riding in a Mart Cart rolled up to her and the United Steel's sales rep.

"I'm sorry to bother you," she said, "but can I use that Amigo? I don't like this cart!"

"Of course, you can!" replied Beebe.

After the lady rode away, the sales rep looked at Beebe with a Cheshire Cat grin on his face and said, "Shirley, did you plant her?"

"No! Honest! I didn't!"

And she really hadn't. It was just a serendipitous moment.

"With that," explained Beebe, "the manufacturers' reps liked them, so they took the line on."

That produced a significant jump in Amigo Shopper sales.

•••

Up to that point, the Amigo Shopper was not a bone of contention with the franchisees.

"We didn't care," Beth explained, "if a franchisee went down to the local grocery store and sold them a Shopper. In fact, we encouraged it."

But the franchisees rarely did that.

"All they thought about," Al said, "was what we had trained them on—selling Amigos to people mainly with multiple sclerosis and polio. They wanted no part of trying to sell a shopping cart to a grocery store!"

All that changed, however, when Amigo Shoppers began showing up in the franchisees' territories—Shoppers that they had not sold, but were sold by Amigo Mobility through national accounts.

"You can't do that!" they all said. "Amigo Shoppers can only be sold through Mobility Centers."

•••

The Thiemes had been in the franchise business a long

time and had been challenged on everything from territory size to what products they could sell, and, up until now, they had prevailed. But this situation was different. The Shopper controversy affected *all* the franchisees, so Al was afraid of a class-action suit. Thus, before he went any further, Beth had an attorney review Mobility Center's franchise agreement to determine who could and who could not sell the Amigo Shopper.

The last sentence of a six-sentence paragraph labeled "Item 16" in the franchise agreement stated: "You are not restricted in the customers to whom you may sell your products and services, except that you may not solicit customers outside your territory."

In other words, as Beth explained, "The franchisees couldn't go after national accounts, and they couldn't prevent us from doing it, either."

Neither Al nor Beth could remember who suggested putting that clause in the franchise contract, but, Beth said nonchalantly, "I believe it was just typical 'boiler plate' stuff."

•••

Confident that the franchise agreement allowed Amigo Mobility to pursue national accounts unhindered, Al called the Mobility Center franchisees to Bridgeport for a sales meeting to discuss that particular sentence in detail. And to stave off as much disagreement as possible, Al called his old friends and longtime devotees, John and Donna Layman, ahead of time to ask them to reread the entire franchise agreement.

"Is there anything in there," he asked, "that *prevents* Amigo Mobility from selling the Shopper?"

When the topic came up at the meeting, and discussions began to get heated, John Layman stood up and squelched the debate.

"Amigo Mobility," he said, "has the right to sell the Shopper."

•••

With a fellow franchisee siding with Amigo Mobility, Al and Beth could relax a bit. But this controversy was just the latest of many, and there were more to come.

"Franchising is a very difficult business," Beth explained, "and it requires a lot of focus and energy. I think it was too hard to have both Mobility Center and Amigo Mobility at the same time. Amigo Mobility is a complex business in and of itself. It was too much for us to have both businesses."

In fact, the Thiemes had been thinking about shutting down the franchising operation altogether for at least two years, ever since John Murphy quit in the early part of 1998. But with twenty-seven lawsuits coming at them all at once, that would have been financial suicide.

It was no different now, but Al came up with an ingenious plan that, if it worked, would allow him to shut down Mobility Center, Inc., without affecting a single franchisee. Instead of shutting down the Mobility Center, Inc., in one fell swoop, he decided to shut down the operation one step at a time.

"It wasn't a particular year that franchising ended," Beth explained. "It kind of happened over time. We stopped selling franchises, and we didn't renew any franchise contracts. We just let them run their course."

Al sent out a letter that notified all the franchisees that he was going to dissolve the franchising program, explaining how he was going to do that.

"You can keep your business," he told them. "You just run it however you want, and you don't have to pay royalties to us."

•••

"I think in hindsight," Al recalled, "what we should have done is, at its peak or right before its peak, we should have sold Mobility Center, Inc. We incorporated our franchise business in Delaware for purposes of maybe someday going public, but we are probably not the right people to run a public company, so we should have put it on the market."

And then he asked an obvious question: "If we had had the right advisors back then, and they had recommended selling, would I have followed their advice? I think I would have! We saw that we couldn't handle it all; there were too many other problems. So, instead of it even coming into my mind to sell it, I just said, 'Well, this didn't work. It's time to close it down.'"

Beth agreed with Al's assessment.

"We should have sold it in 1989," she said. "That would have been really smart and strategic."

"Franchising was just an idea whose time did *not* come," explained John Layman. "Other companies were franchising, but they were in different industries, and this was something new for our industry."

•••

There was no question that the Amigo Shopper market was the one that Amigo Mobility needed to enter, but by phasing out one marketing plan and phasing in another, the company was entering dangerous waters. Al's plan seemed plausible—ingenious, really—but as the franchises phased out, where would sales come from? Al was reluctant to aggressively sell Amigo Shoppers, for fear of reprisal from the franchisees, and the last of the twenty-seven franchise contracts would not expire for another six years! So, he and Beth would have to wait six long years before they could totally and aggressively pursue the potentially lucrative motorized shopping cart market.

But they didn't have six years. They didn't have six months. They didn't even have six weeks!

CHAPTER 22

"Divine Intervention"

"If you don't repay me, you may surrender the company!"
—Frank Martin, investor

After years of falling sales while the franchise agreements were running out, a ray of light appeared in February 2000, when a buyer from Publix Super Markets contacted Amigo to say that he was interested in the Amigo Shopper. Publix had over 1,200 grocery stores throughout the South, so there was the potential for *thousands* of orders. However, nothing happened after that one inquiry, so for the rest of the year, Amigo Mobility teetered on the edge of collapse.

The company did receive an order for 100 Amigos from Amigo du Brazil in February, but that money was quickly used up. Then, in August, there was another ray of hope, although this one had more possibility than the Publix inquiry. A buyer for the Kmart Corporation called to say that he would be ordering $800,000 worth of Amigo Shoppers, but he didn't give a specific time when he would place the order.

As far as Beth was concerned, promised orders or potential

orders are not orders at all. Because they don't bring in money, they do nothing more than build expectations. Thus, Al was forced to borrow another $100,000 from his friend, Bob Zelle. But that, too, was gone in an instant, for the company lost $88,000 in November.

Now the company was not only *low* on cash, it was *out* of cash.

"We are $200,000 overdrawn," Al noted in his journal, "and the bank will not cover our checks."

•••

Desperate for cash, Al sent letters to a dozen well-to-do Amigo owners, asking them for money. It wasn't a handout that he was looking for, he told them, but an "investment opportunity." He dropped the letters in the mailbox and waited.

While he waited, things got worse—if that were possible.

"Having a hard time sleeping," Al wrote in his journal. "We may have to sell our house."

Al had once said, "You aren't a real entrepreneur unless you have faced losing your home!"

But he had made that statement years earlier, and it was somewhat ironical that he was facing that very situation now, after being in business for thirty years. But, as in most of his other challenges, he just took it in stride.

"It was another thing we might have to do," Al explained. "Before the bank took the house away from us, we'd sell it. Our total effort was to get our company growing and profitable again."

Beth, however, was not so nonchalant.

"I do remember," she said, "sitting in tears in the back of the church during a weekday early mass, just thinking, *We're close to losing it all!* It really stands out to me as a memory of my life, because I was stewing about it. I can remember, all of a sudden, just giving it to God, and saying to myself: *You know what? If we lose everything, God gave us brains, and we'll just start something else! We'll work somewhere else. We'll find another way.* It took me much longer to get there than it did Al! I'm not saying he wasn't paying attention and not concerned about it, but he's always thinking he'll find a way."

And, as luck would have it—"Divine Intervention" is the way Mike Galer put it—Al got a call from one of the Amigo owners to whom he had sent a letter. His name was Frank Martin.

•••

A graduate of Northwestern University with a degree in investment management and an MBA from Indiana University, Frank Martin operated his own investment company, called Martin Capital Management, in Elkhart, Indiana. He had multiple sclerosis, had used an Amigo for years, and loved it. In fact, he had visited the company a few times over the years to get his Amigo repaired, or to buy a new one, or to have a trunk lift installed in his latest car. So he was very familiar with the company and its products. Al's letter intrigued him enough to set up a visit.

When Martin arrived, Al explained in detail the situation the company was in and why he needed money.

"You're doing something wrong," he said, "because you've got the best product out there!"

That was undoubtedly true, but with the franchises phasing out, sales were declining, and Amigo Mobility needed cash *now*. Martin was willing to give it—not because of the strength of the product, but because of the character and strength of Al and Beth.

"This couple loves, lives, and breathes Amigo," Martin explained, "and as an investor, there is nothing I enjoy more than seeing somebody who really is passionate about what they do. Some of my best business judgments invariably are bets on people, not on numbers. There was no doubt in my mind that they would practically die before they failed! You can't ask for anything more than that!"

Along with two of his investor friends, Martin agreed to lend Al and Beth $300,000, but not on their good graces alone. While Martin was genuine in his flattering remarks about the Thiemes, he was also a businessman, and he didn't like to lose money.

"If you don't repay me," he told them, "you may surrender the company."

Martin gave Al and Beth one year to pay back the loan. However, if they were unable to do that, then the amount of the loan would be converted into Amigo stock, and he could request the company be put up for sale. If Martin did that, he and his partners would get a pro rata share of the sales price of the company. This was serious business.

Al didn't give the draconian loan stipulations much thought.

"We didn't care what their terms were," he recalled. We just needed the money!"

"When I think back about that time," Beth recalled, "I'm surprised that Frank Martin mentioned he would sell our company, because the one thing I noticed about him was he did it out of friendship, not wisdom. I really think it was to help us succeed, and if we couldn't succeed, help us with a backup plan. He really liked us."

•••

Frank Martin came through just in the nick of time, for the bank was only days away from pulling Amigo's loan, which would have thrown the company into foreclosure.

"It could have been the end," Beth said somberly.

But when Mike Galer walked into Comerica's office with a check for $300,000 from private investors, Beth said, "It gave the bank enough confidence to not pull the loan. It gave us time to get things turned around."

However, time was not on their side, and business was not improving fast enough. The company was able to eke out a modest $22,000 profit in October 2001, but that was more of an

Frank Martin, business investor
(courtesy Frank Martin)

anomaly than a trend.

"I love business and being the owner of a company," Al wrote in his journal, "but it is getting difficult for me to run our company. Beth is getting stronger each month, but our progress is too slow."

•••

One of Al's favorite sayings was, "Want to kill time? Work it to death."

And that is exactly what he and Beth were doing: working, working, working—which made time go by quickly. So much so, that before they knew it, Frank Martin's loan was due, and they had no money to pay it off.

So, as Martin's agreement stipulated, Al exchanged the loan amount for 1,848 shares of Amigo stock, giving Frank Martin and his two investors a 30 percent stake in the company— flipping the switch to start the wheels of a possible sale.

Frank Martin had the Key Bank in Detroit draw up a sales prospectus to give to potential buyers. And it was then that Al realized the gravity of the situation.

"They are all waiting for the bank to stop working with us,"

Al noted in his journal, "and to take over the company."

But then things took a turn for the worse when Alden's wife came down with cancer and died within two months. And just when it seemed that things couldn't get any worse, Alden himself became ill.

It had been nine years since his accident, and he had learned to live with his disability, more or less. In fact, he and Marie and Max, all of them disabled, teased each other every year at Emy's perfectly laid out Thanksgiving table. To lighten things up, according to Alden's son Jim, Max and Alden both pretended to want what the other one had.

"Uncle Max," said Jim, "had one good arm and one good leg, and Dad had two good arms and no good legs, so they wanted to trade!"

That produced great laughter around the table.

Sadly, Alden passed away on October 6, 2002, at the age of 67.

Having lost his brother, and with Amigo Mobility again on the precipice, Al was down. As we have seen again and again, not much affected him over the years, but this time was different. Although there was nothing he could have done for his brother, there was a real possibility that he would lose his beloved company. He prayed for intervention.

"Asked the Lord to help us," he wrote in his journal. "Had a good, long talk."

Then another divine intervention came into play when the sales prospectus was finalized and sent out to potential investors. The economy had just gone into a major slump because of the stock market crash, so no one was interested in investing in or purchasing a company, especially a struggling company.

A few investors who had shown some interest decided to wait until the bank took the company over, so they could pick it up at a lower cost.

Fortunately, by cutting expenses to the bone and increasing

Shopper sales, Amigo Mobility earned the profit necessary to purchase back the stock from Frank Martin and his friends before the company could be sold.

•••

In the meantime, Mike Galer and Beth were approaching every bank in Michigan, trying to borrow money. They made a perfect "pitch" team, with Mike presenting the numbers, and Beth selling the company concept. No one could sell Amigo Mobility better than Beth, not even Al himself. She was articulate and passionate, and her good looks didn't hurt, either.

"We put together a presentation," Galer explained. "It had a beginning, middle, and end, but we always got the same negative response."

•••

In an apparent long shot, one of the company's business consultants mentioned a bank in Ohio that had an odd name: the Fifth Third Bank of Cincinnati. That was the result of a merger in 1908 between the Fifth National Bank and the Third National Bank. The legend was that the original name was *Third Fifth*, but since the merger took place during the growing temperance movement, the bankers settled on Fifth Third because Third Fifth could have been construed as a reference to alcohol.

At any rate, the bank's representative, Cheryl Holm, called Beth and set up a meeting.

"I'm heading north on Friday for the weekend," Cheryl said. "I'll stop at your office at four o'clock."

Although Beth said OK, she didn't have high expectations. First of all, she and Galer had already made presentations to eleven different banks, all to no avail. Second, Cheryl Holmes was going to stop by at the end of the day at the end of the workweek, on her way for a weekend of rest and recreation.

"It didn't sound promising," Beth said skeptically.

But Cheryl Holm showed up right on time, just as she said she would. After Beth and Mike introduced themselves and started their presentation, Holm stopped them after a few minutes. They both thought that they were going to get one more "thanks, but no thanks." But they didn't.

"Give me all your papers, numbers, whatever documents you have," Holm said. "I can read those later. Right now I just want to know why you're in this business, where you've been, and where you're going."

Beth and Mike looked at each other in disbelief!

"Well, I was passionate," recalled Beth, "and Mike was passionate; we just started talking. She could see that we loved what we were doing as a company."

"I like your story," Holm said. "I like what you're doing here. You are all in! You are down in the dirt! You're going to make this thing work. I love that!"

Obviously, Holm sensed the same determination that Frank Martin had felt a year earlier.

"If you go out," Holm said enthusiastically, "you're going to go, kicking and screaming! I'm going to take the numbers with me. I'll review everything this weekend."

It was a long weekend for Beth and Galer, who prepared themselves for the worst as they anticipated Holm's response.

But the worst is not what they got when Holm called.

"I'm going to run the numbers by my people who have to approve this," Holm said. "But I'm going to recommend they do it."

"I think our jaws were on the table!" recalled Galer. "What? A bank is saying yes? You gotta be kidding me!"

A few months later, the Fifth Third Bank gave Amigo Mobility a loan for $818,000, enough to get them out from under the Michigan National Bank with $218,000 to boot!

"So," Galer said, "we were kind of living on a different cloud for a while."

•••

"When we say that God has sent us people," Beth explained,

Cheryl Holm, commercial loan officer, Fifth Third Bank
(courtesy Cheryl Holm)

"we really believe that. The angels in our lives were Bob Zelle, Herb McLachlan, Frank Martin, and Cheryl Holm. I'm not sure we would be here today without those four people."

There is no doubt about that, but Amigo Mobility was going to need more than angels to weather the storm that was about to engulf it.

CHAPTER 23

Power Wheelchairs vs. Scooters

"If you can hold a fishing rod,
then you don't need a power wheelchair."

—Beth Thieme

Medicare existed, of course, to pay for medical services for the elderly, but it was completely caught off guard by the meteoric rise in the demand for power mobility devices. Between 1999 and 2003, for example, sales for those mobility devices increased 450 percent, while overall Medicare payments increased only 11 percent. And by 2009, 175,000 power mobility devices were being sold annually at a cost to the government of $723 million.

By now the Electric Mobility Company, the maker of the Rascal, was all but out of business due to The SCOOTER Store's overwhelming dominance of the power mobility market. That dominance, combined with the astronomical rise in sales of power wheelchairs, raised the eyebrows of people in Washington, so Medicare asked its Office of the Inspector General (OIG) to investigate why the costs had been increasing to such a degree. And what the OIG discovered was mind-boggling.

After randomly selecting 200 claims from people who had received some type of scooter or power wheelchair (both of which the OIG called "power mobility devices," or "PMDs"), the agency found that over 71 percent of those claims did not meet Medicare's "medical necessity" requirements. Ultimately, the agency learned that people who had received nearly $200 million worth of PMDs did not need them because they didn't have some type of physical malady.

Why, then, did those people order PMDs in the first place? Because, the OIG learned, the TV commercials being run by medical equipment companies, especially The SCOOTER Store, were telling people that they could get a scooter for free— paid for by Medicare—"to leave the house, to socialize, to get to bingo."

Shirley Taylor, an Amigo salesperson in Florida, readily confirmed this inappropriate use of PMDs.

"They didn't need a mobility device at all!" she exclaimed. "They use them as cars! They would stand up and walk away!"

•••

All this had happened, even though Medicare officials had what they thought were strict guidelines governing when a doctor should or should not prescribe some sort of PMD. Before there were any commercials for scooters, doctors followed those guidelines. But once the scooter commercials started airing, people began pressuring their doctors to prescribe a PMD for them, whether they needed one or not.

"The ads give people a sense of entitlement," explained an Illinois doctor, "and some have left my practice because I refused to prescribe them a chair. They are led to believe they need them, deserve them, and if we don't sign for them, they get upset and go elsewhere."

•••

If that wasn't disconcerting enough, upon further investigation, the OIG discovered that even when patients legitimately needed a PMD, they were often not sold the right one! What they wanted and what would have served them best was a POV/scooter. What they got instead was a power wheelchair. In fact, the OIG found that 60 percent of the people who had a power wheelchair "did not need them or did not want them."

For example, out of the $886 million spent on PMDs in 2005, only 4 percent of that amount was spent on POVs/scooters.

Allegedly, The SCOOTER Store and other durable medical equipment suppliers, both large and small, were upselling customers to the more expensive power wheelchairs. According to an article in *The Express-News*, San Antonio's local newspaper, "The SCOOTER Store received $5,000 to $7,000 for every power wheelchair it sold. In most cases, though, the customer wanted a less expensive POV at a cost of $1,500 to $2,000."

Obviously, the incentive for the durable medical equipment suppliers to sell power wheelchairs over POVs was that they made more money on them, and Medicare was willing to pay for the more expensive wheelchairs. Irrespective of which powered device the customer wanted, Medicare would pay 80 percent of the cost. For example, for Amigos, which cost $1,200, Medicare would reimburse the customers $960, and the customers would either pay the remaining $240 out-of-pocket or have their supplemental insurance policy absorb it. Likewise, for power wheelchairs, which might cost $7,000, Medicare would pay $5,600, and the customers would have to pay the difference, or $1,400. But since there was so much profit margin built into the more expensive power wheelchairs, the suppliers would absorb whatever amount remained, whether the customer had supplemental insurance or not, which is why the power chairs were free! On the other hand, there wasn't enough profit margin on an Amigo or a similar POV for the suppliers to absorb the difference, so they pushed power chairs.

In many cases, although a customer may have wanted a POV, the salesperson ordered a power wheelchair instead.

An article in the Ft. Lauderdale *Sun Sentinel* of August 5, 2011, gave one illuminating example of this scheme:

> Take the power wheelchair that has become a $4,500 armchair in Marvin Rosen's Coral Springs living room for three years.
>
> Rosen, 81, said he wanted an $800 replacement for a scooter that helped him get around the house because he can't walk well. A supplier told him the power chair would be bigger and better. His doctor signed off, and since Rosen's supplemental insurance policy covered his co-pay, he didn't pay a dime.
>
> Within days, he could see the chair was too big to pass the doorways or maneuver in his house. The company hadn't measured beforehand, as required. The company wouldn't take it back because he missed a three-day-return period he said he didn't know about.
>
> "I ended up with a chair that was useless to me," Rosen said. "I sit in it sometimes to watch TV. What a waste. These salesmen are a fast-talking group. That's their come-on. They tell you it's for your benefit, make it easy to buy, and then you can't give it back."

In a letter that Al wrote to Senator Charles Grassley, chairman of the Senate Finance Committee, he told him an even more egregious story:

> A man in the Midwest was sent home from a rehab center with a power wheelchair (Medicare financed). His need for a power-driven mobility vehicle was legitimate,

but he was given no choice between a power wheelchair and a POV, and no visit was made to his home to see how he could manage. He and his wife found the power wheelchair too big and awkward to use effectively around the house and too heavy to load into their vehicle. During the time he was struggling to use the power chair, the couple invested in an SUV and a lift mechanism to try to make the chair portable beyond their home. But even that didn't work. They finally purchased their own POV/scooter, and the power wheelchair is sitting in the garage unused.

To add insult to injury, when the man contacted Medicare to say that he wanted to exchange his power wheelchair for a POV, he was denied.

"You qualified for a power chair, not a POV," the Medicare representative explained to him, which meant that if he qualified for a power wheelchair, he must *need* a power wheelchair, and therefore he would not be able to use a POV!

•••

Obviously, Medicare officials were not happy with either the amount the agency was spending on PMDs or the fact that people were not getting the mobility device they wanted or needed. But Medicare had no one to blame but itself!

Through a multi-million-dollar lobbying campaign that started in the early 2000s, lobbyists for the power chair companies were able to convince Medicare that scooters were just that—scooters! They were ideal for going outside, the lobbyist said, but inappropriate for indoor use.

"The government listened to them!" Beth exclaimed in frustration. "The difference was that the lobbyists were saying that people who were disabled had to have a power wheelchair with a joystick. The reason those power chairs have joysticks is that people who need them have very limited use of their legs *and* arms. When I see advertisements showing people in power wheelchairs fishing outdoors, I just shake my head. If you can hold a fishing rod, then you don't need a power wheelchair!"

Nevertheless, in September 2004, the government sent out a document that not only defined what a POV/scooter was, but also who was qualified to obtain a POV through Medicare. POVs, the document said, are "motorized devices guided by a tiller with limited seat modification capabilities. These devices have large turning radii and are most suited for outdoor use." And as far as who could best use a POV, the document said that "the person is able to negotiate his or her home environment without power mobility, but requires power mobility outside the home."

Obviously, the power wheelchair lobbyists had done their job, for all those constraints spelled out by the new government regulations were the complete opposite of what they had been thirty years earlier. At that time, it will be recalled, Medicare did not want to pay for POVs because they *might* be used outdoors.

Since power wheelchairs cost significantly more than POVs, Medicare changed the allowable amount that it would pay for both POVs and power wheelchairs. Now the agency would pay up to $8,000 for a power wheelchair, but only $960 for an Amigo-type POV. At that amount, no POV manufacturer, including Amigo Mobility, could make any money selling POVs through Medicare, and that was a devastating blow.

•••

Al tried once again to get Medicare to change the law.

"'It would be so simple,' I said to them. But the power wheelchair lobbyists were more powerful than we were."

In another letter that Al sent to Senator Grassley, he wrote:

Given all the proven physical, psychological, and financial benefits of a POV over a power wheelchair, a critical question remains: Why is Medicare reluctant to level the playing field and encourage a lower-cost mobility alternative as a better mobility solution to individuals with mobility limitations? It would appear logical that the lowest-cost mobility solution would be the first choice as reimbursed medical equipment. Ironically, our current system is exactly reversed.

How ironic that POVs have always offered more mobility and are less expensive than power wheelchairs, but have always been harder to get under Medicare. Amigo Mobility respectfully requests that individual needs, along with home evaluations, be determined and that lower-cost alternatives, such as POVs, be given equal or priority consideration for providing the best solution, based on those findings and Medicare costs.

It is our recommendation that Medicare regulations consider one of two directions: (1) they should be reversed, so that power wheelchairs, instead of POVs, would be prescribed only by a specialist in physiatry, orthopedics, neurology, or rheumatology; or (2) they should be made uniform for all mobility vehicles.

Al's letter was concise, to the point, and presented a well-thought-out argument, but he never got a reply.

To give the matter more punch and publicity, Bob Dorigo Jones, a business friend of Beth's, suggested contacting John Stossel, ABC's conservative news editor. Bob knew Stossel and told Beth that he would contact him to see if he would be interested in airing "the story of what's going on with power wheelchairs versus Amigo-type vehicles," Beth recalled. And Bob's timing could not have been better.

Stossel's third book, *No, They Can't: Why Government Fails–But Individuals Succeed*, had just come out, which argued that government policies meant to solve problems instead produce new ones.

In 2009, Stossel joined the Fox Business Channel to host his own program, called simply *The Stossel Show*, which examined issues that concerned free-market capitalism, individual freedom, and small government—issues such as health care, civil liberties, and free trade.

Stossel's political and economic philosophy aligned almost perfectly with Al's, so with a nationwide audience he might be able to persuade public opinion to change Medicare's mind.

The Thiemes' daughter, Jennifer Thieme Kehres, and longtime Amigo owner, Jean Csaposs, would appear with Stossel on his show.

The program aired on December 16, 2011. Jennifer, dressed in a grey suit, was sitting on a chair; John Stossel was sitting on a new Amigo; and Jean Csaposs was sitting on her well-used Amigo. Stossel pulled no punches about whom he and Amigo Mobility were pointing a finger at:

(A SCOOTER Store ad appears.)

ANNOUNCER: You may qualify for a power chair or scooter for little or no cost to you. Call now! The SCOOTER Store has delivered over half-a million power chairs and scooters at little to no cost to people just like you.

STOSSEL: No cost to people like you! Sounds great, except nothing is really free. Those power wheelchairs cost you taxpayers, via Medicare, about three thousand dollars each! Now, Medicare pays less than a thousand dollars for a scooter like this one. (He drives his Amigo around in a circle.) And I think it's pretty good. It's just as maneuverable. And yet, lots of people, probably most people, get the power chair! Why, when they cost much more? And they're also less flexible. And the US Inspector General said that most of the people who get the power chairs don't need them! Shouldn't have gotten them. Now this is a little complicated, so here to try to explain this to us is Jean Csaposs and Jennifer Kehres. Jennifer's father invented the first version of the scooter that Jean and I are sitting on. So, Jennifer, tell us about it.

JENNIFER: My dad, Al Thieme, invented the first mobility POV scooter, like you're on, back in 1968, for a family member with multiple sclerosis. Forty-three years later, I still work with him daily, and we manufacture all Amigos in Michigan.

STOSSEL: And at the time, people paid for these things with their own money?

JENNIFER: Yes, with cash.

STOSSEL: And most of the customers were people like Jean?

JENNIFER: Yes.

STOSSEL: Jean, you had polio as a child, and you discovered this scooter, and it made a big difference?

JEAN: I saw it demonstrated at an exhibit in Washington, D.C., and I said, "I got to have one of these things!" So I paid nine hundred dollars. I called up Al in Michigan, and he sent it to me, and I've used one ever since.

STOSSEL: What can you do with it? I'll get out of the way. Show me!

JEAN: OK! I can do amazing things with this scooter. (She drives the Amigo around.) First of all, it's got a very, very small turning radius, and I can go forwards and backwards. I can also use my electric seat lift to put me into just about any position that my daily life requires: getting in and out of bed; on and off the toilet; and out of the shower. I use it all of the time! It enables me to move up to the kitchen sink and wash dishes or to the stove where I cook every day. So I find it enormously flexible.

STOSSEL (to Jennifer): So what's your complaint?

JENNIFER: That the playing field is not level right now. So, if you needed a mobility aid, and you went into a medical dealer, you could receive a power wheelchair for free, or you would have to pay about fifteen hundred dollars for a product like an Amigo.

STOSSEL: And this is because the government reimburses everybody three thousand dollars for the fancy power chair, but a thousand dollars for this thing.

JENNIFER: Yes. And federal reports have shown that there's 300 to 400 percent profit being made on a power wheelchair; where people come in and they want to buy an Amigo.

STOSSEL: So you've complained to the government, and they said what?

JENNIFER: We've sent letters and tried to contact them for years, and they don't see a need for the change. To ask them to increase the reimbursement for a product like an Amigo doesn't make sense to them. But when you're looking at the big picture, and to increase the reimbursement for this, it could save millions and millions of dollars for Medicare.

JENNIFER: I think if you gave people a choice on which product they wanted, more people would choose a product like this because it better suits their needs; whereas, right now, the choice is taken away.

STOSSEL (to Jean): But would you choose this? The other thing costs three times as much!

JEAN: Well, I come from an era where you tried to save the government money, not spend government money.

STOSSEL: But isn't the other thing better? It costs three times as much. Wouldn't you rather have it?

JEAN: No. Now, John, you know, just because something costs more doesn't make it better.

STOSSEL: Alright. Well, we asked the two big power chair companies about this ..., they make the three-thousand-dollar chairs ..., they advertise them widely. The SCOOTER Store said, "No comment." Hoveround said the Inspector General report, which said that 60 percent of the people don't use these things, was inaccurate. And Hoveround qualifies only 7 or 8 percent of the people who call after seeing their commercials. They don't want to wrongly qualify anyone, because they get audited frequently, so they say. But I bet lots of people who get their chairs shouldn't have them. On Craigslist, we found lots of ads for power wheelchairs, and the sellers said they were "never used" or "hardly used." So, those people didn't need them. But, Jennifer, c'mon. I bet you're getting a reimbursement. I bet a lot of people get these things, but don't really need them, because the government pays!

JENNIFER: Almost 70 percent of Medicare reimbursements are on power wheelchairs, whereas only about 3 percent of Medicare reimbursements are on products like this (indicating Jean's Amigo). And the reason is not what's the best product for their customer's needs, it's what's the biggest profit margin ..., unfortunately.

STOSSEL: So why would the doctors qualify people for the triple-priced device?

JENNIFER: A lot of times, they don't even realize it, and they don't even know the difference between the two products, and that it's based on profit margin.

STOSSEL: And the people come in and say, "I saw the TV commercial! It's free! I want one!"

JENNIFER: Yes. So, many people are receiving the power wheelchairs that don't need them, which is wasting taxpayer dollars and then frustrating customers who realize that's not the right product for them.

STOSSEL: Thank you, Jennifer. Thank you, Jean.

•••

Al Thieme's son, Joe, confirmed all of these shenanigans in an email that he wrote to Jennifer:

If a study were done on the last 100 power chairs sold to Medicare, the results would be: (1) 90% of the people could use a POV; (2) 80% would prefer a POV, but were told it was not covered or were not even given the opportunities for one; and (3) 70% could not use a power wheelchair, but could use an Amigo. And I bet my numbers are a little low.

I have worked at five different medical supply companies in Florida, and one of them wouldn't even let me sell POVs! It had to be a power chair. Another company pays a commission to their salespeople only on power chairs.

There is sooo much abuse!

•••

The newspaper stories and *The Stossel Show* exposé reinforced what the Office of the Inspector General had discovered—that these bait-and-switch schemes were pervasive throughout the durable medical equipment industry—and Medicare needed to take action. Although the OIG had a staggering budget of $75 million a year to combat fraud and abuse, it only had so many people to do that. So, it decided to go after the biggest fish in the pond, and that was The SCOOTER Store. From its humble beginnings in 1991, by 2005 the Store had become by far the largest distributor of power wheelchairs in the world. Selling approximately 10,000 power chairs and 2,500 scooters a month, by 2008 the company generated annual revenue of upwards of $500 million!

"Al Thieme created the product," explained Doug Harrison. "We created the market."

But as a result of Harrison's alleged sales practices, the US Department of Justice brought a suit against his company, charging widescale fraud.

According to the *San Antonio Business Journal*, "The lawsuit claims that The SCOOTER Store engaged in a nationwide practice of making misrepresentations to Medicare beneficiaries and their doctors about obtaining reimbursements from the government for power wheelchairs, as opposed to less expensive scooters."

•••

While there was no doubt that the commercials drove up the demand for power mobility devices, it was Medicare's own guidelines that promoted the more expensive power wheelchairs over the less expensive scooters. And that was the result of incessant lobbying by the power wheelchair manufacturers and dealers.

"People were happy with Amigo-type scooters," Beth said. "They loved them. They were maneuverable. They were portable. You could put them in a car trunk. And they were less expensive than a power wheelchair. Their tactics took down the POV/scooter industry!"

CHAPTER 24

The Party's Over

"Al's still around and I'm not!"
—Douglas Harrison

The Justice Department did not reveal the exact amount that Medicare had paid for fraudulent reimbursements, just that The SCOOTER Store had submitted claims worth more than $400 million between 1997 and 2005. Whatever the actual amount was, after The SCOOTER Store did an internal audit, Harrison said that his company had overcharged Medicare only $19 million, and that the overpayments were due to Medicare's coding process and confusing claim forms, not fraud.

Perhaps Harrison should have been a little more cooperative, for the Inspector General's Office was not afraid to take action. One medical supply dealer in Houston, for example, was sentenced to forty-one months in prison for submitting fraudulent claims. Another dealer was sentenced to fifty-five months in prison and ordered to pay a $500,000 fine for similar illegal activities. A Los Angeles doctor was fined $200,000 and sentenced to eighteen months in prison for prescribing power wheelchairs to patients who did not need them. Based on what The SCOOTER Store was accused of doing, Harrison could have faced considerable prison time.

After two years of negotiations, however, no one associated with The SCOOTER Store went to prison, but to settle the case with the Justice Department, the company agreed to reimburse Medicare $4 million and forego $43 million in pending claims.

•••

In the aftermath of the OIG's report and The SCOOTER Store's settlement, Medicare began taking steps to prevent future fraud by doing what it did best—namely, reducing its reimbursements for power-operated vehicles. Instead of simply enforcing the rules that were already on the books, Medicare took the easier path.

Ironically, the first drastic reduction in Medicare's reimbursement for a POV was instigated by the durable medical equipment industry itself—specifically, the power wheelchair manufacturers. In an effort to get Medicare to increase the amount that it paid for high-end, joystick-controlled power wheelchairs, the large power wheelchair manufacturers lobbied Medicare to recode POVs and power wheelchairs. What those companies hoped to accomplish was to force Medicare's reimbursements down on POVs and to increase the reimbursements on power wheelchairs.

"The end result," explained Harrison, "was a 35 to 40 percent cut to everybody, including us! There was no warning."

While the reimbursement reduction was "brutal," to quote Harrison, he was still able to weather the storm by severely reducing company expenses and fine-tuning his computerized order-processing system.

•••

The next hurdle that Medicare set up in an effort to slow down the sales of POVs was a rental/purchase program implemented when the Affordable Care Act was passed in the spring of 2010.

Under that new policy, Medicare would not pay the vendor in one lump sum once the POV was delivered to the customer, as it had done in the past, but would pay over a period of thirteen months, which put a significant cash crunch on the suppliers.

With that new policy, as Harrison put it, "We still had 100 percent of the expenses, but only one-thirteenth of the revenue! So that meant that I was going to be millions of dollars in the hole on cash flow! Any business ..., and I don't care if you're a fifty-thousand-dollar-a-year business or a hundred-million-dollar-a-year business ..., when you're out of cash, you're out of cash, and you're dead!"

Harrison knew that he would get paid eventually, but in order to fill the gap, he was forced to go out on the open market to raise cash, and that, as he said, was "ugly." Around that time, the country went into a severe recession—"The Great Recession," as it was called—and there was no money available except from private equity firms, and that was "pretty ugly, too!" he explained.

Harrison managed to raise the necessary funds—at a very high interest rate—and seemed to weather this latest assault by Medicare. But the government agency was not finished yet.

●●●

Since Medicare was having no luck at all reducing the orders for POVs by throwing up roadblocks against suppliers, the agency implemented the Provider Enrollment Chain and Ownership System, otherwise known as PECOS. Unlike all of the previous attempts to reduce runaway health care costs, this system was targeted specifically at doctors. Since they were the ones who were authorized to prescribe a POV, Medicare was going to make it more difficult for them to do so. Now a doctor had to enroll in the PECOS system and obtain a PECOS identification number, and only physicians who had that unique number would be allowed to prescribe mobility devices. So, practically overnight, the number of doctors who could prescribe a mobility device dropped by 80 percent!

"And, oh, by the way," Harrison explained, "if you, as a supplier, accepted a prescription from a doctor who was *not* enrolled in PECOS, Medicare wouldn't pay you for that claim!"

To make matters worse, Medicare also changed the billing process. Unlike the previous method, whereby a supplier could get pre-authorization on a POV, submit the bill, and then deliver the mobility device, now the supplier had to deliver the POV to the customer first, and *then* submit the application for payment. Only then would Medicare determine if it would pay for the device or not.

"The risk with that system," Harrison explained, "was even if everything else was perfect, if Medicare found out later that the doctor did not have a PECOS number, they would deny our claim, and we had already delivered the scooter!"

At first, Harrison thought that this was just another hurdle to jump over, but it turned out to be more daunting than any of the other obstacles Medicare had deployed. All Harrison had to do, he thought, was obtain the list of doctors who had signed up for PECOS from Medicare, enter their information into his electronic database, and *voilà*, he would be back in business.

"The kicker," Harrison said, "was Medicare didn't have a database telling you which doctors were on PECOS and which were not!"

They were working on it, the Medicare representatives told him, but they didn't know when it would be ready.

•••

Since Medicare did not have a database, and the agency had already implemented the new procedure, Harrison had to act *fast*. He found out the name of the company that was compiling the PECOS data for Medicare and, with Medicare's approval, obtained a copy of the database. His computer programmers then incorporated the data into his order-entry program. So, for the time being at least, Harrison had once again avoided disaster.

"When people called us," he explained, "we could look up the name of their doctor in the database, and if they were green, they had a PECOS number. If they were red, they didn't have a PECOS number."

Harrison's system was 100 percent effective, but with only 20 percent of doctors signing up for PECOS, The SCOOTER Store could not process 80 percent of the people who called in. Nevertheless, the company's sales were still far greater than other POV suppliers because of its sophisticated computer-ordering system.

It didn't take long, however, for Harrison's competitors to find out about his list of PECOS doctors and yell foul. Why is it, they complained, that The SCOOTER Store was still selling so many POVs, while their sales had dropped to a trickle?

"Clearly," Harrison said irritably, "if you're Amigo or the other big suppliers, it means only one thing: The SCOOTER Store's cheating! And so some of my 'good friends' ..., and I don't know if Al Thieme was on that list or not ..., whatever my suspicions are, they are nothing but my suspicions ..., a whole lot of them found out that we had a doctors' list that we used, and their assumption was that those are the doctors that The SCOOTER Store pays off to do their paperwork!"

●●●

Medicare's last attempt at reducing costs was to introduce a competitive bidding process, forcing the myriad POV suppliers to bid on the scooter business, with the lowest bidder winning.

"The government," explained Beth, "got this bright idea that manufacturers or medical dealers could bid in a state for sales of Medicare equipment. When people needed a power mobility aid, Medicare would point them to the company that had won the bid. The margins were so tight ..., I'm going to say 10 percent above cost. And once a particular company was awarded the contract, everybody else in the entire state was locked out!"

Douglas Harrison could not agree more with Beth's

summation.

"It was foolishly run, moronically run," explained Harrison. "It was the kind of program that you'd expect from a bunch of government bureaucrats. And it pummeled the pricing on scooters and power wheelchairs across the country."

John Layman did his best to get the Medicare contract in Arizona, "but we couldn't afford to discount our products any further," he said, "because they were already cut to the bone, and we didn't get the contract. With that—not getting the contract—basically, we had to drop out of the system."

•••

All of these schemes and attempts by Medicare to control the cost of power medical devices were not only overkill but ineffective. And the answer to its problem was so simple. All the agency had to do was re-implement, or enforce, its long-entrenched "Clinical Criteria" flow chart. It was a simple one-page document that, when followed correctly, gave a patient a power mobility device that best suited his or her needs, be it an inexpensive POV or an expensive power wheelchair.

The very first question on the flow chart, appropriately enough, was whether or not the patient had a mobility limitation.

If the answer was yes, was a cane or walker sufficient?

If the answer to *that* was no, could the patient use a manual wheelchair?

If the answer to *that* was no, would a POV/scooter serve the patient's need?

If the answer to *that* was no, then and only then would a power wheelchair be prescribed.

Although this procedure was straightforward, Medicare failed to follow it.

•••

In any event, Douglas Harrison had faced every obstacle the government had thrown at the industry, and prevailed. His sales were now much lower than they had been, but through his wits and determination, he had outmaneuvered the government time and time again, and The SCOOTER Store was still in business. But then, out of nowhere, came a fatal blow.

Brian Setzer, one of Harrison's longtime salesmen, had had enough. He had been with the company for nearly five years and was appalled that Medicare had done nothing to counteract what he thought was fraud by The SCOOTER Store. Utilizing the so-called whistleblower law, on January 7, 2013, he contacted newsman Jeff Glor at CBS News to tell him that The SCOOTER Store's main goal was to coerce doctors into writing prescriptions to boost profits. "Bulldoze 'em to get the paperwork done," Setzer charged.

> GLOR: So people could get their wheelchairs?
> SETZER: Yes.
> GLOR: Even if they didn't need them?
> SETZER: Yeah. I'd get a call: "Well, can you get him to do this or get him to do this?" I couldn't feel right in my heart to do that.
> GLOR: Who's telling you to do this?
> SETZER: Corporate office.
> GLOR: Even if you knew they didn't need it?
> SETZER: Uh-huh.
> GLOR: And this happened a lot?
> SETZER: Oh, yeah. They twist the doc so hard that they didn't want anything to do with you.

Up to the time of that TV interview, the government had no proof that The SCOOTER Store was doing anything illegal, but with the CBS exposé, it felt that it had enough probable cause to take action.

In response to Setzer's allegations, The SCOOTER Store's CEO, Martin Landon, told the press that "the company is in full compliance with all federal rules and regulations." Landon thought that would be the end of the story, but both he and Harrison were rudely reminded, a month later, that the matter was far from over.

On the morning of February 20, 2013, just as Harrison's workday was about to begin, a squad of federal and state law enforcement officers, with search warrants in hand, stormed his New Braunfels corporate headquarters. They entered every door simultaneously, thereby preventing anyone from fleeing. They told the employees not to move or take anything. Eventually, all the employees were allowed to leave, but Harrison and his top executives were retained and questioned. The FBI agents told them that they were there to investigate the company's billing practices, which resulted in defrauding the government of $100 million.

The next day, CBS's *This Morning* program aired a live segment with Jeff Glor standing in front of The SCOOTER Store's New Braunfel's office building:

GLOR: One-hundred-and-fifty federal and state agents were part of this raid on The SCOOTER Store here yesterday, and agents remain on the site this morning. We just spoke to an FBI agent who said workers will not be allowed back into headquarters today, as the nation's largest power wheelchair company remains under investigation. The agents came from the Inspector General, FBI, and Texas Attorney General. They held some workers back for interviews and told others to leave the building immediately and leave their desks alone. Outside, employees were handed fliers with contact information for the FBI, as The SCOOTER Store, known for its abundant TV ads, became the subject of this federal investigation. The issue is that once a doctor has written a prescription, Medicare rarely verifies whether the chairs are actually necessary.

And the problem was crystallized when the Inspector General released this report, citing that industry-wide, eighty percent of Medicare payments for power chairs are made in error; most going to people who don't need them or who lack proof they need them. From 2009 to 2012, government auditors found The SCOOTER Store overbilled Medicare by as much as a hundred and eight million dollars. Last month, The SCOOTER Store would not agree to an on-camera interview. They told us it was committed to improving the quality of life for seniors and the disabled, saying its rigorous internal screening process ..., including a Medicare-required, face-to-face doctor examination..., disqualifies eighty-eight percent of them seeking Medicare or private insurance reimbursement for powered mobility devices. But now the scrutiny of the nation's largest power wheelchair company has reached a new level, as federal agents begin their examination of evidence. The evidence selection will take days here, we're told. As of yet, no arrests and no charges have been filed. Charlie, Nora.

CHARLIE ROSE (*CBS newsman in the New York office*): Jeff, I think part of this is simply trying to build a case, so that they can recoup the money for people who spent money on these scooters.

GLOR: Recouping the money is a big part of this. The SCOOTER Store agreed to pay back nineteen and a half million dollars, last year. Medicare says last year they were overbilled one hundred and eight million dollars. So there's some controversy about that because Medicare says: "That was not a settlement; that's just a starting point."

•••

Indeed it was, for the long run, over for Harrison. The

precipitous drop in sales for power mobility products, combined with Medicare's relentless hurdles to getting payments, and now the highly publicized raid on the company, were more than The SCOOTER Store could sustain, so Harrison filed for bankruptcy in the fall of 2013. The SCOOTER Store officially went out of business on a most inauspicious day: September 11.

However, the investigation dragged on for years, but in the end, neither Douglas Harrison nor any of his executives were ever indicted. A government spokesman said, "The Justice Department does not believe it has sufficient evidence to prove criminal liability beyond a reasonable doubt as to senior managers at The SCOOTER Store."

"It took the Feds about five years," Harrison explained sarcastically, "to figure out that Doug Harrison did not invent PECOS, that PECOS was not a system whereby Doug or The SCOOTER Store paid doctors off. It was a Medicare system that said some doctors could prescribe stuff, and some couldn't. But by that time, we were out of cash."

As for Brian Setzer, who started all of the commotion in the first place, he received a $3 million award for notifying the government about The SCOOTER Store's alleged activities.

●●●

When Al and Beth got Medicare to approve the Amigo back in 1977, they not only opened the gates to competitors like Electric Mobility and The SCOOTER Store, but they also unwittingly set in motion the chain of events that led up to the destruction of the POV market that Al had created.

Harrison discovered a market niche, went after it with a vengeance, and after two decades, inadvertently caused its demise.

In his own defense, Harrison said, "I think most entrepreneurs, being eternal optimists, can always rationalize away any decision we've ever made, so we don't see them as a mistake. It's just something you learn from and go on!"

●●●

No one, not even Douglas Harrison himself, could have predicted the swift decimation of the POV market. Harrison had gone into business to build a "company of scale," as he said, and he accomplished that goal. But Medicare's reaction to his marketing techniques surprised him. When Harrison recalls his Horatio Alger story, he is unapologetic for what had transpired over his twenty-two years in business.

"When we were around," he proudly recalled, "The SCOOTER Store sold more than $5 billion worth of scooters and power wheelchairs. And we helped more people to get their mobility back than any other mobility provider before us or since. I don't have hard feelings. I would never have done what I did if Al Thieme hadn't done what he did. You know, the other thing ..., Al's still around, and I'm not!"

CHAPTER 25

The Amigo Shopper

"Praise the Lord!"
—Al Thieme

Fifth Third Bank's loan was indeed a godsend. Then a couple of sizable orders for the Amigo Shopper came in from Publix (600 carts) and Office Depot (1,200 carts). Publix gave Amigo Mobility a blanket order for Shoppers to be delivered over the full year, but Office Depot wasn't so accommodating.

"Office Depot," Beth said, "didn't have motorized shopping carts at that time, and they wanted to do a nationwide rollout, so they gave us an order for 1,200 carts. But the caveat was, we had to deliver them within six weeks of getting the order! Our son, Jordan, worked two shifts per day that entire six weeks. He'd come in early in the morning and work until ten at night every day. We had high school seniors here, building Shoppers, and shipping and moving stuff. It was unbelievable that we could do it! I remember our very last day, putting the carts on the truck and shutting the doors. We had a cooler of beer for all of the production team. We made the date!"

While those orders kept Amigo Mobility going, it still went through another year of "terrible cash flow," Al noted in his journal. "Growth eats cash."

Then, in June 2003, Al heard that another one of his competitors, Ortho-Kinetics, closed its doors. While that seemed like good news for Amigo, it could also mean a precursor of bad things to come. Less than a year later, however, Amigo received four big orders for Shoppers—another one from Publix, the order that Kmart had promised earlier, a new order from Target, and one from Kroger, the large Midwestern grocery store chain.

"Praise the Lord!" Al wrote in his journal.

●●●

Those Shopper orders could not have come at a better time, for the last Amigo Mobility Center franchise—the one located in North Chicago—closed its doors on June 26, 2006. Amigo Mobility now had very little presence in the health care POV marketplace, except for mail orders and a couple of factory-owned stores, one in Grand Rapids and the other at the Bridgeport facility. The company could have tried to sell to medical equipment dealers, but they would not have been receptive in any case, for the once red-hot Amigo type vehicle market was now almost nonexistent.

"*Free* power wheelchairs had taken over the mobility field," Al explained.

●●●

Starting from only a few per month, Shopper sales increased steadily to about $3 million per year! As a reward for Shirley Beebe's efforts, she was promoted to national sales manager, and Frank Gorski was hired to take over Shopper sales.

Gorski worked on the Shopper project for several years and did a good job at increasing Shopper sales, but it wasn't easy for him. He lived in Canton, Michigan, a small town west of Detroit and a good hour-and-a-half drive from Bridgeport.

"He always thought his wife would move," Beth recalled,

"but she didn't want to leave the Detroit area, so he drove in every day!"

Eventually, Gorski quit.

"I'm leaving, and going to go to work for one of your reps in the Detroit area," he told Beth, "and take advantage of the shorter drive."

That was the reason Gorski gave to Beth, although the bigger reason could have been that Beth was pressuring him for more sales. When she asked him what his sales projections were for the upcoming year, 2004, he replied, "Five to 10 percent higher."

"The market is bigger than that!" Beth exclaimed.

"No, it isn't," he replied. "The market is saturated."

•••

After Gorski left the company, Beth hired another man to take his place, but he only lasted a week. That's when Beth decided to see what she could do with that part of Amigo business, for nobody else seemed to see the potential in the Shopper market that she saw.

"There's no reason," she told Al, "this can't be a huge part of our business. Just look at the number of grocery stores out there. I'm going to take over these sales!"

Years later, Beth recalled, "Bells just went off in my brain. I got so excited about the Shopper market."

Next, she recruited Trisha Borch, who had just been hired a couple of weeks earlier to work in the service department.

"You're 100 percent working with me," Beth told her. "We're going to sell Shoppers!"

•••

When Beth and Trish started going through Gorski's files, "there was very little there!" Beth said in frustration. "There was just some notepaper with some notes here and there, and his file drawer had a few files in it. We had to start over from scratch, finding who the buyers were and which retailers he had contacted."

To get the records under control, Beth purchased a state-of-the-art contact management computer program and entered information as she found it. The software kept track of who their sales reps were, who the customers were, what discussions had taken place, and when the next follow-up calls needed to be made.

"I could die tomorrow," Beth explained facetiously, "and somebody could walk into that position and know exactly what to do."

Now Beth and Trish could start setting goals for making contacts and generating sales.

"OK," Beth told Trish, "today, if we get $60,000 in orders, you can go home as soon as we hit that!"

She had picked a huge number because, at $1,200 per Shopper, she was certain they would never reach that goal.

However, Beth said, "Trish and I were bulldogs!"

Shortly after lunch, they hit $60,000!

"You're not going home," Beth told Trish. "I was just kidding!"

Trish knew that. The two of them were just having fun.

"We were on fire!" Beth recalled.

•••

Beth was back in her element. Ever since she had taken over sales from Al, some thirty years earlier, she had been involved with them on and off, but had not been on the phone trying to close a sale in years. Now she was back on the phone, talking to buyers and owners, loving every minute.

"I didn't realize how much I missed sales," she said.

She got to know each and every buyer and store owner, along with the names of their spouses and children. Her new software program made that easy to do. More importantly, they knew her.

Eventually, Beth and Trish divided up the sales tasks. Trish made and took most of the calls in the office, and Beth, now that her kids were old enough to take care of themselves, spent more time on the road.

"Most of my time," Beth explained, "was spent creating relationships with the buyers. I think they could feel the passion I had for our products and the company. We published a newsletter that we sent to the buyers. It doesn't really talk about Amigo necessarily; it subtly talks about industry trends, what to look for when buying these carts, and so on. We had our name in front of them every month, so they knew my name, my picture, our product, our company, and what we do."

Although Trish was in the office and Beth was on the road, Amigo still maintained the manufacturer representative sales force.

"The reps were the boots on the ground," is the way Beth explained it. "We created trusting relationships with our field representatives, so we worked together to land new business."

Most companies that use manufacturers' representatives only pay them when they make sales. In Amigo's case, however, they got paid for any sale made in their territory, regardless of whether they facilitated it, or it came out of the home office. They could hardly believe that!

"You've got to trust me on this," Beth told them. "I will always pay you for the sales in your territory."

At first, they were all skeptical. That is, until she called them.

"I'm flying in," she said, "and we'll go together to finalize this contract."

Beth didn't care who made the sale.

"Because," she said, "if it's a line that they are making money on, that attracts more reps."

That was altruistic of her, but Beth had another more pragmatic reason to keep her sales reps under her wing.

By now Target had been using the Amigo Shopper for years. One time, when the chain wanted to buy additional motorized grocery carts, it put the contract out for bid.

"I know they love our product," Beth's Target rep told her.

"They just have to go through the process. Just place the same bid as before, and we're good to go."

Beth followed his instructions and lost the account!

"So, what did I learn?" she said. "Get on a plane, have a face-to-face with the client, and don't leave it up to a rep. Bring your rep with you, but don't leave it in their hands. I also felt very strongly that I wanted the customer—the retailer—to always know they have a voice at the factory. So, if something wasn't right, or they needed something, they always knew that they could contact the factory directly. Communication did not always have to go through the rep."

It was a hard lesson, to be sure.

"It took ten years to get the Target business back," Beth said.

•••

Beth's approach to the Shopper market obviously worked, because in 2009 she won the Senior-Level Executive Award, one of the "Top Women in Grocery" awards, presented by *Progressive Grocer Magazine*. The industry trade journal offers several awards each year, and the "Women" award winners are selected from thousands of "female movers and shakers in the North American retail food industry." The citation on the award read:

Congratulations, Beth Theme
CEO/VP of Commercial Sales, Amigo Mobility International
You've been chosen by your colleagues for being among
the best and the brightest. By example and direct action,
you have demonstrated outstanding leadership,
inspiration, and achievement in the industry you serve.

•••

Long before the Mobility Center, Inc., was shuttered, Beth had been trying to get Walmart to buy some Shoppers. Using the new computer software that she had purchased, she would call the company on a regular basis, but every Walmart purchasing agent she contacted was unreceptive. Eventually, however, one of them told her that before the company would consider buying her motorized grocery cart, it would need to be assessed by their test lab.

Beth had a Shopper sent to Walmart's headquarters in Bentonville, Arkansas, for analysis, and anxiously awaited the results.

"We're sorry," they said, "but you did not pass the test. It veers to the right a bit."

"What happened," Beth explained, "was when the truckers took the Shopper off the truck, they dropped it and bent the front fork!"

Beth told the purchasing agent that was not normal and begged her to let another Shopper be sent down to Walmart for testing.

"OK," she replied, "but it's got to be here in two days!"

"We couldn't take the risk of putting a Shopper on a truck again," Beth recalled, "because this was our last chance."

So, Al Bussinger, Amigo's chief engineer, and his son, Ben, put a brand-new Shopper in a pickup and personally drove it down to Bentonville to make sure that it wouldn't be damaged.

"We passed the test!" Beth exclaimed.

•••

Not long after that, Beth got a call from the purchasing agent.

"Come on down," she told her. "I want to have a meeting with you."

Beth flew to Bentonville, rented a car at the airport, and proceeded to Walmart's office. She expected to arrive at a big beautiful building, but it was only a large metal warehouse, whose interior was just as bland as its exterior. There were ten red vinyl chairs in the lobby, a security guard, and a lady with a beehive hairdo sitting behind a yellow computer terminal.

When Beth said who she was, the lady looked up her name in the computer and told her to go to Room 9.

"So, I went down this hallway," Beth recalled, "and there were twelve rooms ..., they felt like oversized closets. You could get four chairs and a table in there. I was sitting there ..., a little nervous ..., and the buyer walks in and sits down, and she starts rattling off stuff. It took me a minute to realize that she was saying we had the business. She's explaining what we had to do, and I'm taking notes as fast as she's talking. What the process is, what we had to do, and here's what we had to watch for, and she got up and shook my hand and says, 'Nice meeting you!'"

"I'm sitting there," Beth said, "thinking, *I think we got this!* There was no 'Congratulations, you're a supplier now!' It was kind of funny how it happened, but that's how we started selling to Walmart. We were pretty excited about that."

And so was everyone else in the company.

For the first time in years, the news coming out of the Amigo plant in Bridgeport was good. The community learned that the company was now hiring people and expanding its facilities to handle the growing Shopper sales. Instead of searching for banks and begging for money, Amigo Mobility was now being solicited by banks.

For example, four officers from the Key Bank in Detroit visited Amigo, looking for its business. When they met with Al and Beth, they offered them a line of credit of $2.5 million!

Beth thanked them for their time, but told them the company didn't need the line, since "we have a savings account and no debt."

•••

But not all the news coming out of Bridgeport was good. Marie Emma Thieme, the first Amigo user, stopped breathing on the morning of January 22, 2005, at the age of sixty-seven— after living a full twenty-five years longer than Dr. Chisena had predicted.

Nearly all of Bridgeport turned out for Marie's funeral service, which was held at Faith Lutheran Church, the same one that she and Al had been married in, over fifty years earlier.

"The church holds 400 people," recalled Jim Thieme, "and it was totally filled."

"Al bought a big cemetery plot when John was killed," Emy explained, "and Marie is buried next to him. There is a big stone that says 'Thieme,' and John is on one side, and Marie is on the other. A year ago or so, I bought artificial flowers to put on the graves since I couldn't plant flowers on all of the graves anymore, because my mother, sister, Max, Mary, and Waneta are all at the same cemetery. I got artificial flowers, and one of the kids takes them down there for me. I use them over and over."

•••

A year later, Al got a phone call from Raymundo Bonilla, a businessman in Mexico City, inquiring about selling the Amigo Shopper in Mexico.

Bonilla had been in the grocery store supply business for years, selling ordinary shopping carts, shelving, and other store fixtures to supermarkets, but he had never heard of the Amigo Shopper. Then, in 2006, one of his suppliers in France visited him in Mexico City and told him about the Shopper.

"You should try to do something with it in Mexico," he said.

When Bonilla called Amigo, Beth invited him to Bridgeport to visit the company. When Al and Beth met Bonilla, they were impressed with his amiable personality and years of business experience. The question was not whether they could work together, but whether there was a market for the Shopper in Mexico.

The Thiemes brought up the lack of success that Federico Fleischmann had had twenty years earlier when he tried to sell Amigos in Mexico and failed for two reasons: few people could afford to buy Amigos, and there were no curb cuts in the country. Bonilla understood all that, but he told them that many of the grocery store chains in Mexico were already providing manual wheelchairs to handicapped individuals, elderly people, and pregnant women. Price was always an obstacle in Mexico, he admitted, but selling to grocery stores, which have money, was different from selling to individuals.

After visiting with the Thiemes for a couple of days, discussing the pros and cons, and thinking about what he could do in Mexico with the Amigo Shopper, Bonilla asked Al and Beth: "Well, what do you think? Should we try to do something in Mexico?"

They agreed.

"We began," Bonilla recalled, "by bringing in just a few carts and making a free trial. That's how we began to make the Amigo Shopper more popular."

Bonilla traveled from one end of Mexico to the other, setting up product demonstrations and arranging free trials. Finally, Soriana, one of Mexico's largest grocery store chains, gave Bonilla an order.

"Since then," he said, "it's been very busy."

But not easy logistically.

"Selling in the US is different from selling in Mexico," Bonilla explained, "because in the US there are a bunch of retailers and a bunch of regional stores. The Mexican economy is smaller than the Texas economy, and the Mexican economy is divided into Mexico City, Guadalajara, and Monterey, which are 800 kilometers [500 miles] away from each other. Then you have León, Puebla, and Tijuana. The country is very spread out. In Texas, you have San Antonio, Houston, Dallas, and Austin, all within 400 kilometers of each other. There is more economic power in that small area than in all of Mexico. In the United States, if something happens to the cart, it's easier to order a new one, rather than trying to fix it."

The stores in Mexico, however, with their limited budgets, try to keep their Amigo Shoppers running for as long as possible at the least possible cost.

"Mexicans are very good at servicing whatever it needs,"

explained Bonilla with amusement. "It doesn't matter if we don't have the use of manuals. It doesn't matter if we don't have the correct replacement parts. We are very creative at keeping things going. Imagine: I have seen some carts working at Soriana stores that were sold twelve years ago! They don't change batteries. They don't change seats that need to be replaced. They don't even clean or maintain them! Ten years ago, we had our own warehouse and our own delivery trucks. Then I learned that in Mexico there is something called a *recinto fiscal*, which is a warehouse managed by the government and by the Servicio de Administración Tributaria (Mexico's IRS), so you can bring imported goods into that warehouse and store them there. They will charge you rent, but you don't have to pay taxes on the goods until you take them out. We discovered that about two years ago, and then my life changed. When we were in our own warehouse, and we had our own trucks and drivers, I used to work as a *capataz*, a foreman, for the whole operation. I had to do everything. But this new warehouse arrangement did all those things for me, and then I was able to do what I'm best at: *selling!* Al and Beth gave me the opportunity to sell their products in Mexico, and it's been a great story because we haven't stopped since then!"

•••

In 2008, after more than thirty years in business together, Al and Beth bought a cottage Up North, near Gladwin, Michigan, just as Al had done fifty years earlier when he and Alden owned a cottage on Bud Lake. In fact, their new cottage was only about thirty minutes away from the old one.

From time to time, they would invite members of their immediate families to their cottage. They couldn't invite all the Thiemes, because there were too many.

Beth knows all their names, but Al "has to think about it for a while," she said. We don't get together at Christmas with all of Al's children anymore, because they're all grandparents and have places to go, and it's too hectic."

•••

As the 2000s turned into the 2010s, and Al was entering his seventies, Beth thought it best that he should "slow down." That didn't mean he wouldn't be involved in his beloved company; it just meant that he would not be involved in the day-to-day operations. They hired a president to do that, but that was easier said than done. Over the next ten years, they hired a few key people, but things just didn't work out.

"We weren't able to find a person," Al said, "that had our culture and was able to put in the time the company needed to keep it going in a direction we felt it should go. Then Beth offered to handle the job!"

"We promoted *me!*" she said wryly.

In March 2020, Beth Thieme became president of Amigo Mobility International, forty-five years after joining the company.

"For me," she said, "I would never have come in as president earlier, for two reasons: I was raising a family, and I didn't want to work fifty hours a week or more, which I'm doing now. I think Al would have struggled with it. Now he's OK with it. He trusts me. My most important thing is my relationship with Al, and I wouldn't have wanted to jeopardize that. He's a strong guy, and it would have been hard for him to give up control earlier. But now it's working. It's really working well. I've committed to five years, and I've said to our next generation of leadership here, both family and nonfamily, my mission in the next five years is to teach you how I think, how I arrive at decisions, the *why* of things. My dream was to have kids, and that was my priority for many, many years. And I expected to help with the business, too. I've helped with babysitting the grandkids. I've done that stuff. Now it's time for me to run the business."

CHAPTER 26

Golden Jubilee

"I've learned that there's one difference between people who
are successful and people who are not, and that's persistence."
—Al Thieme

It had been a long, challenging, and implausible journey
for the entrepreneur from Bridgeport. When Al Thieme started
Amigo Company in 1968, little did he know the overwhelming
challenges that lay before him. Where most people would have
given up years earlier if confronted with the problems that Al
faced, he doggedly pursued his destiny of providing Amigos
to people with walking disabilities. Despite the challenges, Al
and Amigo are still around fifty years later, and he attributes his
success to perseverance.

"I've learned that there's one difference between people
who are successful and people who are not," Al explained, "and
that's persistence."

"The word that comes to me," explained Beth "is *relentless*.
When Al makes up his mind to do something, he is relentless.
He never sees a wall. And if he does, he asks, 'How do I get

over it?' He just keeps his eye on the goal, and he doesn't give up! He never thinks day-to-day or week- to-week. He only thinks long-term—the big picture. I think companies that survive have a visionary, and I truly believe that Al has always been the visionary in our company. 'This is going to work,' he'd say to himself. 'Of course, it's going to work, and this is what I have to do to make it work!'"

But as we have seen, things almost didn't work a number of times. Many of the obstacles were external, but some of them Al created himself. Not intentionally, of course, but in the process of building his business, he made decisions and took actions that he thought would be beneficial to the company, when in fact they turned out to be woefully detrimental.

One of those self-imposed problems was hiring the wrong people.

"Al is not a good judge of character," Beth observed. "He falls for people. He trusts *everybody*!"

That trait, while laudable, has worked against Al more than once during his long business career.

And his reluctance to work with bankers was also troublesome.

"Financial people," explained Beth, "don't work well with Al. They don't work well with entrepreneurs! I just don't think they understand them. They're frustrated by people like Al, because bankers function on order and logic."

After analyzing how Al managed Amigo Mobility, Wolfgang Price said that he lacked education and "business savvy," and "impaired the development of the firm, mostly for lack of understanding of what business is like and how to conduct it in building a firm."

There might have been some truth to Wolfgang's stinging assessment, but in the final analysis, it wasn't Al's lack of education or lack of business savvy that prevented him from confronting the likes of Electric Mobility and The SCOOTER

Store. It was the lack of cash flow.

Al knew full well what it would take to build a more formidable enterprise, but Amigo Mobility didn't generate enough cash for expansion, especially when he was reluctant to use banks. He was also unwilling to take the company public or to solicit funds from venture capitalists, for fear of losing control of his beloved company. That forced him to borrow money from friends and family and to sell small amounts of company stock to whomever would buy it. While that strategy kept him well in control of his company, it severely limited his ability to expand the company or to move it quickly in one direction or another, based on market conditions.

"But looking back is twenty-twenty hindsight," Al said.

When he was in the heat of battle, trying to determine which direction to take the company against government bureaucracy, against unrelenting competition in the United States, from low-cost copycats from Asia, and even against people in his own company, he didn't have a crystal ball to see the future. So, he did the best he could, and he finds solace in that.

"The mistakes I made," he said, "have been valuable learning lessons, and the problems I made myself made me a better person. They humbled me. If everything that came to me was easy, and everything fell into place, would I be the person that I am today? I'm thankful that I had those difficulties. They made me a better person and a more understanding person."

That's typical entrepreneurial thinking, putting a positive spin on adversity. But Beth is a little more pragmatic.

"Every company," she said, "gets in trouble some way. You just hit some tough roadblocks. You have to make sure that whoever is running the ship has that passion to fight through anything, because it's *never* going to be perfect and easy."

All the problems and challenges notwithstanding, "it did all turn out," Beth said. "Could it have been an easier life? Yes. But what I've learned over the years is that Al is truly an entrepreneur,

Aerial view of Amigo Mobility International, 2022

and entrepreneurs change the world."

To celebrate Al's entrepreneurial spirit and the longevity of Amigo Mobility, the employees thought it only fitting to throw a party—a once-in-a-lifetime celebration—a Golden Jubilee!

•••

Planning for the big event started two years earlier. Beth, Jennifer, and Jordan talked about what kind of event it should be, from an Amigo Round-Up type of event to one hosted by the Saginaw Chamber of Commerce.

"My dad," Jennifer explained, "is always quite humble about being the center of attention, but he loves a good party!"

The family decided to make it a more intimate event, like the company's annual Christmas party.

Jennifer and Jordan reserved the banquet hall at the Bavarian Inn in nearby Frankenmuth, scheduled a small local jazz band, and sent out more than 200 invitations.

The Bavarian Inn was the perfect venue. Al has known the

owner's matriarch, Dorothy Zehnder, for many years and greatly admired her.

"She's my role model," Al said.

Jennifer instructed the jazz band to play background music without singing.

"If my dad had his way," she exclaimed, "it would have been polka music!"

Jennifer also hired someone to tape Al telling the Amigo story to be shown at the party.

"I called a videographer a few weeks before," Jennifer recalled, "and told him that I just needed a three- to four-minute video to show. But it turned out to be eleven minutes, and he said that I couldn't cut it."

•••

Just like most other days, Al and Beth went to work on the day of the party. Since Jennifer and Jordan had arranged everything, their parents only had to show up. Surprisingly, when Al and Beth drove to the celebration by themselves, they didn't talk at all about what they had gone through for the past decades.

"We were excited about it," Beth recalled, "but we were a little apprehensive. Al and I feel a little awkward getting attention and being in the limelight."

The event was scheduled to begin at 5:30 p.m. to start the cocktail hour, so Al and Beth arrived early in order to greet everyone as they arrived. Al was dressed in a dark suit, a blue button-down shirt, and a burgundy tie. Beth was wearing a stylish bright red dress.

The first one they greeted was Dorothy Zehnder, who hugged Al as she congratulated him on his achievement.

•••

"When guests walked in," Jennifer explained, "the Bavarian Inn staff directed them to the Amigo Fiftieth Party. People were excited about seeing each other for the first time in years. People signed the guestbook, took their name tag, and we had a bowl of yellow Amigo smiley face pins for people to take. When you moved into the room, there were gold balloons with the number fifty on them, a dessert table with Amigo's fiftieth anniversary logo on cookies, and large pictures of my dad throughout history. Onstage, a jazz trio was playing, and waiters were walking around with drinks and appetizers."

As people mingled, got reacquainted, and reminisced, a slide show was projected on a large screen, showing pictures of Amigo owners with quotes from them about the little machine that had replaced their legs and changed their lives. For example:

"Amigo spells freedom for me!"
—Barbara Gratzke

"Having an Amigo lessened my anxiety. I could go to a movie or come home for lunch on my own."
—Sister Karen Zielinksi

"People don't feel sad when they see my Amigo. They feel curious and playful. They smile at me more quickly."
—Sunny Roller

•••

When Jennifer went to the podium to ask everyone to take a seat, she was a little hesitant.

"It just felt like a giant Amigo homecoming," she recalled. "Everybody came in, there were hugs, and people were happy to see each other ..., former employees we hadn't seen in twenty years, and new employees, and people from the community. No one wanted to break up their conversations. The whole event could not have been any more perfect. It was so wonderful. I have never been in a room and felt so much love and pride."

At the head table were Al and Beth, Jim and Janet Thieme, Jennifer and her husband, Dan, and, sitting next to Al, his sister,

Al Thieme with his good friend, Bob Zelle,
at Amigo Company's 50th Anniversary celebration

Emy. When Jennifer looked across that table and saw her dad and aunt, she couldn't help being a little philosophical.

"I just sat there wondering," she recalled, *"Did they think fifty years earlier that this would happen?"*

Many of the employees, particularly the ones from the earliest years, were probably thinking the same thing that night. That is, except for Charlene Zorn, one of Al's original Whiz Kids. Although she had been gone from the company for twenty-five years and had missed most of the adversity and hard times, she could well understand how her old boss could still be in business all these years later.

"It wasn't surprising to me," she explained, "because I just

Al and Beth Thieme, along with Al's sister, Emeline,
at the company's 50th Anniversary

know he was a hard worker. When you think about it, he never finished high school, and because of that he was motivated. His motivation in the beginning, I believe, was that he and Marie had a young family, and he wanted to make her more independent. And out of his love for her, he wanted to make something of the Amigo Company. He was an entrepreneur and businessman. He built the plumbing business, so he knew something about running a business. And he knew that he needed to surround himself with people who could help him. I know he reached out to Bob Zelle and many different people that could help mentor him. So, no, I'm not surprised that he survived fifty years."

•••

After everyone had taken a seat, Jennifer welcomed all the

guests, and then Jim Van Tiflin gave the first toast:

Al, Beth, and Amigo family members:

It is difficult to describe how honored Janice and I are to have been invited to participate in tonight's event. We have been friends for a long time despite the fact that, years ago, I was one of the bankers who said no to an Amigo loan request! In spite of the rejection, Al and Amigo persevered, and look where we are today. Me, a retired former bank president, and Al a thriving entrepreneur.

I could tell you a bunch of stories about how smart or not many of my decisions were during my career, and as I stand here tonight, three come to mind. Today, all three of those companies are multimillion-dollar companies. And the thing they had in common with Amigo was that their initial loan requests were denied as well. The other thing that they had in common was perseverance . . . . They weren't going to take no for an answer. That is the hallmark of successful entrepreneurs, and Al and Amigo had it, and *have* it, in spades. So, my toast tonight is to Al and Amigo and "gutting it out"! Here's to fifty more years of helping people.

Then Mitch Reno, who had once been Amigo Mobility's director of marketing, gave a wonderful extemporaneous toast:

One of my strongest and most powerful memories of Al was from an early Amigo Round-Up. Nearly a hundred Amigo owners, family members, and employees gathered in Las Vegas at Bally's resort. It was an exciting three-day event, filled with accessible activities.

I remember vividly watching Al as he walked over and kneeled down to speak with one of the Amigo customers. As he knelt in front of her, he looked up at the lady seated on the Amigo with care, respect, and a sincere level of interest. He was totally focused on her. As you can imagine, she felt like she was the most important person in the room at that moment.

That night and in that moment, it showed me how much he cared about our customers. I could see it in the way he interacted, the way he looked into a customer's eyes. That customer-centric focus became the culture of the business and the people who work at Amigo.

Later, I noticed that type of behavior from Al many times. And I would see it emulated by so many of the loyal employees who are gathered here tonight. The customers of Amigo have always been more than friends; they are family.

Then Alex, Al's youngest child, stepped in:

For those who haven't known me since birth, my name is Alex Thieme. I am the youngest ..., or as my parents like to call me ..., the grand finale!

We are here today to celebrate an accomplishment unlike any other: fifty years of changing lives through mobility, all because of a man with a dream in 1968 ..., my dad.

When you are young, your dad is your hero. For me, that feeling has never changed. And what's amazing is he's a hero to so many more than just me.

Everything he does, he doesn't just want to be the best at it. He wants to be better than that. We all know the phrase "There must be a better way." When it comes to Al Thieme, the sky's the limit, and he has proven that, time and time again.

His vision, passion, and dedication to helping people are the reason the company has thrived for the last fifty years, and we will continue his legacy for many years to come.

For most people, working with their significant other might cause trouble. Maybe that's why my parents' offices are on opposite sides of the building!

My parents have been working to build a business and a family for over thirty years, and they have been extremely successful. They have taught us to be hard workers. They have taught us to do the right thing. And most importantly, they have taught us what love is.

He has been the greatest father and role model I could have ever asked for.

Al Thieme is a living, breathing testament that working hard, doing the right thing, and caring for customers and employees alike will create a culture of people who truly care, and that's what Amigo is all about.

Please join me in raising a glass: To Al Thieme ..., inventor, entrepreneur, 1981 Small Businessperson of the Year, and, most importantly, my dad.

Fifty years down, fifty years to go!

•••

After the accolades, soup and salad were served, Mike Galer gave the invocation, and then dinner was served. Since the Bavarian Inn is world famous for its savory "Frankenmuth Chicken," that is what everybody had, with roast beef au jus.

After dinner, the lights were turned down, and the video that Jennifer had ordered was played. The video begins by showing various parts of the Amigo, then shopping cart baskets stacked up, then scenes of the production line in operation, and then the warehouse.

Next, Al comes into the scene and proceeds to recount the Amigo story: his and Marie's trip to Mexico, how he had to push her around in a wheelchair, and how he made the first Amigo for her.

"We didn't know what to call it," he continued. "We didn't want to call it a wheelchair. Unfortunately, wheelchairs have such a negative thing about them, so we tried to come up with a name. Marie came up with the name. She said, 'Amigo.'"

Then Bob Zelle enters the scene and sits down next to Al.

"My name," he says, "is Bob Zelle. I live in Frankenmuth. My business is on Zelle Drive, which runs parallel to the expressway. The driveway is just beyond the Speedway station. I started that business in 1965."

Then an unseen announcer asks: "How important is Bob to the story of Amigo?"

Al replies, "I'd say he's number one, because he was there to help me and to give me confidence, business advice, and money!"

Zelle retorts facetiously, "I gave him about twenty-five or thirty dollars! That's it! Al's got the right attitude to be successful. He's got the right work ethic to be successful. He's a 'people person,' and without people, you can't be successful."

The video then goes into a brief montage of scenes within the company, with Beth sitting next to Al.

"What is it about Al," the announcer asks, "that made the business successful?"

"His curiosity and his never being satisfied," Beth replies. "He's just always kind of restless. We just need to keep doing better, faster, keep improving. He's just driving us."

"What would Al have said fifty years ago," asks the announcer, "if he could look into the future to see what he had built?"

Beth replies, "He'd say, 'I would have thought we would have been bigger! Why didn't we do more?' He's never satisfied."

"What," the announcer asks, "do you want the legacy of Amigo to become?"

"I never thought much about what Amigo should become," Al says. "I think I always had a feeling that there's something that I'm here for. There's a purpose."

Then the announcer asks Bob Zelle, "As you look back on the past fifty years of this company, what are you most proud of? What do you remember the most? What is Amigo to you?"

"I've told people," Zelle says, "that I knew Al Thieme before he started Amigo. He was working in a house with a garage behind it. He had a dream, and he built that dream to this. That's what I remember most."

"How does that make you feel, Al?" the announcer asks.

"Humble," Al says. "There's so much more to do. We now have a base and a platform, so that the next fifty years will really be something!"

●●●

Although Jennifer had feared that the video would be too long, "everyone was held in rapt attention," she recalled with a sense of relief. "It seemed to fly by in an instant. I get goosebumps just thinking about it. *You're never going to see this again!* It brought grown men to tears! You could just feel it, like everybody had goosebumps ..., a tangible sense of pride and joy in the room. And my dad was able to look around and see all the lives he had touched ..., not just the Amigo owners, but all the employees where Amigo is such a big part of their lives. I always joked that in Saginaw there are two degrees of separation from Amigo: either you worked there, or you knew someone who worked there. It just had the magical component. Everything just fit together so well."

Surprisingly, and unfortunately, Al Thieme did not stand up to give a talk. With all his years in Toastmasters, his strong voice, and his self-assurance, he could have brought the group to tears, or laughter, or both.

"But he was the guest of honor," Beth explained. "We were honoring him for being in business for fifty years. So that's why he didn't get up to speak."

However, Beth did stand up to give a few words. She spoke

about how far the Amigo Company had come and how proud she was of her husband and the company.

•••

When the night was drawing to an end, Jennifer went up to the podium and thanked everyone for coming, but no one wanted to leave!

"Everyone lingered and hugged and shared memories," Jennifer recalled.

"Who would have thought," Amigo employee Jeff Godi told Jennifer, "that we would all be here, celebrating a man who started this in a garage, ended up changing so many lives with the Amigo, and making his business what it is today?"

"My fiancé, Matthew," said Gabriella Hoffman, another Amigo employee, "loves to tell people, 'Al Thieme invented the Amigo right here in Bridgeport, Michigan! Made the whole industry, right where Gabriella's office is!'"

Stories like those could have gone on forever, but the festivity had come to an end. Jennifer and her husband, Dan, were the last to leave.

"I think my parents were tired," she recalled, "and left a little before us. Some of the other Amigo employees were there with us at the end, too. It could not have gone any better, and it was a gift to have everyone together to celebrate fifty years of Amigo."

•••

That night may have ended, but there was still one more celebration to go.

"I wanted to do something tangible for my dad's anniversary," Jennifer explained, "a long-term physical remembrance of him. We could have planted a tree or done a statue, but I didn't want to spend thirty grand on it, and it would have been kind of weird to have a statue of a living man!"

As Jennifer and her brother, Jordan, were walking through the company one day, they passed by a large storage closet, approximately twelve feet by thirty feet, located between the

The Al Thieme Library

showroom and the machine shop. It was a long and narrow space that was open to the roof.

"I kind of did a double take," Jennifer recalled. "I told my brother, 'Hey, what if we make this into our dad's library?' His whole life, he's learned by reading. He reads four to five books a month. I feel like he's trying to make up for the fact that he didn't do formal schooling. Anyway, he has all these books, and in all these books he writes notes in the front of them and indicates pages that he likes. I didn't want to donate them or get rid of them."

So Jennifer and Jordan had the space turned into the Al Thieme Library.

For eight weeks, the two Thieme children worked with designers and builders to transform the unused space into a library. Al, of course, knew something was going on in that area, but Jennifer did her best to keep it secret. The new library was completed well before its unveiling on November 12, 2018.

On that date, Jennifer announced that there was going to be a special celebration of the unveiling of the secret room. Everyone in the company was invited, she told them, and State Senator Ken Horn would be there to cut the ribbon.

As everyone crammed together in the narrow hallway outside the former storage room, Al asked his daughter, "Jen, you really planned a ribbon-cutting with a senator for a closet?"

"Just wait!" she replied excitedly. "This is better than a closet! I promise!"

•••

After Senator Horn cut the ribbon, Al walked into the revamped space, where he saw on the wall to his left a sign that said, "The Al Thieme Library." On the wall to his right were pictures of ten books, with the titles of Al's top ten favorites:

1. *The 7 Habits of Highly Effective People: Powerful Lessons in Personal Change,* by Steven R. Covey
2. *Good to Great: Why Some Companies Make the Leap and Others Don't,* by Jim Collins
3. *The Power of Positive Thinking,* by Norman Vincent Peale
4. *How to Win Friends and Influence People,* by Dale Carnegie
5. *Steve Jobs,* by Walter Isaacson
6. *Steps on the Stairway,* by Ralph Ransom
7. *The Law of Success in Sixteen Lessons,* by Napoleon Hill
8. *Acres of Diamonds,* by Russell H. Conwell
9. The Bible
10. *Benjamin Franklin: An American Life,* by Walter Isaacson

"This *is* better than a closet!" Al exclaimed. "It's pretty special."

Hanging on the back wall, there are fourteen framed pages copied from Al's fifty-year journal record.

"I literally held my brother hostage," Jennifer laughingly recalled, "to go through all of our dad's early journals, page by page by page, to pick out which ones we wanted to frame. I just felt like they were such a perfect capture of his resoluteness, optimism, and personality."

A page from 1976 caught Jennifer's eye, for it mentions the then Beth Loichinger returning to work at Amigo Company.

"Wow, what a pivotal moment in history," Jennifer exclaimed. "It changed everything! Without that I wouldn't be here!"

It's not a lending library, but, as Jennifer explained, "It's a wonderful sentimental space that was a special part of Amigo's fiftieth anniversary."

Epilogue

"I wouldn't change a thing."
—Al Thieme

The market for Amigos has changed since Marie Thieme contracted multiple sclerosis back in 1966. Now there are treatments for MS that weren't available then, and the number of people who contracted polio decades ago is dwindling.

"There's still a demand for three-wheeled scooters," explained John Layman, who is still selling Amigos and other POVs in Phoenix. "Some customers have disabilities. Some have walking limitations. Typically elderly, but not necessarily. It's the same as it's always been in that regard—it's people who have walking impairments."

However, Layman no longer sells POVs through Medicare.

"We dropped out a long time ago," he said. "That hurt our business some, but not as much as you would have thought, because Medicare is such a pain to deal with for providers as well as for customers. People would rather just pay cash for them."

Customers can still get a POV through Medicare, but the agency makes it very difficult. First of all, the average price for an Amigo in 2022 was $2,800, but Medicare would only pay

$935, or 33 percent, toward that amount, and customers had to pay the balance of $1,865, either through their supplemental insurance or their own cash. Furthermore, Medicare would not pay for any accessories that customers needed, such as headrests or armrests. On a manual or power wheelchair, on the other hand, Medicare would pay 80 percent of the cost in 2022, regardless of price, plus whatever accessories customers needed! Although most power wheelchairs cost around $3,000 at that time, they could get as high as $30,000.

Why would Medicare pay for manual wheelchairs and power wheelchairs, but not for POVs? Because after all the years of buying mobility aids for people with walking disabilities, Medicare concluded that those patients only needed a POV temporarily, and therefore it was an unnecessary expense.

Jason Hurd, the manager of Amigo Mobility's retail store in Bridgeport, explained Medicare's misguided perspective this way: "Even if you qualify for a POV, you're ultimately going to end up in a power wheelchair anyway, so why not just cut out the middleman and push the customer into a power wheelchair? You can't bill for seating, you can't bill for headrests, you can't bill for armrests. So if a customer could use a POV, but they need some side supports, you can't bill for them! That automatically zeros out a POV. That automatically puts the customer in a power wheelchair!"

Ironically, after more than five decades, the most efficient and expedient way for a person to obtain any POV is the same as when Al Thieme introduced the Amigo in 1968—and that is by paying cash.

•••

All Al Thieme wanted to do when he started building Amigos was to provide a friendly-looking motorized wheelchair to people who had walking disabilities—a device that was pleasing to the eye, highly functional, and would allow the user to live an active, productive life. He didn't care if he made a lot of money at it.

"Being the richest person in the cemetery," he said, "doesn't matter to me. Going to bed at night, saying, 'We've done something wonderful.' That's what matters to me."

"To some extent," Wolfgang Price said, "I think he felt good that the family was involved in the business."

For the most part, Al agrees with Wolfgang's assessment.

"Marie was involved in the business," he explained, "my brother; my sister and two of her daughters; every one of my children at one time or another and their spouses; and nephews, nieces, grandchildren, and great grandchildren. The family saw and lived with the change and additional activities that Marie was able to handle, and they were happy to be a part of helping other people continue to have an active life with their newfound Amigo mobility, even if I paid them less than I paid others!"

●●●

Al could not have imagined the journey Amigo would take him on, let alone all the drama. No one could have. When asked fifty years later what he would change on the dramatic journey if he could do it all over again, he replied: "I wouldn't change a thing."

Al is quite pragmatic in that respect, regarding such questions as a waste of time. What happened, happened, and there is nothing that can be done about it, so why speculate? However, he does have some advice for budding entrepreneurs.

Not surprisingly, his first suggestion relates to banking.

"It's more than just the numbers," he explained. "It's important to have a good relationship with a bank. Find a bank that is willing to take a risk on you, and use them before you need them. Be proactive by providing annual business plans and year-end recaps *before* they ask you for them. Meet with them on a regular basis and be at *every* bank meeting."

As a business grows, the owner is going to hire people to help perform all of the functions that the enterprise requires, from salespeople to financial experts. Al's advice about working with all of those individuals is to "trust, but don't *en*trust. Trust is to place confidence in somebody. Entrust is to give trust to the care of others *without* surveillance."

Something else Al learned over the years was the importance of building up a savings account.

"Yes, you need one," he said somewhat hesitatingly. "I always believed in putting all your money into the business ..., to be fully committed. For many years, everything we owned in the business and personally was pledged to the bank. If we didn't make it, we truly would have had to start over from scratch. But we kept going, and maybe knowing there wasn't another option was good for us and the business."

After a business has survived the start-up mode by working with a bank and hiring and managing people well, then the owner must think of diversifying.

"At first," Al explained, "you have to put all your eggs in one basket. But when the company is stable and has consistent profit, you must find other opportunities for growth."

In the case of Amigo Mobility, as we have seen, it diversified into the shopping cart market.

From the perspective of personal development, Al recommends that people keep a daily journal and never stop learning.

"A journal is an opportunity for reflection," he said. "It captures what happened and the people who were part of the story. A journal brings great value to future generations as they enjoy reading about the history of a company. There are so many lessons in history, and it is easier to see what you could have and should have done when you are looking back."

According to Al, the best way to engage in lifelong learning is through reading.

"Books have been the cornerstone of my education," he explained. "I read about thirty books a year. I especially

Al and Beth's family, 2022 (L-R): Alex and Matti Thieme; Dan and Jennifer Kehres with their children Boden, Brecken, Delaney, and Lola; Beth and Al, Kate and Tony Eimers with their children, Hendrik and Stella; and Rachel and Jordan Thieme

appreciate and enjoy books about self-improvement, business books, autobiographies, history, inspiration, and the Bible. All I have read, learned, and have answers for is great for the past, but the ways of business, the world, and people are continually changing. The questions are much different for each generation. Old answers are not sufficient. To stay in the lead, a person must continually read, study, and prepare for the future."

Al's main piece of advice for people to be successful in business or any other endeavor is to follow their dreams.

"Your work is going to fill a large part of your life," he explained, "and the only way to be truly satisfied is to do what you believe is great work. And the only way to do great work is to love what you do. If you haven't found it yet, keep looking. You'll know when you find it. Like any great relationship, it just keeps getting better and better as the years roll on. So keep looking until you find it. Your time is limited. Have the courage to follow your heart and intuition. They somehow already know what you truly want to become."

•••

Obviously, Al Thieme found his passion⌐ a long time ago, when he realized how much the little machine that he invented was changing people's lives. At 85 years old in April 2022, he still loves to be at the office every day, although not at the crack of dawn, as in the old days.

"I can't imagine," he said, "doing anything that is more exciting than what I am doing right now, to see the many different product lines we are getting into due to our knowledge and experience of designing, building, and servicing battery-powered devices that move people and products."

But he becomes contemplative when he thinks about how the market has changed, or how extraneous forces have changed it.

"There was a need and I saw it, and it has been the greatest honor of my life to help other people," he said. "But I just keep thinking, there must be a better way."

Appendix

A few examples of the extraordinary customer letters and testimonials that Al Thieme has received over the years.

7-1-2021

Dear Mr. Thieme,

Enclosed is my picture on my Amigo. We were in Virginia Beach.

You are correct. I got my first Amigo in 1980. I kept it covered up in our garage for a few months so no one would know that I needed it. Then we took it to Virginia Beach. And suddenly I could come and go like everyone. It was like being "free at last." It changed my life and John's life. One night we were in Springfield, OH and my amigo would only go backward. John called your 800 number and a man told him how to fix it. Of course we were happy. Thank you for every thing

Betty Jo Pendleton

Ray A. Kroc
Senior Chairman of the Board
Founder

August 3, 1981

Amigo Sales, Inc.
6693 Dixie Hwy.
Bridgeport, Mich. 48722

Dear Amigo Sales:

I am a totally satisfied customer with two of your
Amigo's.

I apologize for taking such a long time to send a
photo. As you can see, we are not much as photographers.
These were taken at my office at the Padres and in my
private box at the stadium. I sit in my Amigo and watch
the games (or will, now that the strike is over).

Again, please accept my apologies for my tardiness.

Sincerely,

Ray A. Kroc

slm

Encls.

McDonald's Corporation · McDonald's Plaza · Oak Brook, Illinois 60521

AMIGO MOBILITY INTERNATIONAL
6693 Dixie Highway Bridgeport, MI 48722-0492 U.S.A.
(517) 777-0910 TELEX 810-797-636 FAX 517-777-8184

"the mobility company"
Since 1968

RECEIVED JUL 3 1 1989

Dear Allan —
It is great!
It gave me a measure
of independence when
I needed it most
after BI-LATERAL
I'm still using
knee replacement.
It for shopping
trips. Sincerely,
Mary Kay

July 19, 1989

Mrs. Mary Kay Ash
Mary Kay Cosmetics
8787 Stemmons Freeway
Dallas, TX 75247

Dear Mrs. Ash:

      Thank you for purchasing an Amigo. If there is any way
that I can be of assistance, or if you would like any changes,
speciality items or a special unit, please feel free to contact
me.

      I look forward to meeting you personally at some future
date.

                              Sincerely,

                              Allan R. Thieme

                              Allan R. Thieme
                              President

ART:blh

February 18, 2022

Dear Amigo, *(page 1)*

I'm Kathleen Schwertlich (Schwart-lick), and I'd like to thank you for the repairs you did on my Amigo. I have had it since 1974, when I was 19 and at the start of my sophomore year in college.

Thanks to my mom who saw a man with an Amigo at Houston's Galleria, my independent mobility very well could have remained in the low range of pitiful, to none.

I have had Juvenile Rheumatoid Arthritis since 1956, (diagnosed when I was 18 months old); it made getting around really challenging.

By the time I entered college, my deformed legs shaped an upside-down Y. My thighs, and knees were in a locked together fashion, while my calves branched out. I walked on the inside of my ankles and feet. My hips were frozen at a 45-degree angle; so, when standing, I appeared to be starting to sit. Taking regular steps, meant swinging myself forward while moving from left to right.

It was very slow going; so, by the time my Amigo entered my life, I was more than elated.

From that day forward my future trajectories of getting from A to B were forever changed. This inspiring Amigo invention, with its swivel seat, and compact weight, still make a big impact on my life's productivity 48 years later.

I suppose there have been plenty of people who were unable to see this vision, but clearly in 1968 Al Thieme stayed focused on his calling. Again, gratitude is my biggest emotion.

In the latter part of the 19th century when the Methodists were holding a denominational meeting, one leader stood up and shared his vision for both the church and society at large. He told his fellow ministers how he believed that someday men would fly from place to place instead of traveling on horseback. It was a concept too outlandish for many in the audience to handle. One man, Bishop Wright, stood up and furiously protested: "Heresy! Flight is reserved for the angels!" He went on to say that if God intended man to fly he would have bestowed him with wings. Clearly the Bishop was unable to envision what the speaker was predicting. When he finished his protest, he collected his two sons, Orville and Wilbur, and left the auditorium. That's right-his sons were the famous Orville and Wilber Wright! And several years later on December 17, 1903, they did what their father declared impossible; they recorded the first human flight.

Many people prefer the comforts of the past to the risk of the future. I suspect that if Al Thieme had needed everyone's support or approval, he would have never invented my Amigo. I'm grateful he paid attention to his vision.

Your friend,
Kathleen Schwertlich

P.S.: I graduated from college in 1977, when I was 22; I had 4 joint replacements in 1 month (knees & hips), making it possible to walk. My hips are at an 11-degree angle.

Since I now was able to walk, I used my Amigo for big walking events for 35 years. Only for the past 10yr have I used it daily due to replacements of the replacement joints.

Things rarely go as planned; so now I have one leg that's 3 inches shorter, and 1 leg with a titanium rod that won't bend.

I married at 28 years old in 1984 to a Lutheran Pastor. We reside in Katy, Texas where he is the interim pastor for a small startup church. We have no children, and have been married 38 years.

On February 18, I turned 67. Again, thank you for your good work!

"The Amigo has been my best friend for many years. I bought my first Amigo in New Orleans shortly after the World Fair in 1973."

– Ernie Barriffe, Moss Point, Mississippi

•••

"I have been an Amigo owner and user for a good many years. To say that I am satisfied with the Amigo would be an understatement. I have been actively involved with post-polio advocacies and during those years have recommended Amigo to many fellow polio survivors. I can honestly say that I have heard only positive comments about the Amigo from any one of them. And it is not simply the quality of the Amigo. We are all confident in the strength and dependability of the Amigo company to stand behind our purchases. I have had the pleasure to meet Al and Beth Thieme and to spend time with them on several occasions. To know Al explains it all."

– Tim Brown

•••

"I am a non-ambulatory polio survivor. I bought an Amigo motorized POV/scooter in 1978 and used it at work and at home until my retirement. It is my daily lifeline."

– Jean Csaposs

•••

"I've been using an Amigo since I was 12. My Amigo is such an integral part of my life that I decided to become an Amigo Dealer in Israel. I simply cannot imagine my life without Amigo."

– Dan Rashal, Tel Aviv, Israel
– Adriana Grotto, Arezzo, Italy

•••

"I'm sure that a multitude of others, like myself, have been given a whole new life on an Amigo."

– Petchy Sargent, Santa Fe, New Mexico

"I got my first Amigo in 1989 as I have MS. Walking longer distances got harder and harder. That first day out on my Amigo was like getting out of jail."

– Shirlee, Spokane, Washington

•••

"My Amigo is 100% dependable and the sturdiest constant in my life. My 'friend' since 1980, has enhanced my world with every mile it has taken me."

– Cynthia Inman, South Carolina

•••

"Thank you so much for improving the lives of so many people with disabilities. I am able to do my own shopping and get around on public transportation. I have a new found freedom!"

– Helene, Brooklyn, New York

•••

"Thank you for serving others. I don't know what we would have done without you. You've made life better for an untold number of people. Thank you."

– Barbara, Saginaw, Michigan

•••

"Life has been so much fun since getting my first Amigo more than 16 years ago."

– Alice Rodziewicz, Warren, Michigan

•••

"Amigo changed my life. When I bought my first one in 1986 I became 'a real person' with the same possibilities as everyone else to live with freedom. I could find work, study, go out with friends, etc. because I became independent with my Amigo."

– Adriana Grotto, Arezzo, Italy

Interviews

Bob Assadi
Gregory Barber
Shirley Beebe
Robert Boes
Terry Bollinger
Raymundo Bonilla
Grace Berger
Allen Bussinger
Jean Csaposs
Jim Csaposs
Mark Campbell
Keith Christiansen
JoAnn Crary
Jacques Dallery
Jennifer Dixon
Federico Fleischmann
Michael Flowers
Mike Galer
John "Bud" Gilmore
Joyce Godwin
Emeline Thieme Goodman
Carol Hackett
Douglas Harrison
Ray Hodgkinson
Murl Hoppe
Jason Hurd

Jennifer Thieme Kehres
John Layman
William Loeffler
Luc Magnus
Frank Martin
Michael Martin
Herb McLachlan
Itzhak Perlman
Jan Price
Wolfgang Price
Clarence Rivette
Martha Rottiers
Ermin Sallmen
Floyd Schmitzer
Mel Shepard
Robert Shrode
Nancy Thieme Smith
Sue Tate
Shirley Taylor
Allan R. Thieme
Beth L. Thieme
Jim Thieme
Jordan Thieme
Jim Van Tiflin
Brigitte Van Dessel
Robert "Bob" Zelle
Charlene Zorn

Saturday, November 30 (334-31)

□ CLEAR □ RAIN □ SNOW
□ HOT □ COLD □ MILD

9- P—3

Q—5

10-

11-

12- Office misc

1-

Sunday, December 1 (335-30)

□ CLEAR □ RAIN □ SNOW
□ HOT □ COLD □ MILD

9- P—2

Q— 1

10-

11-

12-

Monday, December 2 (336-29)

□ CLEAR □ RAIN □ SNOW
□ HOT □ COLD □ MILD

9- P—1

Q—10

10-

11-

12- Larry Gates was here to

1- learn service for Grand

2-

3- Rapids area

4-

5- Supposed to _____ for TV, but

EVENING